The Turning

The Turning

A History of Vietnam Veterans Against the War

Andrew E. Hunt

NEW YORK UNIVERSITY PRESS

New York and London

NEW YORK UNIVERSITY PRESS
New York and London

Library of Congress Cataloging-in-Publication Data
Hunt, Andrew E., 1968–
The turning : a history of Vietnam Veterans Against the War /
by Andrew Hunt.
p.   cm.
Includes bibliographical references and index.
ISBN 0-8147-3581-9 (cloth : alk. paper)
1. Vietnam Veterans Against the War—History. 2. Vietnamese
Conflict, 1961–1975—Protest movements—United States.
3. Veterans—United States—Political activity—History—20th century.
I. Title.
DS559.62.U6 H86 1999
959.704'31—dc21   99-6137
                                   CIP

New York University Press books are printed on acid-free paper,
and their binding materials are chosen for strength and durability.

Manufactured in the United States of America

10 9 8 7 6 5 4 3 2 1

For Lori

Contents

Acknowledgments

A book is seldom a solitary endeavor. Numerous people assisted me in my effort to conceive and write this history. First, I would like to thank Robert Goldberg, of the University of Utah. I am proud to count him as my Ph.D. chair, longtime mentor, and close friend. Those who know and respect Goldberg's writings will instantly detect his influence in these pages. Without his constant encouragement, criticism, insight, and guidance, this work would have been much poorer. "Bob," as his students call him, made my graduate school years exciting. He steered me to the sixties, and I thank him for that.

Other people deserve thanks for reading the manuscript in its entirety and for giving me constructive feedback. Eric Hinderaker, Edward J. Davies III, Mike Davis, Marvin Gettleman, Rebecca Horn, and Peter Philips read the manuscript and offered invaluable suggestions and insights.

Throughout the research, I benefited from the cooperation of the State Historical Society of Wisconsin. The staff at the SHSW were always courteous and helpful, and they made the job of sifting through the archives a pleasant one. The Hoover Institution at Stanford University and the Bancroft Library at Berkeley yielded additional material. Grants from the Marriner S. Eccles Foundation and the Steffensen-Cannon Humanities Fellowship program sustained me through those difficult years of graduate school.

A number of individuals helped me initiate the research by offering suggestions and advice. The Internet proved a useful starting point. For helping me launch the project, I would like to thank Linda Alband, Paul Buhle, Ben Chitty, Jack Mallory, Barry Romo, Mike Davis, Dave Kohr, John O'Connor, Don Mabry, Vince Gotera, Jonathan Shay, Joe Urgo, Maurice Isserman, and the ubiquitous Jan Barry. Stacks of material at the Vietnam Veterans Against the War national office in Chicago became accessible thanks to Barry Romo. Barry also allowed me to stay at his house when I interviewed VVAW folk in Illinois and Wisconsin. Nikki and Roger Mackenzie, who provided me with a place to stay in San Francisco, deserve thanks for their hospitality.

Other individuals offered me their personal papers. A long and fruitful correspondence with Michael Uhl helped me to better understand the Winter Soldier Investigation, and I thank him for the Citizens' Commission of Inquiry papers. Tom Thompson provided me with original copies of various VVAW publications that he had saved since his days as an Arizona VVAW organizer in the early seventies. Don Donner sent package after package of papers on the Gainesville Eight and Bill Lemmer. Larry Craig furnished pages and pages of material on the Winter Soldier Investigation and other VVAW activities. The numerous VVAW members who consented to interviews added a deeply human dimension to this book. I am also glad I had the opportunity to meet and talk with Richard Stacewicz. Richard compiled a terrific collection of VVAW oral histories, and it was refreshing to exchange ideas and "war stories" with someone researching the same topic.

I reserve a special thank you to Niko Pfund, the director and editor in chief at New York University Press, who upon hearing my project, was consistently supportive and enthusiastic. An equally special thank you goes to Despina Papazoglou Gimbel, Elyse Strongin, and Andrew Katz, whose terrific editing, design, and composition skills greatly enhanced the book. I've been lucky to work with such a caring and high-quality publisher.

Finally, I would like to thank members of my family. My father, E. K. Hunt, and my mother, Linda Hunt, helped in different, yet meaningful ways. Their suggestions, moral support, and love provided the intellectual and spiritual nourishment I needed to even begin work on the project. They introduced me to VVAW when I was too young to understand what the organization meant, but the legacy of their compassion and activism has given me hope for the future. My brother Jeff kept my spirits up by reminding me of the importance of laughter. Monte Bona has been more like a real father than a father-in-law. Our stimulating conversations about history have prompted me to clarify and reexamine my assumptions about the past. My siblings-in-law and their families—too numerous to mention—kept my morale high with their kindness and great senses of humor.

My deepest thanks, of course, go to my immediate family. My daughter, Madeline, provided the smiles, hugs, play, and amazing wisdom that sustained my soul. The recent birth of my son, Aidan, reaffirmed my commitment to tell the story of the men and women who sought to eradicate war from the face of the earth. My principal debt is to Lori Bona Hunt. Lori believed in this project from the beginning and, more important, believed that I was uniquely qualified to tackle it. Her patient ear, level-headed advice, and tolerance of my self-absorption prevented me from dropping out of graduate school years ago. Neither the dedication nor this short acknowledgment can express how much her love and emotional support have meant to me. This book is for her, with all of my love.

Introduction

The 1960s and the first half of the 1970s—an era known as "the sixties" to most observers—has perhaps generated more mythology than any other period in American history. Over time, the standard paradigms of the sixties have become clichés. The scenario is familiar: The decade began with the highest of ideals and aspirations, as embodied by John F. Kennedy's New Frontier and the imagery of Camelot. It ended with Kent State, and then Watergate, and, finally, U.S. helicopters fleeing the rooftop of the American Embassy as Communist troops encircled Saigon. In between those two ends of the decade, a Civil Rights Movement ended American apartheid, the Cold War consensus collapsed in the jungles of Southeast Asia and the streets of the United States, a generation gap widened, a counterculture emerged, a predominantly middle-class New Left drifted left until it triggered apocalyptic confrontations in the streets of Chicago, and a youthful spirit of reform faded into the "me" ethos of the seventies.

For years, historians, writers, and participant-memoirists accepted this version of the sixties without much question or variation. It proved to be a tidy way of summarizing a complicated time in American history. In recent years, sixties chroniclers have shifted their attention increasingly to the "neglected constituencies" of the period. Recently, the spotlight has slowly shifted away from figures who dominated the old sixties narratives—namely, members of Students for a Democratic Society and media pop icons such as Abbie Hoffman—to other activists who exercised just as profound an influence at the time but who have been ignored or delegitimized in most histories. These players include feminists, Chicano power activists, gay militants, American Indian Movement organizers, and antiwar veterans.

Vietnam Veterans Against the War (VVAW) is an organization that has rarely received adequate consideration in the standard sixties histories. The organization could boast everything that SDS claimed: tens of thousands of members (at least on mailing lists); chapters in all parts of the country; sponsorship of social programs, such as drug counseling for poor veterans; and, by 1972, policy papers containing critiques of capitalism that surpassed SDS's founding manifesto, the Port Huron Statement, in scope and sophistication. But VVAWers arrived at their radicalism in different ways from SDSers. Most VVAWers came from working-class backgrounds. Almost none went to Vietnam as radicals. The majority of VVAWers moved to the left as a result of their experiences in Southeast Asia and their subsequent politicization at home. In many respects, VVAWers and other activists of the early seventies confronted entirely different challenges from SDSers. While SDSers resisted the war during its early stages, VVAWers faced the more onerous task of making antiwar activism relevant amid Vietnamization and America's increased reliance on the air war in Southeast Asia. SDSers questioned the contradictions of Cold War liberalism, while VVAWers attacked the legitimacy of Nixonian conservatism and paranoia. Women in many SDS chapters were expected to make coffee and do "shit work"; VVAW issued lengthy position papers condemning sexism and, by 1972, actively recruited women and asked them to serve in positions of power. SDS tapped into youthful idealism, VVAW resisted weary cynicism. The political and cultural icons of SDS's age—the Black Panthers, Abbie Hoffman, Janis Joplin—were either gone or obscured during VVAW's heyday, but the counterculture still resonated deeply in American society.

The emergence of VVAW in the early seventies had a profound impact on the antiwar movement in the United States. VVAW transformed the movement by placing Vietnam veterans in the forefront of the nationwide struggle to end the Vietnam War. The organization attracted a broad spectrum of veterans: officers and GIs; desk clerks, combat veterans and bomber pilots; anarchists, Trotskyists, Maoists, and Democrats. The film footage of veterans casting their medals and ribbons onto the steps of the Capitol in 1971 became a crucial rallying symbol for the antiwar movement, forever etching itself in the minds of millions of Americans. Moreover, VVAW filled a leadership vacuum in the movement, a void created during the late 1960s with the collapse of several key antiwar coalitions. At its height, VVAW attracted between twenty-five thousand and thirty thousand members.

The Turning: A History of Vietnam Veterans Against the War traces the evolution of VVAW, from its inauspicious origins as a six-man speakers' bureau that began in New York City during the spring of 1967 to a mass movement that attracted thousands of veterans from all fifty states and Vietnam, sustained until the war's end by a massive breakdown of morale in the armed forces. Within VVAW's ranks were some of the most talented and perceptive organizers in the antiwar movement. Their protests contained elements of drama and creativity that were lacking in the mass marches and rallies of the period. Moreover, VVAW chapters across the country offered services, including group therapy and drug counseling, that predated similar Veterans Administration programs by nine years. Even as the men and women of VVAW won support from a growing number of veterans, they also stirred fears in the highest levels of government. Indeed, much of VVAW's story consists of protracted battles between the predominantly young, white male veterans, on the one hand, and the Nixon administration, the FBI, and various law enforcement agencies, on the other. Internally, the soul of VVAW became contested terrain between moderates and radicals, men and women, national officers and regional coordinators. Complicating matters were the numerous agents provocateurs within VVAW's ranks, many of whom advocated violent confrontations with police and other authorities.

This account also explores the changing relationship between VVAW and the antiwar movement. At first, demonstrators were either hostile or indifferent to the veterans. With the passage of time and the growth of VVAW, ill will gave way to veneration. Neither tendency, however, promoted a greater understanding of the veterans or their motives for resisting the war. To paraphrase the psychiatrist Dr. Robert Jay Lifton, VVAW-ers were neither "baby killers" nor the angry victims of an unjust policy. They were actors who fashioned their own histories, brought together by the common experience of service in the armed forces during the Vietnam era and a shared assumption that the Vietnam War was morally wrong. Some antiwar veterans arrived at this conclusion by reading books and underground newspapers, other by participating in combat operations. They were young—most were in their early twenties—and blended easily among countercultural youths. But VVAW members, by and large, were angrier and more abrasive than other protesters. Even at the height of the antiwar movement, the veterans complained that they were misunderstood by authorities and radicals alike.

An organization is only as intriguing as its constituents. Integral to VVAW's story are the numerous biographies of leaders and rank-and-file activists. Not all of their stories are included here. This narrative contains fragments of selected demonstrations, rap group sessions, national steering committee meetings, and acts of camaraderie and betrayal. The various war crimes hearings, medal-throwing ceremonies, guerrilla theater, and marches provided a much-needed human face to the "Vietnam syndrome." Still, it is important to remember that VVAW members were inexperienced activists who made countless mistakes and had few mentors to guide them. Impatience, uncompromising militance, and selfishness undoubtedly undermined VVAW's effectiveness on a number of occasions. Tensions were always palpable. National officers and regional coordinators were overburdened with unreasonable workloads, which often led to burnout. Joiners engaged in petty personal disputes with one another. Women were subordinated until VVAW's decline. Organizers missed opportunities to tap into new constituencies.

Still, VVAW grew steadily until 1973, and members came to see themselves as the inheritors of a legacy of radical resistance in the United States dating back to the American Revolution. The antiwar veterans, motivated in most cases by the carnage they had witnessed in Vietnam, sought to narrow the gap between the ideals and the reality of American society. Their search for redemption in a world beset by war is compelling because it teaches us the potential for political awakening among a segment of the population where one would least expect to find it. Those who built VVAW regarded their commitment as an extended tour of duty, a struggle to find meaning and compassion in the human experience.

1

The Highest Form of Patriotism

In the summer of 1967, J. Edgar Hoover, the aging director of the Federal Bureau of Investigation, received a memorandum from FBI field agents in New York City concerning the formation of a new organization, Vietnam Veterans Against the War (VVAW). The agents described it as a loose-knit, "non-membership organization" based at 17 East 17th Street in New York City.[1] As the group's name indicated, participants consisted of Vietnam veterans, thus amounting to "possibly the first antiwar group formed by veterans of an American war still being waged."[2] The impetus behind VVAW, Hoover was told, dated back to the spring of 1967. On April 15, 1967, a group of Vietnam veterans in New York City had marched from Central Park to the United Nations building in the massive Spring Mobilization demonstration against the Vietnam War. The ex-servicemen gathered with three-hundred thousand other people to hear the Reverend Dr. Martin Luther King Jr.'s impassioned speech condemning the Vietnam War. A month and a half after the protest, six of the veterans met in New York City to form VVAW. Field agents assured Hoover that the group would be the subject of "an instant case" to "determine whether the organization is a target for Communist infiltration."[3]

Hoover categorized the case as part of the bureau's sweeping Counter-Intelligence Program (COINTELPRO) investigation of New Left groups. Accordingly, agents collected information about the antiwar veterans and monitored their activities. A thorough, two-month investigation of VVAW resulted in a confidential, sixteen-page FBI memorandum, issued at the end of October, announcing that there was no "evidence that the [Communist Party] or any other subversive organization directs, dominates or controls the VVAW or that it has been a target for CP infiltration."[4] Agents concluded that the group had only one chief goal: to end the war in Vietnam. Still, perhaps sensing the potential damage that such a group could inflict, Hoover ordered agents to continue monitoring

VVAW. He was not convinced that just because the organization was not communist dominated, it did not constitute a threat.[5]

Tens of thousands of demonstrators began assembling in New York's Central Park on the chilly, overcast morning of April 15, 1967, for what was called "The Spring Mobilization to End the War in Vietnam." Under the close scrutiny of plainclothes police officers and the media, a crowd of young men, including a uniformed ex-Green Beret, gathered in the southeastern corner of the Sheep Meadow and burned two hundred draft cards, formally launching the draft resistance movement. Meanwhile, a steady stream of protesters continued to fill Central Park. By noon, they were ready to leave the park and follow a route through the streets of Manhattan to the United Nations building.[6]

An estimated three-hundred thousand people participated. Never before had such a large crowd met to protest the war. Two years earlier, the Students for a Democratic Society (SDS) had organized the first large-scale antiwar demonstration in Washington, which had attracted more than twenty thousand protesters. The Committee for a Sane Nuclear Policy (SANE) had sponsored a similar gathering in November 1965 that drew thirty thousand people. The peace movement had declined the following year. The biggest demonstration in 1966, the November mobilization, drew only fifteen thousand marchers in New York City. The Spring Mobilization, however, bolstered by Martin Luther King Jr.'s presence, revived the ailing peace movement.[7]

By all accounts, the gigantic crowd in Central Park was diverse. Marchers included housewives, grandparents, children, businessmen, high school teachers, priests, nuns, university professors, a small bridal party, African Americans, whites, Hispanics, and a Native American contingent. Young people seemed to be everywhere, some with long hair, others dressed conservatively. Local chapters of SANE, Women's Strike for Peace (WSP), and Clergy and Laymen Concerned (CALC) were represented. Planning for the demonstration began in the fall of 1966, and the huge crowd in Central Park exceeded the expectations of the organizers. "The mobilization was so vast and amorphous," wrote a Quaker demonstrator, "that one could get a host of different reports on it from as many different individuals."[8]

Hundreds of veterans, nearly all of World War II and Korean War vintage, gathered at the southern end of Central Park. The veterans, members of an organization called Veterans for Peace in Vietnam, carried signs bearing antiwar statements such as "Vets Demand Support the GIs, Bring Them Home Now!" and "Cease Fire Now! Negotiate with the NLF."[9]

Veterans had participated in earlier antiwar protests, but the large number at the Spring Mobilization was unprecedented. Just a few years earlier, antiwar veterans were rarely seen at demonstrations; prowar organizations, such as Veterans of Foreign Wars, attracted far more veterans than the fledgling antiwar protests. On October 30, 1965, more than twenty thousand people had marched down Fifth Avenue in a prowar parade sponsored by the New York City Council, the American Legion, and Veterans of Foreign Wars. The parade proved to be a somber event in which thousands of participants "counted to cadence" as they marched. The Johnson administration, encouraged by the protest, hoped that this and other prowar rallies would help solidify public support for the war. The administration later helped organize prowar parades, including one on May 16, 1967, which attracted more than twenty thousand enthusiastic demonstrators.[10]

When veterans took part in protests, their participation was usually isolated and minimally reported. In January 1966, fifty veterans from World War I, World War II, and the Korean Wars participated in a "Veterans March to End the War in Vietnam," at the Gettysburg Civil War battlefield, where they held a "speak-in." The earliest veterans' group to call for peace in Vietnam was the Ad Hoc Committee of Veterans for Peace in Vietnam, which ran a full-page ad in the November 24, 1965, *New York Times*, endorsing the November 27 antiwar march in Washington. When President Johnson ordered the resumption of the bombing of North Vietnam on February 1, 1966, following a temporary pause, the Ad Hoc Committee staged a demonstration that drew seventy-five veterans. Approximately one hundred veterans from various wars returned their medals and discharge papers to President Johnson on February 5 in protest against the war. During the summer of 1966, a small organization known as Veterans and Reservists Against the War, based primarily in New York, organized a march from Valley Forge, Pennsylvania, to Washington, D.C., that attracted some forty people. The march received little media attention.[11]

These early veterans' protests paralleled similar, though more highly publicized, actions within the military. At a time when the antiwar movement was still in its infancy, dissent within the armed forces was isolated and risky, often carrying penalties of dishonorable discharges and imprisonment. In November 1965, Lieutenant Henry Howe was arrested and later court-martialed for attending an antiwar protest at Texas Western College. The following year, three soldiers fresh from basic training at Fort Hood, Texas, refused to serve in Vietnam. The Fort Hood Three, as they came to be known, declared, "We want no part of a war of extermination."[12] The three privates announced their plans to file a lawsuit challenging their orders on the grounds that the war was illegal. The actions of the Fort Hood Three attracted journalists, as well as federal agents. The government launched an all-out campaign of harassment against the men and eventually imprisoned them in the Fort Dix, New Jersey, stockade. The Fort Hood Three were court-martialed and jailed for two years. Yet their determination in the face of adversity inspired antiwar activists to organize rallies from New York to Berkeley. In October 1966, army doctor Captain Howard Levy was similarly court-martialed in a much publicized case for refusing to go to Vietnam to train Green Beret (U.S. Army Special Forces) medics. Military and government officials were beginning to realize that such cases attracted considerable media attention and provided inspiration for the growing antiwar movement.[13]

Antiwar Vietnam veterans were difficult to find in the mid-sixties. Like most Americans, veterans strongly supported the president's policy in Vietnam. Those who questioned the war remained cautious. Many were subject to recall for six years after joining the military and feared retaliation for resisting publicly. They sought examples of ex-soldiers who returned from Vietnam and became outspoken opponents of the war. One of the first and most influential Vietnam veterans to embrace antiwar activism was Donald Duncan. In September 1965, Duncan resigned from the United States Army to devote his energy to the peace movement. Duncan had an impeccable record as a soldier. His decade-long career in the army included eighteen months in Vietnam in the elite Green Berets and four medals for bravery. But, in March 1965, Duncan refused a field promotion to captain, and, in September, while under consideration for the Silver Star and the Legion of Merit (the first enlisted man in Vietnam to be nominated for the Legion of Merit), he resigned from the army. On returning to civilian life, Duncan joined the effort to end the war in Vietnam.[14]

Duncan used his unique status as an ex-Green Beret to legitimize his resistance to the Vietnam War. A few months after Duncan resigned from the army, *Ramparts* magazine, the Berkeley-based leftist monthly, named him its military editor. Duncan appeared on the cover of the February

1966 issue in full dress uniform, with a green beret crowning his head. Ironically, he bore a striking resemblance to Sergeant Barry Sadler, whose single "The Ballad of the Green Berets" was a big hit in 1966. In a piece he wrote for *Ramparts*, Duncan presented a thoughtful indictment of U.S. involvement in Vietnam, based on his experiences. He wrote of Special Forces officers murdering Vietnamese prisoners, documented racist attitudes within the U.S. military toward South Vietnamese allies, drew attention the growing support for Viet Cong guerrillas among peasants, and described the pain of watching his buddies die for a futile cause. "The whole thing was a lie," he concluded. "It's not democracy we brought to Vietnam—it's anticommunism. . . . Anticommunism is a lousy substitute for democracy."[15]

In addition to his duties as military editor of *Ramparts*, Duncan became a full-time activist, touring the country, spreading the antiwar gospel at protests, debates, college campuses, fairs, and Veterans' Day parades and on radio and television programs. His actions, including a series of articles he wrote for the *New York Times*, attracted media attention. The activist David Dellinger wrote that he was "inspired" by Duncan's "heroism" and "courageous patriotism."[16] Meanwhile, the growing antiwar spirit among the nation's youth encouraged Duncan. "When I returned from Vietnam I was asked, 'Do you resent young people who have never been in Vietnam, or any war, protesting it?'" Duncan wrote at the time. "On the contrary, I am relieved. I think they should be commended."[17]

Other veterans joined the antiwar movement. On January 28, 1966, a group of veterans, mostly of World War II, gathered in Chicago and formally founded Veterans for Peace in Vietnam. The idea behind Vets for Peace originated at the November 27, 1965, antiwar march in Washington, where the World War II veteran Ed Bloch, wearing a faded Marine Corps uniform with a bronze star and purple heart, led a contingent of protesting veterans. "No one is better qualified than veterans to make the public aware that it is patriotic to oppose the war in Vietnam," declared the members of the new organization.[18] In the group's first show of strength later that month, several hundred veterans of the Korean War and the two world wars led an antiwar parade of more than twenty thousand demonstrators. The organization expanded rapidly, and, within two years, it boasted thriving chapters across the country and scores of members. The ranks of Vets for Peace consisted mostly of World War II and Korean War veterans, with relatively few Vietnam veterans joining.[19]

By 1967, Veterans for Peace published its own newspaper, *Veterans Stars and Stripes for Peace*, a slick publication aimed at veterans and GIs. Veterans for Peace members kept busy. They organized rigorously, recruiting new members everywhere and attracting an impressive list of high-ranking officers, including retired Rear Admiral Arnold E. True of the United States Navy and retired U.S. Army General Hugh B. Hester. In spring 1966, Vets for Peace joined the Fifth Avenue Peace Parade Committee, the largest antiwar coalition in New York City. The blue Veterans for Peace garrison caps and "Vets for Peace" signs became familiar and increasingly widespread at demonstrations. Even the most pugnacious hawkish hecklers backed off when crowds of Veterans for Peace members, with their aging war uniforms and numerous medals, marched past. Like Donald Duncan, Veterans for Peace members used militaristic symbols (uniforms, arm stripes, medals, Armed Forces–style Vets for Peace caps, the title of their newspaper) to reinforce their opposition to the Vietnam war. Moreover, Veterans for Peace provided cohesion for vets of varied political shades. Members ran the gamut, according to the *Veterans Stars and Stripes for Peace* editor Donald Mosby, from "card-carrying communists" to "ultraconservatives."[20]

When Veterans for Peace officers learned of plans for the April 15 Spring Mobilization, they placed advertisements in the *New York Times* encouraging veterans to attend. It was expected to be the largest antiwar protest ever. The evening before the event, an activist created a banner with bold letters that proclaimed, "VIETNAM VETERANS AGAINST THE WAR!" The following morning, organizers rushed the banner to the Veterans for Peace members, hoping that Vietnam veterans would show up at the protest.[21]

Some did. One Vietnam veteran who went to the demonstration was twenty-four-year-old Jan Barry,* who had dropped out of West Point in 1965 because of concerns about a war that "made no sense whatsoever." Barry was working as a free-lance journalist and employee of the New York Public Library at the time of the Spring Mobilization. A few weeks before the protest, he overheard some of his fellow employees at the library, mostly students, discussing an upcoming antiwar march. The young veteran was troubled by nagging doubts about whether he should participate. While opposed to the war, Barry was not certain whether he was "prepared to go join whatever this crazy stuff was that was 'the peace

---

*Jan Barry has also used the names Jan Crumb and Jan Barry Crumb.

movement.'" He changed his mind after he saw a sarcastic Veterans for Peace advertisement in the *New York Times* inviting veterans to the demonstration. The ad featured a quotation from President Lyndon Johnson that declared, "The bombing will end when the other side is ready to take equivalent action." Beneath the president's quote, Veterans for Peace announced, "We appeal to North Vietnam, if they really want peace, to stop bombing the United States, or else get the hell out of Vietnam." Barry was impressed. "I thought, 'I like that way of turning the rhetoric around and the imagery around and making you have to think about who's doing what to whom.'"[22]

The idea of meeting other antiwar veterans excited Barry, so he went to Central Park. When he arrived, he found himself overwhelmed by the massive crowd and a sea of signs. Barry reached the Veterans for Peace contingent when a voice called out, "Vietnam veterans, go to the front!" A few minutes after noon, a small group of veterans carrying the banner "Vietnam Veterans Against the War!" walked out of Central Park toward the UN building. Barry felt "naked" being toward the front of such a huge march, like a forward observer in Vietnam. But along the route, he realized the impact of the veterans' participation. Right-wing counter-demonstrators who had screamed at dignitaries leading the march quickly quieted down when they saw signs indicating that among the marchers were veterans. The veterans dispersed before Martin Luther King Jr. delivered his speech at the UN Plaza, leaving a disappointed Barry with "no idea who they were, where they went to or where they came from."[23]

Barry had reservations about joining Veterans for Peace. Following the April 15 protest, he attended the organization's meetings. He also went to Veterans for Peace demonstrations in Philadelphia and Washington. Yet he could find no other Vietnam veterans in Veterans for Peace. Barry decided to concentrate his efforts on forming a new organization, which displeased Vets for Peace members in the New York City area. The Veterans for Peace "would have preferred that we stay under their umbrella," Barry recalled. "But I felt that we would be losing that direct ability for us to say, 'We've been there. This is the experience.'"[24]

Barry spent the next several weeks contacting other veterans, following up on leads, writing letters, making telephone calls. On June 1, 1967, he and five other veterans met in downtown New York City and formally established "Vietnam Veterans Against the War." What transformed Jan Barry, a Vietnam veteran and former West Point student, into a dedicated antiwar activist? His odyssey had begun four and a half years earlier, in the jungles of Vietnam.

Jan Barry joined his unit in Nha Trang on Christmas Eve of 1962. Located on the coast of the South China Sea in Khanh Hoa Province in II Corps, Nha Trang had once been an exclusive French resort. When Barry stepped from the prop plane that had brought him from Saigon to Nha Trang, he found himself standing in the middle of a small, crude base camp. The area appeared to be deserted until the drunken commander of quarters (CQ), the guard for the entire base, drove up to Barry in a jeep. The CQ instructed him to change into civilian clothes, and the two men rode bicycles into town and went bar-hopping until Barry was abandoned by his erstwhile host. In the early hours of the morning, Barry found his way back to base camp. He awoke in a room full of drunken men. "That was my introduction to the war."[25]

Barry was born in Ithaca, New York, on January 26, 1943. Shortly thereafter, his father, an automobile mechanic, moved the family to Interlaken, "a cowtown outside Ithaca where everyone votes Republican."[26] Barry's boyhood fascination with the military led to his teenage ambition to attend West Point. "I had grown up on all the World War II stories of my family," Barry remembered, "plus those of my teachers, plus those of the society at large."[27] Failing to get a civilian appointment to West Point, he joined the army in May 1962. When Barry completed radio school, he opted to be sent to Vietnam at a friend's prompting. "You get combat pay in addition to overseas pay. You can really clean up," the acquaintance reported.[28]

At Nha Trang, Barry maintained radio and navigation equipment for a unit of planes that linked Vietnam with Thailand and flew personnel and supplies to all the Special Forces and Military Assistance Advisory Group Vietnam outposts. In late 1962 and 1963, Barry later observed, "the entire contingent of Americans in Vietnam was so thinly spread out that there probably weren't more than five hundred in any one place."[29] When he reached Nha Trang on Christmas Eve of 1962, there were approximately eleven thousand U.S. advisory and support troops in Vietnam, including twenty-nine Special Forces detachments.[30]

Little time passed before Barry concluded "*we* were the war."[31] He felt that he was "being had," and he quickly developed "more of an affinity with the Vietnamese people than with Americans."[32] He could not help comparing the U.S. presence in Vietnam to "the British imperial army in India." Over time, he became acquainted with the servants who "kept our little hooches spick-and-span," the students who feared for their lives because "they knew . . . that the Saigon government was a police state," America's "nasty allies" in the South Vietnamese Army, and the history of a people who were used to "seeing armies come and go."[33] The time he spent in Nha Trang amounted to "an education in colonial military policy."[34]

Before leaving Vietnam, Barry witnessed an event he would never forget. While strolling through the streets of Nha Trang in May 1963, Barry observed a crowd of demonstrators carrying banners. The march was the first in a series of Buddhist protests in Nha Trang that he saw, but not the last. Other marches occurred throughout the summer, and Barry found himself appalled that the Saigon government "would turn loose tanks and machine guns and barbed wire all over the country."[35]

Barry came home in the fall of 1963 upon completion of his tour. His "focus still remained on getting into West Point." In the spring of 1964, despite some second thoughts, he learned that he had been accepted, the first student to arrive at the institution who had been in Vietnam. He enrolled in courses shortly after the Tonkin Gulf incident of August 1964, in which North Vietnamese torpedo boats allegedly attacked, without provocation, American vessels patrolling international waters. Following the attack, Congress approved the so-called Tonkin Gulf Resolution, which enabled President Lyndon Johnson to escalate steadily the American presence in Southeast Asia.

The president ordered air strikes against North Vietnam in February 1965. On March 8, two Marine battalions landed on the shores of Danang to protect the giant U.S. air complex there. Disgusted by this turn of events, Barry dropped out of West Point in 1965 and found himself among "people [who] did not want to know" and "did not want to discuss" what was happening in Vietnam. He became a journalist for a few years, then went to work at the New York Public Library. Though deeply troubled by the war in the mid-1960s, Barry "couldn't imagine myself going out there, marching through the streets, making a fool of myself." His attitude changed after he marched alongside the Veterans for Peace at the Spring Mobilization.[36]

After the April 15 demonstration, Barry "asked everybody I would run into, 'Do you know a Vietnam veteran?' Then I would contact that person."[37] He began collecting signatures from antiwar Vietnam veterans to place on a statement that would later appear, in a slightly different form, in the *New York Times*. The statement declared:

> We believe that the conflict in which the United States is engaged in Vietnam is wrong, unjustifiable and contrary to the principles on which this country was founded. We join the dissent of the millions of Americans against this war. We support our buddies still in Vietnam. We want them home alive. We want them home now. We want to prevent any other young men from being sent to Vietnam. We want to end the war now. We believe this is the highest form of patriotism.[38]

The statement proved to be a starting point for the Vietnam Veterans Against the War. "Being very legalistic and formalistic in those days, we drafted bylaws and had an actual formation meeting on June first," Barry recalled. Six people, including Barry, attended the meeting. "But there were other people signed up on the statement and willing to do something in forming some kind of organization." The veterans created a group with perfunctory bylaws and a small bureaucracy. Membership criteria were simply drawn: Those who had "served in Indochina as a member of the armed forces of the United States, regardless of rank or branch of service," and had indicated opposition "to the involvement of the United States in military action of any kind in Indochina" were eligible. Members unanimously elected Jan Barry president.[39]

VVAW, like Donald Duncan and the Veterans for Peace, transformed war symbols into peace symbols. One of Barry's first acts as president was to design an insignia for VVAW that strongly resembled that used by Military Assistance Command Vietnam (MACV). Unlike MACV's upturned sword, however, Barry created an upside-down rifle with a G.I. helmet hanging on the butt. The insignia conveyed a powerful image of betrayal in a war regarded as unjust.

For his part, Barry continued to collect names of antiwar Vietnam veterans. The process involved a great deal of detective work and resulted in numerous dead ends. But there were exceptions. When the twenty-four-year-old Vietnam veteran Carl Rogers, fresh out of the army, held a press conference announcing his opposition to the war, Barry telephoned him immediately. The two hit it off at once, and Barry convinced Rogers to join VVAW. Eventually, Rogers would serve as the organization's vice president.[40]

Rogers became an effective spokesman. His outgoing personality, All-American Boy Scout looks, and simple eloquence generated widespread publicity for VVAW. A devout Christian from conservative small-town Ohio, Rogers took pride in his church activities and the numerous awards he had received as a square dance caller. In Vietnam, Army Specialist Fourth Class Carl Rogers had been a chaplain's assistant, with the 1st Logistical Command at Cam Ranh Bay. In Vietnam, he met countless soldiers, listened to their stories about the ravages of war, and eventually concluded that the Vietnam war was immoral. One evening, Rogers taped a poignant and reflective "living letter" that he sent to the Central Presbyterian Church in New York City, where he taught Sunday school. Rogers told his fellow Presbyterians that he was most disturbed by the concept of the "kill ratio" in Vietnam.

> The figures we receive are often distorted and not accurate, but even so, the emphasis, you see, is on the number of men that we're killing each day. And it's thought of in terms of . . . well, how can you say it? . . . like going out on a hunt and getting your quota of lions or whatever it may be.[41]

Upon his return to the United States, Rogers went straight to the peace movement: "I wanted to do whatever I could to end this war." Publicity always seemed to follow the young veteran. "Rogers, who could step tomorrow into a Wheaties ad (he wears a crew-cut and teaches Sunday school at New York's Presbyterian Church) has been in the news since his return from Vietnam," observed *Commonweal* magazine in 1967.[42] He marched alongside Martin Luther King Jr., appeared on numerous radio and television programs, and became the subject of feature stories in the *New York Post*, the *New York Times Sunday Times Magazine*, *Redbook*, and *Eye*, a magazine oriented toward the nation's youth. So impressed was VVAW with its new young star that it published a handsome brochure about him and distributed it to the media and to various organizations.[43]

Together, Barry and Rogers provided dynamic leadership. "Jan was a writer and a poet," recalled Sheldon Ramsdell, a founder of VVAW. "Carl was a real wizard at public relations. He could organize a press conference in half a second. Jan was the articulate intellectual, always referring to Tom Paine and Thoreau." Ramsdell, a photographer, had been stationed with the navy off the coast of Vietnam, monitoring the movements of Communist guerrillas. Like Barry, he developed doubts about the war before the deployment of large numbers of U.S. troops. In the mid-1990s, battling the debilitating effects of AIDS, an ailing Ramsdell remembered the early months of VVAW as an exciting period. "It was a thrilling time to be alive."[44]

Despite the charged atmosphere in New York, VVAW organizers faced difficult challenges. In Vietnam, the war dragged on through 1967, with no end in sight. With each passing month, the Johnson administration deployed more U.S. troops. During 1966, the United States increased its forces in Vietnam from 180,000 to 280,000, with an additional sixty thousand American servicemen aboard ships operating off the coast. In early 1967, the U.S. contingent jumped to 380,000. By the end of the year, half a million U.S. troops were stationed in Vietnam. Many antiwar activists were discouraged that large-scale protests such as the Spring Mobilization seemed to have had little or no effect on the Johnson administration. During the summer, many activists devoted themselves to projects such as Vietnam Summer and the Student Mobilization Committee, but burnout often followed. Doug Dowd, cofounder of the National Mobilization Committee to End the War in Vietnam, recalled that many activists suffered from "quick disillusionment." He added: "In the United States we've got such a screwy notion of what constitutes success. For one thing, success has got to be dramatic and quick and so on. We don't see success as making progress toward something."[45]

Having served in Vietnam, VVAW members plunged into the antiwar movement with a strong sense of urgency and purpose. On October 21, a small group of VVAW activists joined a crowd of two thousand veterans from World Wars I and II, the Spanish Civil War, and the Korean War at a huge protest in Washington, D.C. They listened to speeches by Dave Dellinger and Dr. Benjamin Spock before marching from the Lincoln Memorial, across the Memorial Bridge, to the Pentagon. The VVAW and Veterans for Peace marched together in military formation, careful to avoid confrontation with the civil or military police. At the Pentagon, while army sharpshooters waited nervously, military brass and Secretary of Defense Robert McNamara watched the marchers funnel into the parking lot.[46]

The press paid little attention to the antiwar veterans. If Martin Luther King Jr. had overshadowed the veterans at the Spring Mobilization, this time their efforts were obscured by young militants, particularly Abbie Hoffman, a former Student Nonviolent Coordinating Committee volunteer. Hoffman's flamboyance was seldom overlooked by journalists and television cameras; before the protest, he had announced his plans to levitate the Pentagon into the heavens. During the demonstration, shouting by protesters escalated into violent confrontations, and the police began clubbing protesters. By the time the crowd cleared, the militants had grabbed the spotlight, while the antiwar Vietnam veterans were largely ignored.[47]

The veterans persisted in their efforts. Jan Barry's drive to collect signatures from Vietnam veterans and raise funds resulted in a full-page advertisement in the *New York Times*. The ad, originally scheduled for Veterans' Day, was inexplicably delayed until November 19. "VIET-NAM VETERANS SPEAK OUT," announced the headline at the top of the advertisement. "We are veterans of the Viet-Nam war. We believe that this 'conflict' in which our country is now engaged is wrong, unjustifiable and contrary to the principle of self-determination on which this nation was founded."[48] The advertisement further outlined the principles of VVAW, all of which emphasized the right of the Vietnamese to self-determination, and listed the names of sixty-five Vietnam veterans, including Donald Duncan. After the ad appeared, bundles of mail swamped VVAW's post office box, membership lists swelled, calls came in from newspapers and radio and television stations.[49]

One telephone caller was Senator Ernest Gruening, the maverick Democratic senator from Alaska. Gruening, one of the earliest congressional critics of American involvement in Vietnam, had won the applause of dissidents when he, along with Senator Wayne Morse of Oregon, voted against the Tonkin Gulf Resolution in 1964. Three years later, Gruening congratulated VVAW on a job well done and invited Carl Rogers and Sheldon Ramsdell to his Washington office. The senator told the two young veterans of his efforts to persuade Senator J. William Fulbright, chair of the Senate Foreign Relations Committee, to meet with VVAW members and to invite them to testify at future Senate hearings. Rogers and Ramsdell left the senator's office with an important ally. But Senator Fulbright would have nothing to do with VVAW members, fearing any association with the group would undermine his credibility.[50]

The *New York Times* advertisement also had an impact at the highest levels of government. The day the ad appeared, Secretary of Defense Robert McNamara, chief architect of American intervention in Southeast Asia under Presidents Kennedy and Johnson, saw it and "became very incensed."[51] He telephoned the FBI and demanded an expeditious investigation of "40 to 50 of the signers," requesting that all "background data" be sent to him via "special courier."[52] The following morning, McNamara discussed the matter with President Johnson. Meanwhile, the FBI investigated the signers. The next month, J. Edgar Hoover personally couriered the background checks to McNamara's office.[53] McNamara's assistant, William C. Hunt, responded by expressing "great appreciation" for Hoover's "efforts."[54]

In the months that followed its creation, VVAW remained an organization in search of an identity. Its purpose, to end the war in Vietnam, was never in question. The most effective means of ending the war, however, was an issue with which early members ceaselessly grappled. Would it be better to concentrate efforts on the national or local level? Should local chapters be autonomous? Would it be wise to maintain a decentralized national office? What would be the most effective way to reach out to new veterans? Should the focus be on demonstrations or media exposure?

The young activists hoped their advertisement in the *New York Times*, coupled with new offices at 17 East 17th Street in downtown New York City, would enable VVAW to establish contacts with veterans, not just in the New York area but around the country. They believed such links would foster mutual assistance and support between VVAW and other groups and individuals. But, unlike large-scale organizations such as SDS and the Socialist Workers Party, early VVAW members had little desire to build a nationwide mass movement. Francis R. Rocks, a former soldier and the first secretary-treasurer of VVAW, announced the group's plans:

> We do not envision ourselves or intend to become a national organization. We feel that, at this stage anyhow, the impetus should be at the local level—Vietnam vets working to influence and educate people in their own area. Hopefully, we can provide an overall coordination for this.[55]

Rocks, echoing the opinions of most VVAW members, conceived of the organization as "a coordinating body and clearinghouse, based in New York, for actions by antiwar Vietnam veterans across the country." The purpose of the national office, he added, was to set "general guidelines, plans and sponsors area, regional and national actions, and aids in setting up local groups of Viet-Nam vets against the war."[56]

VVAW activists understood the challenges of convincing veterans to join an antiwar organization. "A veteran, after two years of organization, doesn't want to be part of any organization again. He doesn't want to subject himself to ideology anymore," conceded Nick Friedman, who linked up with VVAW shortly after returning from Vietnam.[57] Jan Barry,

Carl Rogers, and Sheldon Ramsdell encountered many veterans who harbored strong doubts about U.S. involvement in Vietnam, yet seemed reluctant to join VVAW. Some were pessimistic about the prospect of collective action, while others remained too upset to focus on their experiences in Vietnam. Several veterans wandered in and out of VVAW's headquarters before completely disappearing. Angry and suspicious of all authority, these men were not about to pay dues to any organization. Barry remained keenly aware of this:

> These were people who felt they had a perfect right to just stand up in Times Square or wherever and say what they thought about the world and they didn't need an organization to do it for them. And so I spent a great deal of time convincing people with that kind of attitude toward the world that we could be even more effective as an organization. But not everybody accepted that. Some people would drop out very quickly and go do their own thing.[58]

With so many obstacles to building a strong local VVAW, organizing nationally appeared impossible. In most American cities, Veterans for Peace would continue to be, for the next few years, the only viable organization for antiwar veterans. VVAW did form chapters in Alabama, California, Ohio, and Oregon during its early months. Energetic student-veterans organized similar antiwar groups at the University of Indiana, the University of Texas, and Columbia University. Many of the early New York area members were Columbia University students. In Los Angeles, veterans under the capable leadership of the Vietnam veteran Jim Boggio formed a thriving and highly visible chapter.[59]

Still, organizing a VVAW chapter in 1967 and 1968 was a lonely and often unrewarding activity. In February 1968, William Crandell joined VVAW after seeing an ad in the *New Republic* similar to the one printed in the *New York Times*. Crandell had served as an infantry lieutenant in the Americal Division and then returned home still a supporter of the war. He "believed in the war" until General William Westmoreland declared the bloody Tet Offensive a "great American victory."[60] After seeing the VVAW ad, Crandell took action. "I wrote in and another guy from the . . . midwest wrote in," he later remembered, "and we were the two members of the entire midwest VVAW. The 'coordinators for the midwest' was the title. And we essentially could do whatever seemed appropriate, which, for a couple years, was largely writing and giving speeches and taking part in a few demonstrations, reading the names of the dead." Membership lists grew slowly. Crandell communicated with prospective members throughout the Midwest, but he never created a formal organization in 1968 because he "hoped that ending the war would not take that long."[61]

Crandell and other early VVAW members tended to be moderate politically, and most felt ambivalent about the antiwar movement, particularly with regard to the younger militants. "I don't want radical change," declared Dave Braum, an ex-helicopter crew chief who became VVAW's treasurer in 1967 and appeared on the *David Susskind Show* with Carl Rogers. "I'm against all political extremes because they don't leave a back door to walk out of. Yes, the military industrial complex is a natural outgrowth of unchecked free enterprise, and at this point it's running rampant. But with the proper controls, it could be a good thing." Braum went on to attack the "radical and irresponsible elements who were receiving the bulk of publicity." Braum was not the only VVAW member reluctant to embrace the radical left in 1967.[62] Sheldon Ramsdell, too, felt uncomfortable at many antiwar demonstrations. "I was a conservative Republican who happened to be opposed to the war," he later remembered.[63] "I don't have a political line," announced Jan Barry at the time. "What seems to be the cement in the peace movement is the radical left, but the radical left also sets up barriers between the movement and other people."[64]

Like his "brothers" in the movement, Carl Rogers distanced himself from the militants. In the fall of 1967, Rogers went to work full time as a publicist for Negotiations Now, an organization of prominent liberals who urged the Johnson administration to stop bombing North Vietnam and to negotiate a "reasonable" peace settlement with Hanoi and the National Liberation Front (NLF). Negotiations Now circulated petitions, hoping to collect one million signatures for its cause. Its roster included such prominent names as Victor Reuther of the United Automobile Workers, University of California President Clark Kerr, presidential adviser Joseph Rauh, the economist John Kenneth Galbraith, and the historian Arthur Schlesinger Jr. Rogers joined the staff of Negotiations Now hoping, as he put it at the time, to appeal to people with centrist political beliefs. "Negotiations Now is the most realistic organization I know for reaching the uncommitted millions who are concerned about the war, but don't think they can identify with the peace movement any more than they can with the hawks," he declared.[65] Rogers later admitted that he had some regrets about working for Negotiations Now. He found the politics of the organization too moderate, its sense of purpose watered down. "I wish I would've worked more closely with people like [prominent and more radical antiwar intellectuals] Noam Chomsky and Howard Zinn," Rogers recounted.[66]

Rogers and most of his fellow antiwar veterans not only distanced themselves from radicals politically but also rejected the countercultural fashions of the era. When they appeared at debates or interviews or on TV shows, VVAW representatives usually wore short hair and dressed in suits and ties. They had no desire to experiment with drugs or carry NLF flags. Street battles with police and civil disobedience appealed little to them. "I prefer to work within the system," said Dave Braum, "to vote out people who can't work with reality and elect those who can."[67] One VVAW member from Maine who "wasn't ready for political activism" avoided the militants and marched through the streets of Washington "with the middle-class types, the families and the well-dressed."[68]

To be sure, the antiwar movement contained a fair number of zealots. On more than one occasion, Vietnam veterans who spoke against the war encountered choruses of boos and jeers. "There were many in the antiwar movement who dismissed us initially as baby killers, and they didn't think we had any redemption and should not belong to anything they were espousing," one early VVAW member recalled.[69] Jan Barry added: "In the early days, the peace movement had great contempt toward GIs and I kept trying to say to them, 'These guys might agree with you if you'd listen to them, if you'd stop calling them baby killers.'"[70] Still, for years older antiwar leaders such as David Dellinger, Sid Peck, Norma Becker, and Fred Halstead had understood the importance of making GIs and veterans feel welcome within the movement. "In a sensible world," Dellinger wrote in 1966, "it would be obvious that there is a natural alliance of sympathy and common interest between the men whose lives and limbs are threatened in a dishonest and unnecessary war and those who are trying to bring that war to an end."[71]

VVAW activists usually encountered more bitter hostility from war supporters and veterans. In the fall of 1967, a VVAW member, Robert Armstrong, contacted every Vietnam veteran attending the University of Oregon with the hope of organizing an antiwar veterans' group. "At the first meeting I realized what I had done," Armstrong later wrote. "My dovish soul had flown into a cage of hawks. I honestly thought these guys would have seen the light, but apparently twelve months of Uncle Sam's red, white and bluism has them thoroughly convinced the slaughter is necessary."[72] The antiwar veterans often touched a raw nerve in the war's supporters. An ex-G.I. who participated in a radio call-in program fielded a barrage of negative comments, including a listener who likened him to Benedict Arnold. The shaken youth returned home to find a note from his father: "Your kind isn't wanted around here."[73]

One evening late in 1967, a blizzard shut down the airport at Fargo, North Dakota. One of the passengers stranded at the airport was Thich Nhat Hanh. In Vietnam, Hanh was a highly respected Buddhist intellectual. He had come to the United States in 1961 and had studied comparative religion at Princeton and taught at Columbia. His pacifist beliefs, coupled with his advocacy of negotiations and "peace," resulted in the South Vietnamese government's issuing an edict in 1966 prohibiting Hanh's return to Vietnam. He went into exile in Paris, writing books and articles, including *Vietnam: Lotus in a Sea of Fire*, and expressing his opposition the war. A speaking tour of the United States toward the end of 1967 brought him to university campuses across the country, including a small college in Moorhead, North Dakota.[74]

At the snowed-in Fargo airport, Thich Nhat Hanh granted an interview to Mike McKusker, an Associated Press reporter. For a long while, the eloquent Buddhist answered questions about his writings, plans, and activism. The discussion turned to the Vietnam War. It was a subject with which McKusker, a Vietnam veteran, was well acquainted. McKusker had been an award-winning combat reporter and photographer with the 1st Marine Division in I Corps in Vietnam in 1966 and 1967. While talking to Hanh, McKusker began to recall his experiences in Vietnam. "I wound up talking with him, spilling my soul out to him, really," McKusker remembered. McKusker and Hanh walked up and down the airport concourse several times while plows attempted to clear the runway. McKusker revealed the troubling things he had witnessed in Vietnam, while the Buddhist, dressed in a saffron robe and McKusker's jacket, listened intently. "I liked him instantly. He was the only priest I've ever confessed my war sins to," McKusker said. Before the two parted ways, Hanh pulled out a book of his poems and gave it to McKusker.[75]

McKusker was already on thin ice back at the AP bureau, where nervous editors felt he devoted too much attention to the antiwar movement. When McKusker's story on Thich Nhat Hanh went out over the wire, the reporter received an angry call from his editor, who fired him. McKusker then took a job with the *Today Show* in New York in January 1968. He also contacted Jan Barry and Carl Rogers, two names he had discovered while still in Fargo, and told them he wanted to join VVAW. "We didn't have very many people in the organization," McKusker recalled, "but we always had enough to show up at the demonstrations."[76]

The demands of the antiwar movement in New York afforded little rest. McKusker spent much of his spare time with his VVAW comrades, organizing rallies and speaking engagements. In February 1968, VVAW moved to larger offices on the sixth floor of 156 Fifth Avenue. The national office strongly encouraged members to write letters about their experiences in Vietnam to Senator Fulbright, and many did; yet Fulbright continued to ignore them. At demonstrations, VVAW members distributed copies of the recently launched newspaper *Vietnam GI*. The creation of Vietnam veteran Jeff Sharlet, the first issue of *Vietnam GI* appeared in January 1968. Its articles and editorials focused primarily on GI resistance and on the war itself, while largely ignoring veterans' issues. *Vietnam GI* soon became the most influential GI newspaper in the country, and Sharlet accumulated a mailing list of thousands of G.I.s in Vietnam.[77]

Jeff Sharlet worked "an endless succession of 18-hour days" putting together *Vietnam GI*.[78] Like other veterans, his opposition to the war grew from his experiences in Vietnam. In 1963, Sharlet went to Vietnam as a Vietnamese language translator-interpreter, assigned to the Army Security Agency. He spent most of his time monitoring, decoding, and translating North Vietnamese radio messages. He also had an opportunity to speak to Vietnamese peasants and students and gradually turned against the U.S. presence in Vietnam. Upon returning home, he went to Indiana University, where he joined the local chapter of Students for a Democratic Society. He also joined Vietnam Veterans Against the War during the summer of 1967 and used the money from his prestigious Woodrow Wilson Fellowship to launch *Vietnam GI*. An acquaintance of Sharlet's described his politics as close to that of the "SDS milieu."[79]

Vietnam GI appeared at a time when more veterans were gravitating toward the antiwar movement. The Tet Offensive had resulted in a series of gory battles that lasted into early March, with terrible casualties on both sides. Antiwar veterans, well versed in the facts and history of the war, were invited to attend debates. "While VVAW was very small in the beginning," recalled Barry, "we could go out there and debate the State Department, on their own turf and we could debate people the Pentagon sent out."[80]

Carl Rogers, in the meantime, met with his friend Allard Lowenstein, head of the "Dump Johnson" campaign and the driving force behind

Senator Eugene McCarthy's decision to enter the 1968 presidential campaign. McCarthy had officially announced his intention to run for president on November 30, 1967, and he won widespread support among young, liberal activists, men and women who, according to one McCarthy speech writer, "reacted against the violent anti-Americanism of the New Left, whom they far outnumbered."[81] Rogers, with Lowenstein's support, founded Vietnam Veterans for McCarthy and immediately went to work. Both activists believed that a McCarthy victory in November offered the best hope of bringing a quick end to the war in Vietnam. Rogers rallied support for McCarthy among his antiwar veterans.[82]

With the New Hampshire primaries just weeks away, Rogers and a group of other Vietnam veterans joined thousands of young activists who flooded the state in February to work on McCarthy's campaign. "There have been estimates that as many as 2,000 students were campaigning full time in New Hampshire in the ten days before the election," McCarthy later wrote, "and that as many as 5,000 joined the effort on the weekends."[83] Rogers remained highly visible, walking around Manchester with a large sign that read, "I'm a Vietnam veteran. I'm for McCarthy. Ask me why."[84] Repeated attempts by the Johnson administration to smear young McCarthy supporters as "communists" failed. In fact, locals treated the Vietnam veterans with glowing reverence. Recalled one Vietnam veteran who volunteered for the campaign: "In Manchester, women my mother's age were concerned about us and kept bringing us hot soup and coffee. In Portsmouth I received several invitations for dinner."[85]

Pro-Johnson Democrats in New Hampshire nervously watched the heated primary race unfolding. They placed advertisements in newspapers across the state warning that "the communists in Vietnam are watching the New Hampshire primary. . . . They are hoping for a divided America. Don't vote for fuzzy thinking and surrendering. Support our fighting men . . . by writing in the name of President Johnson."[86] Rogers was so angered by the pro-Johnson campaign that he collected signatures from more than a hundred Vietnam veterans and placed them on an advertisement reminiscent of Barry's original VVAW ad. "VIET-NAM VETERANS SPEAK OUT," declared bold letters at the top of the ad, then below: "Viet-Nam Veterans for McCarthy." "We . . . endorse the candidacy of Senator Eugene McCarthy in the belief that he is the man most able to lead the country out of war in Viet-Nam and to unite the country to meet the challenges at home." The advertisement featured the names of the top VVAW leaders, including Jan Barry, Dave Braum and Sheldon Ramsdell.[87]

On March 12, Johnson's write-in campaign defeated McCarthy by a mere 230 votes, a gap so narrow that Johnson considered New Hampshire a defeat. McCarthy's near-victory encouraged his followers and, on a broader level, signified a victory for the peace movement. Other VVAW activists turned their energy to the McCarthy campaign. Sheldon Ramsdell went to work for McCarthy as a full-time staff member. Mike McKusker also joined the national staff and worked for the candidate in Los Angeles. The VVAW national office distributed contribution cards with a photograph of McCarthy beneath the words "Politics is the Art of Making it Possible." Most VVAW members who returned questionnaires to the national office answered "McCarthy" to the question "Which presidential candidate(s) do you prefer actively?"[88]

Not all antiwar veterans rushed to join the McCarthy campaign. Robert Wilkinson, a VVAW activist from Madison, Wisconsin, went door to door promoting the Socialist Workers Party presidential candidate Fred Halstead. Wilkinson, a leader of the Madison Committee to End the War in Vietnam, also ran as the SWP candidate for governor of Wisconsin in 1968. When Robert Kennedy entered the presidential race on March 16, a Vietnam veteran from New Jersey named Robert Bradley Kennedy (no relation) started Vietnam Veterans for Kennedy, an organization that Kennedy's staff originally asked Carl Rogers to head. Rogers refused. Robert Bradley Kennedy, who had served in Vietnam as a forward observer in the army, campaigned around the country as head of Vietnam Veterans for Kennedy until Kennedy's assassination on June 5.[89]

Few veterans defected from the McCarthy to the Kennedy camp, however. Most of the Vietnam veterans in the McCarthy campaign had become involved prior to the New Hampshire primaries, weeks before Kennedy entered the race. When Kennedy announced his decision to run for president, few had any reason to switch allegiance. Although RFK quoted Camus, met publicly with his admirer Tom Hayden, of SDS, and campaigned in impoverished ghettos, he was more cautious than McCarthy when it came to the Vietnam War. Some activists and intellectuals supported RFK because they felt McCarthy was too stiff. Indeed, McCarthy's long-winded recitals of Robert Frost poems left many supporters struggling to stay awake. Norman Mailer, a Kennedy backer, sarcastically likened McCarthy to the chair of a fine English department. But McCarthy took a more decisive stand on Vietnam than Kennedy. Both wanted a bombing halt and negotiations with the enemy. McCarthy, however, supported a coalition government in South Vietnam that would

include the NLF and called for swift troop withdrawals. RFK had no intention of undermining America's commitment to Vietnam, and he even
advocated retaliatory responses if negotiations with the NLF failed.[90]

One name absent from the Viet-Nam Veterans for McCarthy ad was
Jeff Sharlet, the editor of *Vietnam GI*. Sharlet, whose politics more closely
paralleled those of SDS militants than those of VVAW, had serious misgivings about the effectiveness of electoral politics in general, and Eugene
McCarthy and Robert Kennedy in particular. His *Vietnam GI* editorialized:

> If peace is to come, it will be ordinary men and women who bring it
> about. If we cast ourselves (and our votes) at the feet of the first politician
> who sounds good, we'll pay for it in spades. Our job is to tell the truth
> about what is going on, to organize others and to work with them to keep
> the heat on, to use every tactic we can think of to force those who run
> things in this country to come across.[91]

A small but growing number of VVAW members shared Sharlet's concerns. After all, it had been a Democratic president, John Kennedy, who
increased military aid to the Ngo Dinh Diem regime and stepped up the
number of U.S. advisers in Vietnam to more than sixteen thousand. It
had been a liberal Democrat, Johnson, who pushed through the Tonkin
Gulf Resolution, committed combat troops (five-hundred thousand by
early 1968), and initiated Operation Rolling Thunder, the intense aerial
bombing of North Vietnam. And it had been a Democratic-controlled
Congress (including Senator McCarthy) that approved the Tonkin Gulf
Resolution. Some Vietnam veterans remained skeptical about McCarthy's
commitment to ending the war, as well as his efforts to distance himself
from the peace movement. These veterans spoke of "taking the struggle to
the streets," and they embraced militant tactics. Murray Polner wrote of
one antiwar Vietnam veteran who "joined every peace march he could"
and "enjoyed taunting cops and . . . incessantly defying the legitimacy of
any authority."[92] The conflict, early in 1968, over whether to support Mc-
Carthy or to engage in "street politics" led to the first VVAW split. "Where
we more or less split was over presidential politics," recalled Mike
McKusker. "We had a lot of urban guerrillas who just said, 'Screw this
presidential politics, let's take our crap out in the streets.' Others just said,
'Let's give him [McCarthy] a chance.'"[93]

The Tet Offensive marked the beginning of a year of turbulence and
upheaval. President Johnson's announcement on March 31 that he would

not run for re-election stunned many but sparked a generally positive re-action throughout the peace movement. Martin Luther King's assassina-tion on April 4 led to rioting in 125 cities nationwide, while the murder of Robert Kennedy on June 5 bewildered the young peace activists who sup-ported him. The takeover of five buildings at Columbia University by SDS militants in late April resulted in hours of stark television footage of police frantically tear-gassing and clubbing demonstrators and innocent bystanders alike. Many stunned television viewers felt as if they were viewing a nation in meltdown. The spring of 1968, wrote Kirkpatrick Sale, "mark[ed] the emergence of political violence on a significant scale around the country."[94]

Amid stormy events and growing frustration, VVAW leaders set their sights on the upcoming Democratic National Convention in August. Shortly after the assassination of Robert Kennedy, Allard Lowenstein or-ganized the liberal Coalition for an Open Convention (COC), an um-brella group intended to bring together those opposed to the nomination of Vice President Hubert Humphrey for president. Lowenstein objected to Johnson's use of shady backroom politics and his heavy-handed meth-ods of pressuring delegates. He wanted a more open and democratic process, and he announced plans to hold a peaceful demonstration in Chicago during the convention. To Lowenstein and other liberal antiwar activists, the prowar Hubert Humphrey, who entered the presidential race in late April with Johnson's support, represented little more than an ex-tension of the president. VVAW, along with Rogers's Vietnam Veterans for McCarthy, immediately joined the COC. Rogers and Barry also recruited eighteen other Vietnam veterans to participate in COC-related organiz-ing. "We are adamantly opposed to the nomination of Hubert Humphrey and will not support him under any circumstances," the veterans de-clared. "As veterans of the war he has so long defended we are convinced that we can have an enormous effect—man for man—on the minds of the uncommitted to help prevent Humphrey's nomination."[95]

Meanwhile, Barry and Rogers initiated their most ambitious plan yet. The two leaders of VVAW worked around the clock, contacting Vietnam veterans across America. They hoped to enlist fifty Vietnam veterans, one from each state, to travel to the Democratic National Convention. Once the fifty veterans reached Chicago, they would lobby convention dele-gates to adopt an antiwar platform and to support Eugene McCarthy. Other VVAW organizers joined Rogers and Barry in their effort, includ-ing Los Angeles VVAW coordinator Jim Boggio. Eventually they located a

Vietnam veteran in each state willing to travel to Chicago, including John Fitzgerald, a McCarthy delegate and a Purple Heart recipient from Massachusetts. While Barry and Rogers spent weeks traveling and contacting people by telephone, candidate McCarthy slowed his campaign. He warned his supporters to stay away from Chicago, calling it "the wrong place for the Democratic convention of 1968."[96] Mike McKusker, who campaigned for McCarthy in California, later noted, "We had a long, two-month hiatus in the summer where McCarthy had retreated. Kennedy's death really scared the hell out of him."[97]

Activists began trickling into Chicago the weekend before the convention, with a steady stream arriving on the opening day, Monday, August 25. A pugnacious Mayor Richard Daley vowed that he would not tolerate unrest in his Chicago. "As long as I am mayor," he proclaimed before an American Legion meeting, "there will be law and order in its streets."[98] Authorities guessed that fifty thousand, perhaps as many as one-hundred thousand, activists would come to Chicago. Ultimately, ten thousand did. The mayor placed his twelve-thousand-man police force on twelve-hour shifts and stationed six thousand Illinois National Guardsmen outside the city. Authorities warned police to watch for hippies, the flambouyant Yippies led by Abbie Hoffman and Jerry Rubin, SDS militants, and anyone who appeared subversive. An estimated ninety million Americans watched on television what seemed a city under siege. For the Vietnam veterans who drove, hitchhiked, flew, or traveled by rail to Chicago, the troops, with their rifles, gas dispensers, grenade launchers, .30-caliber machine guns, and bazookas, served as stark reminders of the war in Vietnam. Some veterans, including Bernard Harrison, a twenty-three-year-old Philadelphian who went to Chicago to support McCarthy, had fresh memories of the Tet Offensive revived on the streets of the Windy City.[99]

The veterans hoped their unique status would help them influence delegates, yet they went to Chicago with few expectations. Before the convention began, John Talbott, a physician who served in the Army in Vietnam and joined the pro-McCarthy lobbying effort in Chicago, wrote an open letter to the delegates expressing his pessimism. "I feel that the Democratic Convention is all but over, that Humphrey has all but taken control of the convention delegates and there is no way for the electorate to be heard." He concluded his letter on an even darker note: "I see us heading down the same old road to more disasters, more aluminum caskets, more craters in rice paddies, more murdered leaders, more 'blue-ribbon' commissions on riots, and more dehumanization of us all."[100]

The convention was a disaster for the Vietnam veterans. The Democratic Party, still under the firm control of Johnson, Daley, and Humphrey, adopted a decidedly prowar statement by a decisive vote of 1,567 3/4 to 1,041 1/4. The antiwar platform went down, and with it went McCarthy. In the streets of Chicago, meanwhile, police turned on protesters with clubs, tear gas, and mass arrests. Mike McKusker recounted:

> It was Wednesday night in Chicago. Sometimes I thought it was as bad as anything I'd seen in Vietnam, except they weren't popping rounds at us. But they came at us and they came at us hard, those Chicago cops, man. It was kind of funny, I had a friend who was with me almost the entire time. We were in Vietnam together and he had no sympathy for my antiwar attitudes. He thought I was an idiot. At the same time, he also thought I was being an idiot [for] sticking my neck out around the Chicago cops with whom he grew up. It was one of the worst police forces in the world. And so he was out there with me almost every damn day to make sure I don't get hit, so he's out in the middle of it, too.[101]

On Thursday night, August 28, following Hubert Humphrey's nomination as the Democratic Party presidential candidate, the battle moved from the convention auditorium to the streets as many of McCarthy's young campaign workers joined the militants in battles with the police. McKusker and other Vietnam veterans found themselves in the midst of the chaos. They had received an invitation to attend a function at the home of the comedian and activist Dick Gregory. "If you were in the streets, and you moved, you were a Yippie," Gregory later said.[102] The police arrested Gregory and a group of pro-McCarthy delegates, then tear-gassed McKusker and other observers. Along the way, McKusker "got clubbed in the ribs by a National Guard rifle butt." "If they hadn't gassed us, I thought some of us would've been killed," McKusker remembered. "The mob pushed in one direction, then being pushed back in another, people were going to get trampled. Then they [the police] hit the gas and everybody turned around and walked away, so it saved a lot of lives, at least."[103]

A former helicopter crew chief and VVAW member who went to Chicago hoping to persuade a few delegates to support McCarthy found himself in the middle of a street battle, complete with a police helicopter buzzing overhead. He later recounted:

Seeing those guys up above, looking at the troops and the cops, and knowing they were against me—for me this was as terrifying as anything in Vietnam. Somehow I had become the enemy, the Vietcong of the United States, when all I am is a human being that wants to be human. Just because I hate this war and the kind of things that forced us into it, they've made me the enemy of my country.[104]

The veterans left Chicago feeling depressed and powerless. Their non-violent efforts were completely overshadowed in the press by the battle in the streets. After the tear gas cleared, a frustrated Carl Rogers dumped a large box of campaign literature out of a high office window in downtown Chicago and watched it flutter through the air to Daley Plaza below. Several dedicated VVAW activists simply disappeared following the convention and never resurfaced. "That was like the end of it for many guys. They were angry about what happened in Chicago," Rogers recalled.[105] Sheldon Ramsdell decided to "lay low" after the convention, and others did the same.[106] "I tried to forget Chicago," a VVAW member later said, "I never really expected anything else, anyway. America has a cancer."[107] Jan Barry remembered that VVAWers returning home from Chicago "were totally discouraged."[108]

For some antiwar Vietnam veterans, the unrelenting demands of activism exacerbated existing health problems. Following a trip to Fort Hood in the fall of 1968, *Vietnam GI* editor Jeff Sharlet complained to his friends that he felt "really beat." Sharlet later experienced sharp pains while visiting friends in Boston. He flew home to Florida and checked into a VA hospital in Miami, where physicians discovered cancer in his kidney. Doctors removed Sharlet's kidney and subjected him to massive radiation treatment and drugs. While in the hospital, Sharlet turned *Vietnam GI* over to his fellow veterans. Various GI antiwar newspapers tried to raise funds to help Sharlet.[109]

VVAW was in trouble after the convention. The organization, now financially insolvent, abandoned its offices on Fifth Avenue. VVAW never enjoyed a substantial treasury, but it usually had enough money to keep one permanent staff member (Barry) in the office and pay for telephone calls and mimeographing. According to one account: "They [members] took money out of their pockets, or sold newspapers, or gave up smoking cigarettes to support this fledgling organization."[110] But VVAW's finances had dried up by summer's end. To make matters worse, Barry had lost contact with many members. Telephone numbers had been disconnected, addresses changed. Barry and Rogers tried to revive the exhausted organization, but with little success. "Carl Rogers and I called a meeting that fall and nobody came," Barry remembered. "We sat there looking at ourselves thinking, 'Now what are we doing?'"[111] Carl Rogers added: "There wasn't anybody who wanted to provide the leadership." Rogers left shortly thereafter to organize his own group, GI-Servicemen's Link to Peace, which offered support to antiwar GI coffee houses located near military bases and served to connect the growing GI movement with national antiwar activity.[112]

VVAW entered into what Barry called a "period of minimal activity." Veterans for Peace filled the void left by VVAW's absence, helping to organize a series of well-attended antiwar demonstrations during the summer. In the fall, Veterans for Peace sponsored its own demonstration, GIs and Vets March for Peace, where, on October 12, five hundred active-duty G.I.s joined some fifteen thousand civilians in San Francisco to protest the war. Fred Halstead called it "the most effective fall 1968 antiwar action in the United States."[113] Speakers at the march included Lieutenant Hugh Smith, General Hugh B. Hester (ret.), Donald Duncan, and Lieutenant (j.g.) Susan Schnall. Schnall, a nurse, faced court-martial for dropping antiwar leaflets from an airplane over naval installations and the aircraft carrier U.S.S. *Ranger*, anchored at Alameda, California. "We must bring our boys home now!" Schnall told the spirited crowd of demonstrators.[114] Veterans for Peace joined other organizations in planning similar G.I.-civilian marches in New York, Chicago, Atlanta, and Los Angeles. Along the way, they recruited antiwar Vietnam veterans. "They [Veterans for Peace] worked actively to get the young Vietnamese veterans involved," remembers the *Veterans Stars and Stripes for Peace* editor Donald Mosby.[115]

Richard Nixon's narrow victory over Hubert Humphrey in November mattered little to the majority of peace movement activists. As far as they were concerned, the battle had been fought and lost in Chicago. "We have no choice for president," Donald Duncan grimly told a crowd of antiwar demonstrators before the election. Nixon squeaked past Humphrey by less than 1 percent of the popular vote, largely due to his promises of "law and order" and his "secret plan" to end the war in Vietnam.[116]

By the early winter months of 1969, only the Los Angeles chapter of VVAW showed signs of life, occasionally cosponsoring rallies with other antiwar groups. "There was no active VVAW on the east coast," Barry remembered. Another blow came on June 16, 1969, when Jeff Sharlet died of cancer in a Miami VA hospital. For months, Sharlet had been suffering the debilitating effects of cancer, and when the end came, he was penniless and emaciated. Antiwar G.I.s and veterans across the United States and Vietnam mourned his passing. VVAW had lost one of its most articulate and energetic spokesmen. His fellow veterans published a few more issues of *Vietnam GI* after Sharlet's death, but without him, the paper had lost much of its vitality and spirit. It soon folded.[117]

As the turbulent sixties drew to a close, VVAW seemed to be yet another defunct antiwar organization. It had begun as an informal "clearinghouse," sending antiwar Vietnam veterans to speak at debates, demonstrations, fairs, and on radio and television programs. Within months, a handful of chapters had emerged around the country, but their existence was tenuous at best. When Eugene McCarthy entered the presidential race in late 1967, his campaign absorbed the energy and creativity of the incipient organization. The antiwar veterans believed a McCarthy victory in 1968 would bring an end to the Vietnam War. Yet McCarthy's defeat in Chicago killed the hopes of the veterans and dashed their faith in electoral politics. Many disappeared after the convention, succumbing to burnout. VVAW was in a stupor. Nobody, during the early months of 1969, not even Barry, could have predicted that future events would revive it. The G.I. movement had grown bolder and stronger. Many of its supporters would join VVAW after leaving the military. Following Nixon's decision to invade Cambodia and the tragic killing of four students at Kent State University in Ohio in May 1970, a new generation of veterans would join VVAW. The organization would fall under the control of activists who shunned political campaigns and embraced street protest and guerrilla theater. VVAW would return, but in a new and different form.

2

To Redeem the Promise Lost

Throughout most of 1969, VVAW was moribund. Its remains—posters, pamphlets, address cards, stationery, photographs, and buttons—lay boxed in Jan Barry's apartment. But renewal was forthcoming. The participation of veterans in the Vietnam Moratorium protests in the fall of 1969 revived VVAW. The American invasion of Cambodia and the shootings at Kent State energized other antiwar veterans to get involved. By the summer of 1970, VVAW boasted more than two thousand members, and its leaders were planning one of the most highly publicized actions of the antiwar movement, Operation Rapid American Withdrawal (RAW).

A few days after the first Vietnam Moratorium, Jan Barry received a telephone call from one of its planners. "Didn't there used to be a Vietnam veterans' organization?" the caller asked. "Can you get it going again because we have all these veterans who showed up at the Moratorium and we don't know what to do with them."[1]

The October 15 event had been an enormous success. An estimated two million citizens had participated in activities around the country. They marched, listened to speeches, distributed pamphlets, read the names of Americans and Vietnamese killed in the war, showed films, joined candlelight vigils. Church bells tolled for the dead, and flags hung at half staff. In Boston, more than one-hundred thousand people flooded Boston Common for the largest demonstration in the city's history. Jubilant organizers were planning a second event for mid-November.[2]

Scores of Vietnam veterans went to the protests. The October Moratorium exposed many for the first time to the antiwar movement. In Los Angeles, one VVAW member, Rayford Henderson, worked full-time for the Vietnam Moratorium Committee. VVAWer Bruce Ford, a student at the University of South Dakota, spoke "informally at moratorium activities."[3] Lewis Delano, a VVAW activist and editor of the GI antiwar newspaper *Left Face*, arranged speakers for the Birmingham, Alabama, Moratorium Committee. Mike McKusker addressed crowds in Portland, Oregon. The nationwide outpouring of dissent sparked renewed interest in VVAW, and Jan Barry considered reviving it.[4]

Ironically, while VVAW languished, the antiwar movement was experiencing dizzying growth, and dissent within the military was flourishing. Near military bases, activists opened coffeehouses that brought G.I.s into contact with military counseling, antiwar literature, countercultural music, and other soldiers. The earliest coffeehouse, the UFO, in Columbia, South Carolina, opened its doors late in 1967 for soldiers at Fort Jackson. Its founder, Fred Gardner, a reservist and a former *Harvard Crimson* editor, left Columbia to open another coffeehouse, the Oleo Strut, in Killeen, a few miles from Fort Hood, Texas. Despite persecution by local officials and military authorities, nineteen coffeehouses were operating by 1970.[5]

The emergence of a strong G.I. press was another indicator of the antiwar movement's growth. Early publications such as *Veterans Stars and Stripes for Peace* and *Vietnam GI* gave way to newer, more radical periodicals, usually targeting local military bases. The G.I. activist David Cortright described them as "often short-lived and appearing in the form of barely readable mimeographed sheets."[6] Two pioneering efforts were *FTA* at Fort Knox, Kentucky, and *Fatigue Press* at Fort Hood. Imitators emerged everywhere. With titles such as *Open Sights* and *The Ally*, G.I. newspapers provided a crucial forum for dissent and kindled resistance within the military. A series of demonstrations in April 1969, sponsored by the G.I.-Civilian Alliance, drew thousands of soldiers into the peace movement. Organizations such as the American Servicemen's Union (ASU), the United States Servicemen's Fund (USSF), and the Pacific Counseling Service (PCS) offered guidance and support to antiwar military personnel. In the United States and Vietnam, activists in the armed forces planned protests, distributed literature on bases, and hung political posters in barracks.[7]

When antiwar soldiers left the military, they searched for outlets for their newfound activism. Jan Barry again launched VVAW, hoping the renewed organization would absorb many of the growing number of veterans who opposed the war. In late October 1969, Mobilization (or Mobe) leaders donated space to the VVAW in their office complex at 150 Fifth Avenue. Barry was back in business, opening boxes of old VVAW files and literature, making telephone calls, and writing letters. During the previous year, the Los Angeles VVAW chapter had, in the words of Mike McKusker, "quietly reinforced."[8] Jim Boggio, the energetic head of the chapter, was "no where to be found," leaving the twenty-three-year-old Peter Martinsen "to reorganize and reactivate a Southern California branch."[9] McKusker and other activists spent months recruiting new members. "I didn't organize any chapters so much as I'd go into Navy bars in Long Beach and start talking up this stuff," McKusker remembered. "And it was perilous at times, but I ran into some very, very interesting characters and actually got some members out of that experience."[10]

Gradually, veterans began trickling into the VVAW offices. Scott Moore joined VVAW in November 1969 and became its vice president. For Moore, VVAW was a family affair. Weeks earlier, his mother, Madelyn Moore, an activist in the Fifth Avenue Peace Parade Committee, had begun working as a full-time organizer in the national office of VVAW, at Jan Barry's request. Madelyn often referred to herself as "the VVAW den mother."[11] Scott Moore came from a respected upper-class family in Easton, Pennsylvania. He had been a lieutenant with the 9th Infantry Division in Vietnam. His brother claimed conscientious objector status, and his parents had strongly opposed the war from the outset. Moore had had no reservations about joining the army, but his experiences in Vietnam had transformed him into a critic of American involvement in Southeast Asia. Particularly troubling to Moore was the "inhumane attitude in general" within the armed forces, especially toward the Vietnamese. "These people were subhuman, and, well, they were—the expression is 'gook,'" he explained.[12] When Moore returned in the summer of 1969, he attended antiwar demonstrations. "My main interest when I got back," he recounted, "was getting . . . [Americans] out of Vietnam."[13]

VVAW organizers were about to encounter their first test. In November, Scott Moore and the other veterans read a series of reports written by the *New York Times* reporter Seymour Hersh about a massacre in the hamlet of My Lai. On March 16, 1968, soldiers under the command of Lieutenant William Calley Jr. had allegedly herded perhaps as many as five hundred Vietnamese civilians—men, women and children—into My Lai and systematically slaughtered them. The Army brass had concealed the story for more than a year. When Hersh's story appeared, new members flocked to VVAW.[14]

Hersh's My Lai stories appeared in more than thirty U.S. newspapers on November 13, two days before the second massive Mobilization antiwar march in Washington. Public reaction was mixed. Many Americans distrusted Hersh's accounts or agreed with White House Press Secretary Ron Ziegler, who regarded the occurrence as an aberration. Others insisted My Lai was merely a microcosm of the war. "My Lai was not a criminal incident in an otherwise 'just' war," editorialized the *Christian Century*. "It simply represents the ultimate logic of a criminal war."[15] A handful of antiwar activists called for war crimes investigations. "Up until the revelation about My Lai, we could not talk about war crimes," remembered Jan Barry. "No audience would believe that this was true. Even the peace movement audiences would not believe that these things went on. So we just left it as something that was never discussed. There were plenty of other issues to bring up."[16] By the end of 1969, a group called the Citizens' Commission of Inquiry on U.S. War Crimes in Vietnam (CCI) announced plans to conduct hearings involving veterans and soldiers in cities across the country. The first was scheduled for Annapolis, Maryland, in March 1970. "Individual soldiers should not be made scapegoats for policies designed at the highest levels of government," CCI organizers explained.[17] Some VVAW members participated in CCI activities, and the two groups would eventually join to coordinate national hearings. But the VVAW national office initially refrained from such investigations. "I mean, this is really heavy-duty," Barry said. "We're almost charging our fellow veterans with war crimes."[18]

Allegations of widespread atrocities in Vietnam were not new. In 1967, the Bertrand Russell Peace Foundation had held the so-called International War Crimes Tribunal. The Russell tribunal declared the United States "guilty" of "aggression, civilian bombardment, the use of experimental weapons, the torture and mutilation of prisoners, and genocide involving mass burial, concentration camps and saturation bombing of unparalleled intensity."[19] It further accused American leaders of violating several international treaties, including the Hague Convention of 1907, the Kellog-Briand Pact of 1928, the Geneva Convention of 1949, and the UN Charter. The proceedings of the tribunal—which included testimony from respected scientists, doctors, activists, writers, and three Vietnam veterans (two of whom later joined VVAW)—were published in 1968 in a 650-page volume titled *Against the Crime of Silence*. Despite the impressive collection of evidence, the findings of the Russell tribunal failed to arouse public opinion against the war.[20]

Reports of outrages committed by U.S. troops in Vietnam were one of many issues that VVAW activists confronted. When it was founded in

1967, the organization's sole purpose had been to bring an end to the war. Its founders spoke of little else. By the winter and spring months of 1970, VVAW had undergone crucial changes. "We began taking on much broader issues," Barry explained, such as "the drug situation, which had become an epidemic by the late sixties in Vietnam, attitudes toward veterans, and something we couldn't quite put our names on. At first it was called post-Vietnam syndrome."[21] Later, psychiatrists coined the term "posttraumatic stress disorder." Other topics came to the fore. For the first time, VVAWers openly discussed race and class and the ways in which they influenced the treatment of veterans. They picketed Veterans Administrations' hospitals, protesting horrendous conditions and attempted to mobilize homeless veterans.[22]

The transformation of VVAW into a multi-issue organization reflected power shifts within the national office. A new generation of Vietnam veterans had assumed control of the group. Joe Urgo typified the shift in leadership. Urgo joined VVAW late in March 1970. Members elected him secretary of VVAW, and he served on the board of directors. He was young, intelligent, energetic, and angry. He had gone to Vietnam to fight communism and returned thoroughly disillusioned with the war. As a teenager growing up in Queens, New York, Urgo, from a middle-class Italian family, considered himself intensely patriotic. He joined Young Americans for Freedom in 1964 and worked in Barry Goldwater's presidential campaign in New York. "I stuffed envelopes, and I read all his position papers, and I read some of the bibles of that time, *None Dare Call It Treason*, all these political, right-wing . . . analyses of history," Urgo recalled. At his Catholic high school, teachers showed him maps marked with red arrows emanating from the Soviet Union. In 1966, Urgo received his draft notice. "I can remember thinking . . . that I could not be alive at this time in history and not partake in what was the central fact of my generation, this Vietnam war," he explained.[23]

Urgo entered the air force and volunteered to go to Vietnam. He arrived shortly after Christmas 1967 and was assigned to guard the far west end of the gigantic Ton San Nhut Air Force Base, near Saigon. During the Tet Offensive, Viet Cong forces penetrated the base, sparking a terrifying firefight in which some of Urgo's close friends were killed. "I always had this feeling throughout the whole night that they came pretty close to taking the base," he remembered. Nervous and bewildered after Tet, Urgo concluded that "nobody was proud of what they were doing, nobody cared." He walked around the base in a daze, stunned by the deaths of several close friends. "There was a literal all-night crying session on my part," he said, "this catharsis, whatever you want to call it, that physically represents the beginning of the breaking with all these illusions I had." Only one month into his tour, Urgo began to oppose the war. He remembered:

> I later learned . . . that nobody believed in what they were doing. In order to get to that point, though, I had to go through a lot of other transformations. I basically had to confront my own racism—you know, these Vietnamese 'gooks.' I was using the language like everybody else. . . . And I'd go downtown and see the tremendous poverty, the starvation, and I knew about the enormous prostitution. The whole thing was this huge conglomeration of corruption, crime, lack of ideals, poverty, racism, and I'm in the middle of this.[24]

Urgo returned to the United States at the end of 1968 and spent his last year in the air force in a small detachment assigned to guard nuclear-armed aircraft at the Atlantic City airport. In his spare time, he organized G.I. antiwar activities and read "all the radical newspapers that were in New York at the time, the *East Village Other*, the *Rat*, . . . and I'd sit on the bus, pouring over them, . . . taking all this antiwar stuff back to my base, and I'd be sitting there thinking, 'I can't believe it, these people are talking about revolution!'" Urgo regularly attended antiwar protests, including the massive October 15 Moratorium demonstration in Washington, D.C. "This time, I'd be in the streets instead of on the side booing people." Urgo returned to civilian life and briefly affiliated with Veterans for Peace in March 1970, but he found the group was "not driven by what I was driven by. They weren't angry enough, they weren't going for the throat enough." At the same time, he joined VVAW and started "hanging around" the national office.[25]

Several new recruits entered the VVAW at the time Urgo appeared. One, Al Hubbard, immediately assumed mythical status. He accepted the position of "executive secretary," making him the group's most visible representative. "Al—tall, thin, goateed and slightly Afro'd—is intense and thoughtful," wrote a reporter for the *New York Daily News*.[26] A CBS News employee who was "impressed personally by his leadership qualities" described Hubbard as "calm and soft-spoken."[27] "Al Hubbard was really some kind of a genius," remembered Madelyn Moore. "His mind was wonderful, just click-click-clicking, all the time. [He knew] how to get the press."[28] The two years Hubbard had spent in Vietnam as an air force captain—including a harrowing plane crash he survived in Danang—became the subject of conversation among many VVAW activists. They appreciated his unpretentious and self-effacing personality. He felt more relaxed in his green fatigues than in a suit and tie, and his rhetoric was decidedly more militant than that of earlier leaders. "Resist the war in every way possible," Hubbard advised members, "and when you do, be prepared to put your own body on the line. . . . Don't go off on an ego trip and fancy yourself as a leader possessed of inherently superior abilities. Nobody can relate to an elitist."[29]

Hubbard and Urgo envisioned VVAW's becoming a mass movement. When they joined late in the winter of 1970, the structure of VVAW had changed very little since its inception. While it boasted 1,500 members and, at times, a few unstable chapters, it remained, as it had been when it was founded, a clearinghouse for antiwar veteran orators. "We had contacts in cities around the country," Urgo said, "the names and telephone numbers of antiwar Vietnam vets who would be willing to speak at protests."[30] Hubbard and Urgo believed that a nationwide organization, with autonomous, self-sustaining chapters, each run by a regional coordinator, could wield enormous power and influence. "Nobody had any real job at being coordinators, but we were recruiting everywhere," explained McKusker, who had relocated to Portland, Oregon.[31]

Numerous obstacles slowed VVAW's growth. In the spring, the organization moved to a larger space in a nearby building, leaving the national office in disarray. "Inside, crowded together, are desks, tables, filing cabinets, stacks of papers, posters, camp chairs and people," wrote a journalist.[32] On one of the desks, Joe Urgo found a shoe box containing pieces of papers with names and addresses, some typed, some handwritten. "That was the VVAW's mailing list," he said.[33] Urgo and Madelyn Moore devoted countless hours to structuring the mailing list, verifying telephone numbers, and locating antiwar veterans. "There was a lot of work, I'm talking about now from early in the morning till ten or eleven o'clock at night—Joe may've slept there," Moore recalled.[34] Complicating matters was a developing rift between newcomers and earlier members. "Essentially what happened was the old guard, who had done . . . debating, [campaign work for] McCarthy, that sort of thing, . . . fell away," Urgo explained. "Now it's Hubbard who's beginning to show up more, Scott Moore begins to show up more, and me. And these guys are talking more activist stuff."[35]

The spring thaw brought an increase in VVAW activism. VVAWers addressed crowds at antiwar protests, staffed literature tables at universities, participated in teach-ins, and searched for potential members. Veterans' Administration hospitals proved fertile recruiting grounds. As *Life* magazine noted:

> The VA hospital system . . . is disgracefully understaffed, with standards far below those of an average community hospital. Many wards remain closed for want of personnel and the rest are strained with overcrowding. Facilities for long-term treatment and rehabilitation, indispensable for the kind of paralytic injuries especially common in this war of land mines and boobytraps, are generally inferior.[36]

Patients at VA hospitals across the country told their horror stories. The VA's showcase hospital in Washington, D.C., assigned one registered nurse to eighty patients. Sophisticated new equipment sat idle at Miami's VA hospital for lack of trained personnel to operate it. Doctors at the Wadsworth VA hospital in Los Angeles described conditions as "medieval" and "filthy." At the infamous Bronx VA hospital, one nurse watched over three wards containing 140 patients, kitchens were "ill-kept and littered," a quadriplegic slept alongside trash cans, and rooms were "so full of rodents that a trap set on any given evening usually produces a mouse or rat by morning." Vietnam veterans in VA hospitals, outraged by conditions, joined VVAW in large numbers.[37]

Meanwhile, VVAW leaders grew tired of sponsoring other groups' rallies and speaking at demonstrations they did not organize. Such behind-the-scenes activism often proved burdensome and unrewarding and obscured the unique status that members felt they brought to the VVAW. By April, Hubbard, Scott Moore, and others began discussing the possibility of a national demonstration they hoped would focus attention on the growing number of Vietnam veterans who opposed the war. The events of May 1970 would provide them with the new members and determination they needed to mount such a protest.

In a live televised speech on April 30, President Nixon announced, "In cooperation with the armed forces of South Vietnam, attacks are being launched this week to clean out major enemy sanctuaries on the Cambodian-Vietnam border." With that speech, Nixon publicly confirmed the invasion of Cambodia, which he had formally ordered two days earlier. The president emphasized that the mission's purpose was "ending the war in Vietnam and winning the just peace we all desire." Pointing to maps of Cambodia, President Nixon explained, "American and South Vietnamese units will attack the headquarters for the entire Communist military operation in South Vietnam." The invasion was a test of America's will, Nixon argued.[38]

During the speech, Nixon neglected to reveal that the United States had been clandestinely bombing Cambodia since March 1969. President Nixon hoped the bombing would demonstrate his decisiveness to the enemy; yet he feared widespread domestic criticism. The president repeatedly told Americans that he sought "peace with honor." He planned to achieve it by "Vietnamizing" the war, which involved, in his words, "strengthening the South Vietnamese so that they could defend themselves when we left."[39]

Protesters immediately expressed opposition to Nixon's announcement. The evening of his speech, demonstrations erupted at Oberlin College and at Rutgers and Princeton universities. Nixon angrily lashed out, referring to student activists as "bums blowing up the campuses."[40] Within a few days, strikes were under way at more than a hundred schools. VVAW members "led student strikes on major campuses throughout the country," noted one account.[41] At Kent State University in northern Ohio, the journalist I. F. Stone encountered "veterans of the Vietnam war radicalized by their experiences and frustrated by their parents' unwillingness to listen to them."[42] Five hundred students participated in a protest at Kent State the day after Nixon's Cambodia speech. They applauded as the Vietnam veteran Jim Geary, a history major and a Silver Star recipient, burned his discharge papers.[43]

Tim Butz had had little time for the antiwar movement. Between his job at B. F. Goodrich in Akron, Ohio, and full-time classes at Kent State, Butz ignored "the social aspects of school." "Being older than most of the other freshman, I didn't hang out at the usual freshman haunts or rush a fraternity or whatever it's called," Butz recounted. "I was totally divorced from that part of the world." A former air force crew chief who had volunteered to go to Vietnam in 1966, Butz returned to the United States in the summer of 1968 and enrolled in Kent State the following year.[44]

On the morning of Monday, May 4, 1970, he attended an antiwar demonstration at the campus commons. He watched National Guard troops encircle the crowd of 1,300 people. At 12:25 P.M., while standing at "the west side of Taylor Hall," Butz heard the crack of gunfire from the opposite side of the commons. Members of Troop G of the 107th

Armored Cavalry Regiment of the Ohio National Guard, responding to taunts and rocks, opened fire for thirteen seconds, killing four students and injuring nine. Butz knew three of the people involved in the tragedy. One of the slain students, Allison Krause, dated his roommate. Two of the National Guardsmen later indicted for murder, Sergeant Barry Morris and Sergeant Lawrence Shafer, had gone to Butz's high school. The incident forever transformed the young veteran. "[After serving in Vietnam] I thought, 'Well, I'm gonna go home. Fuck this whole thing, I'm just gonna get on with my life.' And then, after what happened at Kent State, it was clear to me that I just couldn't get on with my life." Butz joined VVAW a few months later.[45]

The killings had a similar impact on other Vietnam veterans. At a memorial service held for one victim, Jeffrey Miller, Al Hubbard and Joe Urgo watched in awe as thousands of mourners outside Manhattan's Riverside Chapel silently raised their fists while pallbearers carried Miller's coffin out of the building. "The cops were just scared," Urgo said. "It was one of those moments where I began to get a sense of the power of the people."[46] Ron Kovic, a twenty-three-year-old paraplegic, heard about Kent State over the radio. "For a moment, there was a shock through my body," he later recalled. "I felt like crying. The last time I felt that way was when Kennedy was killed. I remember saying to myself, 'The whole thing is coming down now.' I wheeled out to my car. I didn't know where I was going but I had to find other people who felt the way I did."[47] W.D. Ehrhart, a student at Swarthmore College, in Pennsylvania, who had received numerous medals as a combat marine in Vietnam, "cried until I couldn't cry anymore." Ehrhart concluded:

> The war was a horrible mistake, and my beloved country was dying because of it. America was bleeding to death in the rice fields and jungles of Vietnam, and now the blood flowed in our streets. I did not want my country to die. I had to do something. It was time to stop the war. And I would have to do it.[48]

The student uprising spread following the shootings at Kent State. Students at 350 universities went on strike, and protests closed nearly five hundred campuses, fifty for the remainder of the academic year. Thirty-five university presidents called for withdrawal from Cambodia, and 225 student body presidents demanded the impeachment of President Nixon. Students and police clashed at traditionally placid campuses such as Alabama, Eastern Michigan, New Mexico, and South Carolina. More than thirty ROTC buildings were burned or bombed. On May 14, police at Jackson State opened fire on black students, shooting three hundred bullets into a dormitory, wounding twelve and killing two coeds watching from their rooms. The Jackson State incident fueled days of aftershocks. VVAW members on college campuses cautioned their fellow strikers against provoking violence.[49] At Ohio State, strike leaders asked Bill Crandell and other Vietnam veterans to serve as "strike marshals." Crandell recalls:

> Because of our ability as former soldiers to accept leadership and act together, we knew how to direct activities at several critical points. If a cadre of disciplined militants sought to stampede a large, amorphous crowd of student strikers into confrontations with armed and ill-led guardsmen, the vets' disciplined cohesion and experience tipped the scales away from violence.[50]

New applications from veterans arrived daily at the national office of VVAW during the May campus unrest. Membership rolls rose above two thousand. "The invasion of Cambodia and Kent State was *the* big organizing tool for VVAW," said Robert Hanson, who joined days after the invasion.[51] Hanson believed the presence of U.S. troops in Cambodia deepened America's military commitment to Southeast Asia and broadened the scope of the war. While watching television, Hanson heard the actress Jane Fonda tell a talk show host, Dick Cavett, about her efforts to raise funds for VVAW. Hanson rushed to the group's headquarters in New York City. He was excited to learn that VVAW leaders were planning a march for Labor Day weekend. Dubbed Operation Rapid American Withdrawal (RAW), it was to be a four-day, simulated search-and-destroy mission between Morristown, New Jersey, and Valley Forge, Pennsylvania. "One of my great memories of that time," recalled Hanson, "was every weekend we would set up a table in Washington Square Park, Greenwich Village, and ask for donations, from the time I first started coming to the office till [Operation RAW]." The table's staffers found much support among local residents.[52] Around the country, however, antiwar activists experienced the public backlash against student unrest. Polls indicated that a majority of Americans supported the invasion of Cambodia, and three-fourths opposed protests against the government. In St. Louis, twenty thousand residents attended a prowar march. On May 8, more than two hundred construction workers, prodded by sympathetic police, attacked a group of peaceful demonstrators in lower Manhattan. Some Vietnam veterans intervened to protect the protesters. Two former Green Berets pulled assailants away from a bloodied young man. Danny Friedman, wounded in Vietnam, "got into an argument with some construction worker who called me a draft-card-burning, welfare-collecting hippie. . . . He knocked me down and I bounced up, and there were some police standing around laughing, and I went at them."[53] Witnesses described two men in gray business suits, carrying walkie-talkies, directing the hard hats. "They went through those demonstrators like Sherman went through Atlanta," noted one observer.[54]

The incident was a major coup for the Nixon administration. Many Americans cheered the May 8 assault, believing that it pitted a frustrated "silent majority" against a minority described by Vice President Spiro Agnew as an "effete corps of impudent snobs."[55] White House Chief of Staff H. R. Haldeman thought it was "nice to see our side dishing some of it back."[56] Days later, Peter Brennan, president of the New York Building Trades Council, called upon construction workers to attend a prowar demonstration later in the month. (President Nixon later made Brennan his secretary of labor.) Television news footage of hard hats marching in support of the administration crystallized in the minds of millions an image of working-class citizens rallying against pampered college kids. It was a myth that VVAW members, most with blue-collar backgrounds, tried for years to refute.[57]

VVAW activists spent most of their summer planning for Operation RAW, but other issues drew their time and energy. On May 20, VVAWers reunited with Veterans for Peace for a highly publicized gathering in Syracuse, New York. In an action that prefigured Operation RAW, two hundred veterans from across the state marched through the town toting toy rifles. They smashed the rifles in a ceremony at the downtown War Memorial, then erected a statue to those who had died in the war. During the protest, a former marine lieutenant revealed that his division had experienced combat in Laos. The march received enthusiastic endorsements from U.S. Senators Jacob Javits and Charles Goodell. "I share your bitterness and frustration," telegrammed Goodell. "Yours will be a voice that will have to be contended with."[58]

While VVAWers paraded in Syracuse, Vietnam veterans at Manhattan's VA hospital on First Avenue circulated a petition to protest the war. "The Cambodia and Kent State things really triggered it," explained David Jiminez, the twenty-two-year-old veteran who started the drive. "When the guys in the psych and amputee wards heard about it, they had to do something."[59] After the demonstrators had gathered two hundred signatures, the hospital director, John V. Sheehan, confiscated the petition. "It is our considered judgment that controversial activities of any kind will be detrimental to the care and health of a variety of patients within our hospital," Sheehan announced. VVAW offered support and advice to the VA patients, but the patients faced continued harassment from hospital authorities.[60]

The My Lai incident still haunted Americans. For months, the Citizens Commission of Inquiry on U.S. War Crimes in Vietnam (CCI) had been conducting hearings in various cities. On March 11–12, 1970, veterans had presented two days of harrowing testimony before CCI investigators in Annapolis, Maryland. They openly spoke of the systematic torture and murder of Vietnamese prisoners by American soldiers. Some had even participated in the atrocities. CCI convened similar sessions in Los Angeles, New York, Boston, Baltimore, and Buffalo throughout April and May. Jan Barry followed the group's activities with interest. "CCI did a very good job of finding veterans who could back up what they had to say," Barry recounted, "usually by finding somebody else in the same unit who could say, 'Yes, I was also there and this indeed took place.' And they had West Point graduates and people with the military credentials that you'd have to listen to them. It wasn't just people who maybe ended up in the stockade."[61]

Barry believed it "made sense" for the VVAW to help organize war crimes hearings. He met with CCI leaders Tod Ensign and Jeremy Rifkin, two adept nonveteran activists. Ensign and Rifkin encouraged Barry and the VVAW to assist CCI. Thanks to the tireless efforts of antiwar Vietnam veterans such as Michael Uhl and Bob Johnson, CCI had assembled a sizable list of men who had served in Vietnam and were willing to share accounts of atrocities. Barry returned to the VVAW offices encouraged by his conversation with Ensign and Rifkin. By August, VVAW began collaborating with CCI to organize a large-scale national hearing, the Winter Soldier Investigation.[62]

Still, Operation RAW remained VVAW's highest priority. Weeks into planning it, however, coordinators encountered hurdles. Finding veterans willing to commit to a four-day march proved a painstaking task. "We requested the Pentagon release to us a list of people discharged from the military," Mike McKusker recalled. "They came back and said they cannot release those lists for political purposes. And we said, 'You're releasing those lists to the American Legion.' And they said, 'We're only doing that for insurance purposes.' The American Legion and the Veterans of Foreign Wars always got the lists of whoever was getting out and we weren't able to get any."[63] In late July, VVAW, along with the District of Columbia Veterans Association and the Reservists Committee to Stop the War, brought suit in the U.S. District Court against the Defense Department in an effort to obtain lists containing addresses and telephone numbers of veterans. For the remainder of the war, VVAW fought unsuccessfully with the Pentagon to receive the information. But members continued their searches. "It was word of mouth, tracking people down, step by step, phone call by phone call," said McKusker. "I remember, more than once, tracking a single person through five or six states before I nailed him or her."[64]

Other impediments hindered activists. At Valley Forge, wary commissioners did not want the VVAW to hold the climactic Operation RAW rally in the park. Hubbard and Moore would not compromise. They believed the area symbolized America's revolutionary heritage. In their effort to obtain a permit, VVAWers found a strange bedfellow in the fundamentalist Reverend Carl McIntire. The conservative radio commentator was a staunch supporter of the First Amendment, and he had encountered repeated harassment from the Federal Communications Commission. When the park commissioners met on July 31 to settle the issue, Reverend McIntire pleaded on the VVAW's behalf. "I represent just the opposite of what these veterans are calling for," he proclaimed, "But the more they talk, the more people will turn from the defeat and surrender they champion and demand our nation win the peace by victory and honor." Following a two-hour meeting "punctuated by raised voices," the commissioners reluctantly approved the gathering at Valley Forge Park.[65] As the event drew closer, law enforcement officials warned Scott Moore to make sure the marchers remained on the right side of the road. "We'll walk on either side of the road," replied Moore. "That's how we were trained. We'll use all the methods, except killing people, that we were trained to use in Vietnam."[66]

Moore coordinated the route from Morristown to Valley Forge. Meanwhile, Hubbard met with the Philadelphia Guerrilla Theater to discuss Operation RAW. The actors enthusiastically supported the march. They, along with Quaker peace activists, volunteered to dress in civilian attire and allow VVAW members to use them in reenactments of search-and-destroy missions. "We'll have actors mingling with the crowds we hope to attract," Hubbard explained. "They'll be dressed in ordinary clothes, but they will symbolize the Vietnamese peasant. We plan to demonstrate how, when troops move into a town, they sometimes snatch people out of a crowd and search them to see if, for example, they're carrying proper ID cards, or because they're suspected of harboring Viet Cong."[67] Operation RAW was VVAW's first encounter with guerrilla theater. To Hubbard, it seemed to be an economical yet effective strategy. The tactic had been embraced by various radical activists, often with successful results. In 1962, the San Francisco Mime Troupe, a cooperative whose repertoire extended far beyond mime, began performing plays laced with social commentary in the parks of San Francisco. With the rise of the New Left and antiwar movements during the sixties, so-called Radical Arts Troupes (RATs) emerged on college campuses across the country. They performed brief, usually humorous political skits in public places. Some players wore masks or face paint; others used puppets. Whatever the method, guerrilla theater often attracted crowds of curious onlookers. Hubbard recognized its potential to attract attention.[68]

The national office had high expectations for Operation RAW. It was VVAW's first national demonstration. "We anticipate this to be one of the greatest marches in the last decade," predicted Scott Moore weeks before the event.[69] Senators George McGovern and Edmund Muskie sent supportive telegrams. Retired Army General Hugh Hester was named honorary commander of the action. Volunteers from Nurses for Peace and the Medical Commission for Human Rights agreed to assist the participants. The motion picture celebrities Jane Fonda and Donald Sutherland, along with the antiwar luminaries Bella Abzug, the Reverend James Bevel, and Representative Allard Lowenstein, committed to speak when the troops reached Valley Forge on September 7. VVAW also asked the Vietnam veteran John Kerry to address the crowd.[70]

Operation RAW represented Kerry's first exposure to the organization. A Yale graduate from a well-to-do household, Kerry enlisted in the navy in 1966, despite "doubts about the war in terms of policy." His father, a Boston attorney, had been a Foreign Service agent, and the idealistic young John adhered strongly to a belief "in the code of service to one's country."[71] He became a lieutenant assigned to "swift boats"—short, fast aluminum craft that patrolled Vietnamese rivers. His involvement in life-threatening firefights with enemy sampans and huts reinforced his antiwar beliefs. During one charge on enemy positions, Kerry shot and killed a Vietnamese man at close range. "It was either going to be him or it was going to be us. It was that simple."[72] Wounded three times in battle, the recipient of three Purple Hearts, as well as Bronze and Silver Stars, Kerry had a spotless reputation.[73] His rugged, handsome features and strong communication skills made him an ideal spokesman. He gravitated toward the peace movement during the October 1969 Moratorium. "It was just incredible, seeing all those people, and I said to myself, 'that's it,'" Kerry remembered.[74]

Before Operation RAW, Kerry had entered the race for Congress on an antiwar platform from his home district of Waltham, Massachusetts. When his campaign fizzled, Kerry endorsed the antiwar Catholic priest Robert F. Drinan, who triumphed at the polls. VVAW organizers contacted Kerry after watching him on the *Dick Cavett Show*, and he agreed to speak at Operation RAW. His involvement in VVAW would sharply escalate after the march; yet he repeatedly distanced himself from the Left. He considered himself "still a moderate—I'm not a radical in any sense of the word. I guess I'm just an angry young man."[75] Joe Urgo explained Kerry's decision to participate in Operation RAW and eventually to embrace VVAW: "He was . . . beginning to understand the importance of having a more mainstream voice in this crowd. And so that's what he represented, the mainstream Democratic Party coming in."[76]

Reports from FBI field agents indicated that VVAW had resurfaced, and its leaders were planning a march dubbed Operation RAW. The Philadelphia and Cincinnati offices sent teletypes to FBI headquarters in Washington expressing concern about the nature of the march, which was rumored to include "amputees from the Vietnam War" who would perform "search and destroy skits . . . along the way."[77] Such a march, Justice Department officials feared, might heighten the antiwar movement's momentum in the aftermath of Kent State. Watch VVAW carefully, the bureau advised agents in New York, New Jersey, and Philadelphia, in order to "determine the identities of organizations and radical, violent-prone [*sic*] participants" in Operation RAW.[78] Federal investigators discovered that the Youth International Party, or Yippies, a flamboyant youth group headed by Abbie Hoffman and Jerry Rubin, originally planned to participate in VVAW's mock search-and-destroy missions along the march route. The Yippies had agreed to portray Viet Cong captives but opted out at the last minute because of concerns that Operation RAW would be "too passive" and, ultimately, a "bore" and a "drag."[79]

Ironically, the FBI shared the Yippies' subdued appraisal. Agents who were initially expecting to unearth extremist, "violent-prone" behavior in

VVAW's plans for Operation RAW found that the organization intended "to retain respectability and does not want violence."[80] Cincinnati informants told the FBI that VVAWers would be equipped "with C-rations . . . and something that resembles an M-16 rifle. They are to carry their DD-214 forms [discharge papers] to prove they are actually veterans." An army surplus store in New York City offered to supply material and apparel to the marchers.[81] The New York office informed J. Edgar Hoover that FBI agents did not expect trouble from VVAW.[82] Still, the FBI decided not to take any chances. Agents in New Jersey and Philadelphia were assigned to monitor the marchers twenty-four hours a day and to file regular reports with the bureau.

At dawn, on September 4, FBI agents watched as men in olive fatigues began assembling in the Jockey Hollow area of Morristown National Historical Park in northern New Jersey. Like Valley Forge, Morristown played a significant role in the American Revolution: George Washington and his army were quartered there in the winters of 1776–77 and 1779–80. Marchers and a crowd of supporters gathered on a flat, grassy area surrounded by dense woods. By eight-thirty A.M., buses, vans, and automobiles dotted the landscape. A police helicopter whirred overhead while a documentary camera crew filmed veterans collecting toy M-16 rifles. Al Hubbard spoke into a public-address system: "We're leaving the park here with some seventy-five people. There will be people joining us en route, and we'll be en route for three and a half long days. . . . Let's move out." With those words, Operation RAW was under way.[83]

Early VVAW members, such as its founding members Sheldon Ramsdell and Dave Braum, trekked with recent recruits. VVAWers came from as far away as California and New Mexico. The column expanded daily. "Every day, every mile, more and more guys would come in," remembered one participant, Joel Greenberg.[84] They traveled from Morristown to Valley Forge for a variety of reasons. "I felt like putting my fist in someone's face, so the march was the next best thing," wrote Jerry Hultin of New Haven, Connecticut.[85] Greg Makota, from Pittsburgh, Pennsylvania, believed "the American public would take more notice of the peace movement . . . if the men who actually participated in the war actively protested against it."[86] Joseph Bremman added that he "wanted to march for peace instead of war, and the nurses weren't bad either."[87] Looking back on the march, Don Saunders concluded: "Four days and a few blisters were not too much to invest attempting to redeem the promise lost."[88]

During the first day, the marchers, carrying canteens, sleeping bags, and supplies, walked along the routes of lush Morris and Somerset Counties, New Jersey. Red arm bands worn by many indicated that they were Purple Heart recipients. In New Vernon and Bernardsville, the marchers selected actors from groups of bystanders and reenacted tense village sweeps. The results were often terrifying, as VVAWers in combat attire feigned kicking, punching, tying, torturing, stabbing, and shooting suspects. Some of the mock detainees were bruised and battered. During one terrifying moment, veterans restrained a traumatized ex-marine who snapped and tried to cut a civilian with a K-Bar knife. "Most of us revisited Vietnam at some point during Operation RAW," Bill Crandell later wrote.[89]

Crandell and twelve other men staged an incident outside Palumbo's Pharmacy in Bernardsville, in which they kidnapped a twenty-seven-year-old nurse and demanded the location of the community's arms. During the first day, marchers encountered little resistance. At one point along U.S. Route 202, they were stopped by Ernest Cummings, a forty-eight-year-old former paratrooper and veteran of the Battle of the Bulge in World War II. He held an American flag across his chest and shouted: "You men are a disgrace to your uniforms. You're a disgrace to everything we stand for. You ought to go back to Hanoi."[90]

The veterans reached their first campsite at five o'clock, a farm near Interstate 78. For the men in Operation RAW, the evenings became bonding experiences. Participants sat around lanterns, ate pork and beans, and talked. Some laughed, others recounted their experiences in Vietnam. A few wept. "Collectively, guys are talking about how we're going to fight sexism and racism," Urgo recalled. "It was really an astounding experience, looking back on it. Here you've got the epitome of the American males: bloodthirsty, John Wayne killers, who've just done all this shit to the [Vietnamese] people. Now here they are, talking a totally different language."[91] Added Bill Crandell: "There was a terrific need to get together and a terrific need to talk, particularly to talk to other people who had been there."[92]

The veterans, rested and refreshed, resumed their march at six A.M. on September 5. In western New Jersey, they recreated war scenes at the Whitehouse Station train depot, the Flemington Court House, the Sergeantsville fire station, Stockton's Main Street. In each town, they distributed a flier that announced, "A U.S. INFANTRY COMPANY JUST CAME THROUGH HERE. If you had been Vietnamese, we might have burned your house . . . shot your dog . . . shot you . . . raped your wife and daughter . . . turned you over to your government for torture. . . . If it doesn't bother you that American soldiers do these things every day to the Vietnamese simply because they are 'Gooks,' then picture yourself as one of the silent victims. HELP END THIS WAR BEFORE THEY TURN YOUR SON INTO A BUTCHER OR A CORPSE."[93] The marchers then crossed the Delaware River into Pennsylvania. The second day left several of the weary members feeling discouraged. They repeatedly encountered apathy or hostility among locals. Tensions ran high. Each night, perimeter guards patrolled the camps to make sure that threats from local veterans groups never materialized. In one town, a seventeen-year-old youth aimed a rifle at VVAWers. "I . . . was very surprised when I heard some watchers shouting, 'Why don't you guys go back to Russia!,'" wrote one marcher, Jeffrey Kirk.[94] Complained an observer: "This is the kind of thing that's causing riots in Chicago and other cities."[95] Another onlooker glumly declared, "If these are the kind of soldiers we have in Vietnam, then we'd better give up now."[96] One spectator even chided the veterans for their untidy appearance. "If they want to protest, they could at least look a little bit nicer," she said. "They looked like a motley crew."[97]

Many encounters were positive, however, and VVAWers found numerous sympathizers. "Kids in their parents' cars would give us the peace sign all the time," Robert Hanson recounted.[98] In some towns, "mayors would come out to greet us," added Jan Barry.[99] Three New Jersey residents searched the highways for the Operation RAW contingent. "We knew you were going to be on Route 202," said one of the supporters, "and we were driving along hoping to catch up with you and we have, and we're all for what you're doing." The guerrilla theater performances caused some watchers to reconsider their opinions. "It doesn't feel like a simulation, it feels like the real thing," appraised a bystander. "Maybe I've changed from a hawk to a dove now," one viewer said.[100] Friendly motorists in Bucks County, Pennsylvania, honked and shouted "Good luck" and "God bless you."[101]

The media provided extensive coverage. The *New York Times* offered daily updates, while local newspapers and television stations interviewed the veterans. "Pretty soon, they were driving us crazy," remembered Madelyn Moore, "with the newspapers, television, and what-have-you, all following this march."[102] News of the action garnered front-page headlines in the town newspapers along the route. "I guess for the local . . . media it was an interesting happening," said Hanson.[103] The FBI had scrutinized the march since Morristown, and the White House regularly received field agents' reports on the event.[104]

The final day of Operation RAW revealed the profound gap that existed between VVAW and conservative veterans' groups such as the American Legion and the Veterans of Foreign Wars (VFW). The organizations had clashed since the VVAW's inception, with hostilities occasionally escalating into shouting matches. Two weeks before Operation RAW, VVAW sponsored the "People's Army Jamboree" demonstration during the American Legion's national convention in Portland. A massive force of National Guard and police gathered in downtown Portland to monitor the activities of protesters, and a division of the army bivouacked in neighboring Vancouver, Washington. Despite numerous threats against the Jamboree planners, the event occurred without disturbance.[105]

Prowar veterans confronted the VVAW at the end of Operation RAW. Before reaching Valley Forge, the marchers approached counterdemonstrators from VFW Douglas A. McArthur Post 1507. The chaplain of the post announced: "Many of these in the march today, I feel from my heart, are blinded by none other than Satan, anti-Christ, anti-God, anti-America."[106] David McQueen, a forty-eight-year-old World War II veteran, held a sign that said: "Only the depraved want peace at any price."[107] "Why don't you go back to Hanoi?" heckled a VFW member. Another proclaimed, "I don't blame those fellows for not being proud. We won our war. These fellows didn't, and from the looks of it, they couldn't win."[108] Most marchers ignored the taunts. They whistled "Yankee Doodle" or flashed peace signs or middle fingers. Detrimental to the VFW's credibility was its inability to find Vietnam veterans who would publicly demonstrate in support of the war. "You couldn't find prowar [Vietnam] vets to debate," explained Urgo. "We looked for them . . . on this march."[109]

At eleven A.M., the column completed the eighty-six-mile trip, moving into the Grand Parade Ground in Valley Forge. Nearly two thousand rallygoers cheered them. Of the 150 Vietnam veterans who reached Valley Forge, 110 had been awarded Purple Hearts. Some of them carried body bags with large white numbers indicating the 43,419 men killed in the war. Speakers, including Jane Fonda, Allard Lowenstein, the author Mark Lane, and amputees from a neighboring army hospital, praised the marchers. The actor Donald Sutherland read the stirring final pages of Dalton Trumbo's *Johnny Got His Gun*. A few children of antiwar activists played war games with the plastic rifles used by VVAWers. At the end of the gathering, the crowd chanted "Peace Now!," while the haggard participants smashed the toy machine guns they had carried the previous four days. "I think we've raised some questions. I don't think we converted anyone. I think we've caused them to think a bit, and . . . that's what we set out to do," concluded Hubbard.[110]

"I could not bring the people to Vietnam, so I helped bring the Vietnam War to the people," wrote one marcher, Manuel Dones.[111] The creators of Operation RAW had reason to be pleased. The event attracted men who would later become the VVAW's most committed and energetic leaders. It served as a prototype for future VVAW protests. The march provided members with the impetus to continue organizing and provoked interest in creating new chapters around the country. Operation RAW also inspired an exhausted, discouraged, and divided peace movement. "The antiwar people were just stunned by it," Urgo recalled, "and they loved us. They really appreciated the truth and the strength of our convictions in this action." The organization received its largest infusion of new members since President Nixon had announced the invasion of Cambodia.[112]

One of the marchers, Ed Damato, later a national coordinator of VVAW, described what he called "the magic" of Operation RAW:

> In 1969, I went to Woodstock. That was one of those once-in-a-lifetime experiences of camaraderie, and common cause, and fun. And I had a twice-in-a-lifetime experience with Operation RAW. To me, it was like a small, veterans' Woodstock in many ways. . . . I've never seen such camaraderie between a group of people as that group. By the end of the first day, it was like we knew everybody for twenty years. For me, it was just, 'Jeez, look at all these people that feel the same I do, Vietnam veterans that are against this war. . . . It was like in the early sixties, another chance, another possibility, that things can change. . . . It was one of those magical, rare times when you felt open and trusting, and that you had a purpose in life.[113]

In spite of their success, VVAW leaders remained frustrated. While President Nixon had ordered a rapid removal of American troops from Cambodia on June 30, the war continued, with no resolution in sight. The invasion of Cambodia transformed the Vietnam War into the Indochina War. The president vowed to persist in Southeast Asia. American bombers daily pulverized Laos and Cambodia. Between the time of Operation RAW and the end of the year, nearly a thousand full body bags would return to the United States. As Jan Barry recalled: "Coming out of

[Operation RAW], people were angry that it was an enormous effort and it didn't seem to make a dent in the momentum of the war."[114]

At the end of 1969, a few activists had recognized VVAW's potential and spent months building and fortifying it. They updated mailing lists, located other antiwar veterans, and participated in local protests. These diligent organizers envisioned a nationwide movement, with autonomous chapters in all fifty states. Their hard work paid off. Hundreds of new members joined VVAW after the American invasion of Cambodia and the shootings at Kent State. Even more sent in their dues after Operation RAW. Although VVAW's strength remained concentrated in New York City, it was expanding by the summer of 1970, attracting newcomers across the country.

Altered tactics reflected the changing personalities of joiners. No longer did clean-cut VVAWers work on political campaigns and appear on televised debates. The new adherents were angrier, more confrontational. Unlike their forebears, they embraced militant action, such as the guerrilla street theater performed during Operation RAW. Most avoided suits and ties in favor of fatigues and combat boots. Long hair replaced crew cuts. Many members had been politicized amid the squalid conditions in VA hospitals. The veterans forged a new identity, rooted in the common experience of having served in Vietnam and reinforced by their shared disillusionment with the war.

After Operation RAW, VVAW leaders joined antiwar activists in planning hearings on American atrocities in Vietnam. Jan Barry, Scott Moore, Al Hubbard, and others hoped that uniting with CCI to organize the Winter Soldier war crimes investigation would help galvanize public opinion against the war. However, the alliance between VVAW and CCI proved short-lived. Personality clashes between leaders, coupled with legitimate political conflicts, undermined the efforts of the two groups. Nevertheless, VVAW would receive a vital boost from a high-profile source, resulting in the organization's largest growth spurt yet.

3

The War Itself Is a War Crime

While sitting around the evening campfires during Operation RAW, veterans shared stories about Vietnam. For many of them, talking about the war marked the beginning of the long healing process. Their accounts often dealt with death, pain, and guilt. Most of the participants simply could not reconcile their actions in Vietnam with their individual codes of ethics and humanity. It was a troubling realization, yet the marchers discovered they were not alone. Others felt the same remorse. In the process of describing their experiences, the veterans concluded that acts of brutality were not necessarily isolated aberrations but the inevitable outcomes of U.S. military policy in Southeast Asia.

VVAW leaders understood the intense emotional power of members' recollections. Activists in the national office believed that such stories, if presented in a proper forum, could convey the tragedy and senselessness of the war. After its highly successful Operation RAW in September 1970, VVAW allied with the Citizens' Commission of Inquiry on U.S. War Crimes in Vietnam (CCI), to initiate the Winter Soldier Investigation, hearings on atrocities in Southeast Asia. Both groups worked to locate veterans who would be willing to come forward. Most witnesses had yet to fashion a comprehensive critique of the war, but they felt the same inner conflict as the marchers of Operation RAW. The Vietnam War had evoked anger, resentment, self-loathing. The Winter Soldier Investigation would be but a beginning in rousing America's conscience and healing its veterans.

Typical of the joiners who wrestled with the war, and who eventually gravitated toward VVAW during the Winter Soldier Investigation, was a Florida native, Scott Camil. Camil was a man of contradictions. As a youngster, his grandmother had told him stories about relatives who had been murdered in Nazi concentration camps. "I never understood why soldiers would round up civilians and put them in concentration camps and kill them," he recalls. "And I didn't understand why people would kill people just because they were Jewish. So I developed a feeling for the underdog, the downtrodden." Neighborhood bullies in Camil's hometown of Hialeah, a suburb of Miami, Florida, regularly beat young Scott for "killing Jesus." Yet his grandmother continued to instill in him a belief in forgiveness and compassion.[1]

But there was another side to Camil. In high school, he took part in several fistfights with Cuban students, particularly when the immigrants cheered President Kennedy's assassination. His stepfather, a policeman and a leader of the local John Birch Society chapter, taught Camil obedience to authority and duty to the United States. Recruiters at Camil's high school convinced him to join the marines. "Part of my motivation was really a searching for who I was," Camil explained, "and trying to prove to my peers, 'Hey, . . . I'm a real man, I ain't gonna stick around here. I'm gonna go to war, I'm gonna fucking kill commies, I'm gonna win medals, and I'll show you guys.'"[2]

In Vietnam, Camil served as a forward observer with the 1st Marine Division. He lost many good friends in the war, and he grew to "hate the Vietnamese intensely."[3] He later remembered that G.I.s in his unit routinely burned villages and tortured and murdered peasants. They held beer parties, he claimed, celebrating the soldier responsible for the highest body count. Returning to the United States in 1969, Camil sought attention and praise for his service in Vietnam. He recalled:

> When I came back from Vietnam, the first thing I did was I went to the Pizza Palace, which was the hangout that we'd go to on Friday nights after the dance, after dates and stuff. Everybody would go in their cars. . . . And I went back there with all these pictures that I took in Vietnam of the people I killed, pictures that I still have, pictures of me standing on top of dead people, holding my rifle and smiling. And I'd show those pictures to everybody. I was pretty proud of them.[4]

So enthusiastic was Camil that the Marine Corps asked him to travel to college campuses to defend the war. But his stint as a speaker proved short-lived. At Western Carolina University in Cullowhee, North Carolina, Camil defended killing women and children before a shocked audience. "I said, 'Look, when you kill cockroaches, do you just kill the males or do you kill them all?'" he remembered. "I said, 'We're trying to wipe out communism, and the women are communist baby factories. If we don't kill them, they'll continue producing communist children. If we don't kill those children, they're going to grow up and fight our children.'" The Marines immediately canceled Camil's other speaking engagements.[5]

Shortly thereafter, late in 1969, Camil left the marines. He still despised the Vietnamese and distrusted antiwar protesters, but his attitudes about the war were beginning to change. He did not want to see more Americans die in a conflict that he believed generals and politicians had no intention of winning. More than a year after leaving the Marine Corps, Camil attended a speech given by the actress Jane Fonda at the University of Florida because he "wanted to see what a movie actress looked like."[6] She announced plans for a public inquiry into U.S. war crimes in Vietnam, scheduled to take place in Detroit, Michigan, in January and early February 1971. Camil spoke to Fonda at length about his experiences. Despite his ambivalent feelings, he decided to testify at the hearings. "The real reason, in my heart—not the reason I told people—but the real reason that I did this was because I was looking for recognition. We didn't have any parades. We didn't have shit. I wanted recognition, and I had lots of documentation from Vietnam because of my job as a forward observer."[7]

Camil joined more than a hundred other veterans from each branch of the armed forces at the Howard Johnson's New Center Motor Lodge in downtown Detroit, on January 31 and February 1–2, 1971. On the eve of the Winter Soldier Investigation, VVAW had approximately 8,500 members. The months leading up to the gathering had been tumultuous. For a brief time, VVAW and CCI had forged a united effort to plan national hearings, but a bitter split had occurred between the two groups. As a result of the rift, CCI planned its National Veterans' Inquiry for Washington, D.C., on December 1–3, 1970, while VVAW conducted the Winter Soldier Investigation two months later. The hearings generated little media attention. Nevertheless, the event would prove an important step toward the creation of a mass organization. Thousands of new members flocked to the organization as a result of a high-profile advertisement for VVAW in *Playboy* magazine, which hit the newsstands prior to the Detroit inquiry. For VVAW, the turbulent road to Winter Soldier began in August 1970, a few weeks before Operation RAW.

In a small, suburban house in Toronto, Ontario, Canada, two military deserters from the United States recounted atrocities they had observed in Vietnam. The young men had served in the 173rd Airborne Brigade, and they "described, in horrifying detail, . . . some of the human carnage they'd witnessed." No longer able to tolerate the war, the two joined a growing network of G.I.s who had fled to Canada. On a frigid January afternoon in 1970, the two ex-soldiers gathered with CCI's founders, Tod Ensign and Jeremy Rifkin. The meeting produced the first of Ensign and Rifkin's taped interviews. Thereafter, scores of soldiers and veterans cooperated with Ensign and Rifkin, providing testimony on brutal acts committed by Americans in Southeast Asia.[8]

Ensign and Rifkin had spent months preparing for the interviews. By documenting atrocities and planning hearings, the two activists hoped to organize antiwar Vietnam veterans and turn public opinion against American involvement in Southeast Asia. They received encouragement and guidance from Ralph Schoenman, the American leftist who had helped plan the Bertrand Russell International War Crimes Tribunal in 1967. With assistance from the Center for Constitutional Rights, Ensign, an attorney, investigated "the legal implications of veterans publicly admitting to criminal acts which they had witnessed or participated in." He discovered that the armed forces could not punish veterans for alleged crimes committed while they were on active duty. Having familiarized themselves with U.S. and international law, Ensign and Rifkin needed veterans willing to discuss American transgressions.[9]

They approached veterans' groups. They knew that the largest ones—the American Legion, Veterans of Foreign Wars, and Disabled American Veterans—were, in Tod Ensign's words, "rabidly prowar" and would be of little help.[10] Late in 1969, the two men visited the offices of VVAW in New York and Veterans for Peace in Chicago. Both were disappointed to find that VVAW consisted "of only a few active members and no regular staff. The Midwest group was larger but many of its members were veterans of earlier wars—not Vietnam."[11] Jan Barry had joined CCI's National Coordinating Committee by January 1970, but VVAW proved too small to provide much help. Nevertheless, Barry offered copies of the VVAW's short mailing list, which gave a few leads. A VVAWer living in Brooklyn, "who had long hair and smoked dope," showed Ensign, Rifkin, and Barry slides of him posing alongside heads taken from the bodies of Vietnamese victims.[12]

The Vietnam veterans Bob Johnson, a U.S. army captain, and Michael Uhl, a former military intelligence officer with the Americal Division, joined CCI as full-time staff. Endless hours of searching for testimony yielded results. In the spring and summer of 1970, CCI conducted nine hearings in cities across the country, which drew widespread publicity.

"We were trying to blast out this message across the country, making the point as broadly as we could, using the only means we had, which was the media," Ensign recalled.[13]

But the organization operated on a shoestring budget, and its bank account was empty by August 1970. That month, VVAW executive secretary Al Hubbard approached Ensign and Rifkin and proposed that CCI join forces with VVAW; the Reverend Dick Fernandez, head of Clergy and Laymen Concerned about Vietnam (CALCAV); ex-Green Beret Donald Duncan; the attorney Mark Lane; and the actress Jane Fonda to organize national war crimes hearings. "It was the old story," Ensign explained. "We were hurting for money. . . . And they [VVAW] wanted to film it. See, in those days you didn't have video, . . . a documentary film was a major undertaking. . . . And [Fonda] had all these connections, she knew all these people, she could get people on the phone."[14] On August 27, Jeremy Rifkin wrote to Michael Uhl in Paris to inform him that CCI and VVAW were "planning an International Inquiry into War Crimes to be held . . . in Detroit and Windsor, Canada. It will involve Vietnamese victims and over 100 Vietnam vets. The Inquiry is being called 'Winter Soldier Investigation.'"[15]

The name "Winter Soldier" had been derived from the stirring opening lines of Thomas Paine's *The American Crisis*: "These are the times that try men's souls. The summer soldier and the sunshine patriot will, in this crisis, shrink from the service of his country; but he that stands it *now*, deserves the love and thanks of man and woman."[16] The idea behind the name came from the New York City attorney Mark Lane. During the summer of 1970, VVAW had contacted Lane, who agreed to ask his good friend, Jane Fonda, to speak at the closing rally of Operation RAW. Fonda had just finished filming *Klute*, a thriller in which she portrayed a prostitute (a role that would land her an Academy Award). Fonda not only agreed to speak at the VVAW march; she took a strong interest in the organization.[17]

Jane Fonda's conversion to radicalism was swift. During the sixties, she had shown no interest in New Left politics or radical movements. In early 1970, she sailed to Alcatraz island, defying a Coast Guard blockade, to deliver supplies to militant Native Americans who had taken over the famous site of the former maximum-security prison. Following her visit to Alcatraz, Fonda attended a party at the Malibu home of Elliott Gould, where she learned about the Black Panthers from one of their most ardent supporters, Shirley Sutherland, wife of the actor Donald Sutherland.

At a Hollywood party honoring the Italian filmmaker Michelangelo Antonioni, she met Fred Gardner, the activist who had launched the G.I. coffeehouse movement. The two became close friends, and Gardner introduced her to Mark Lane, a lawyer and the author of *Rush to Judgment*, a controversial book, published in 1966, that criticized the Warren Commission's findings on the Kennedy assassination.[18]

On March 25, Fonda embarked on a two-month automobile trip across the country, in which she visited Indian reservations, addressed soldiers at military bases, protested the invasion of Cambodia, and marched in front of stores that sold nonunion lettuce. Fonda quickly earned the respect of activists. "That lady was out there working in coffeehouses without telling anybody who she was," Jan Barry recalled.[19] She often traveled with Lane, speaking at demonstrations and marching at rallies. While Fonda was wrapping up *Klute*, Lane met with VVAW executive secretary Al Hubbard in Fonda's New York City apartment to discuss the possibility of conducting war crimes hearings. Lane had just completed a book, *Conversations with Americans*, to be published by Simon & Schuster, in which he interviewed twenty-two servicemen and veterans who professed to have personal knowledge of American atrocities in Vietnam. He hoped a national inquiry would illuminate the horrors soldiers described in his book. VVAWers offered encouragement and support to Lane, who marched alongside the veterans from Morristown to Valley Forge. "After Operation RAW," Lane recalled, Fonda, Hubbard and he "had some meetings, and I suggested calling the inquiry 'the Winter Soldier Investigation,' after Paine. What happened in Vietnam was the summer, and now this was the difficult winter period."[20] Fonda wanted to raise funds for the undertaking, and she "realized that—given its track record—CCI had to be brought in to organize the effort," remembered CCI staffer Michael Uhl.[21]

Following Operation RAW, VVAW activists turned their attention to the Winter Soldier Investigation. A newcomer, Michael Oliver, who would prove one of the VVAW's most creative and enduring organizers, dedicated his time and energy to searching for cooperative veterans. In the fall, Tim Butz, busily building a VVAW chapter at Kent State, received a telephone call from Mark Lane. "He introduced himself and said, 'Look, we need some guys to work full-time on this thing, can you come to Detroit and work with us?'" recounted Butz. "And I said, 'I don't know.' And he said, 'Hang on,' and he put Jane Fonda on the phone, and I'll be honest, my head was turned by someone who was a movie actress saying, 'We need you to help us out.' So I said, 'When do you want me there?'" Butz immediately joined the Winter Soldier staff in Detroit.[22]

VVAW had much to gain from its alliance with CCI. Many of the witnesses who testified at CCI hearings, according to Ensign, were "drawn into the VVAW orbit."[23] At times, VVAWers seemed more interested in luring new recruits than in tracking down accounts of atrocities. "I had driven with Jeremy Rifkin . . . in September 1970 from Columbus to Minneapolis," wrote Bill Crandell, "organizing new chapters as he collected testimony."[24] Shrewd activists recognized that planning the Winter Soldier Investigation presented the perfect opportunity to restructure VVAW. As Crandell recounted:

> WSI was very important for its effect on VVAW's growth into a nationwide, mass organization. The search for testimony had led organizers . . . to crisscross the country looking for anti–Vietnam War vets. . . . [Michael] Oliver made it a point to organize and appoint state coordinators wherever he went.[25]

Crandell characterized the interaction between CCI and VVAW as "disharmonious," but others recall a more positive relationship.[26] Participants shared offices on the tenth floor of 156 Fifth Avenue. "There wasn't a day that went by that we weren't all mixed together," remembered Uhl, "in the coffee shops, the lobby, the elevators, meetings, demos, rallies, street theater, each other's offices."[27] Despite their preference for conducting the Winter Soldier Investigation in Washington, D.C., CCI representatives agreed to VVAW's choice of Detroit as the site for the hearings so that Vietnamese refugees could testify from neighboring Windsor, Canada, via closed-circuit television. VVAWers admired CCI's skilled organizers. Jan Barry thought Ensign and Rifkin "were both very good at fund-raising and coalition building."[28]

The effort was financed primarily by Jane Fonda, who maintained a hectic pace traversing the country to solicit donations. In October, Fonda embarked on a lecture tour, which eventually took her to fifty-four college campuses and brought in more than $10,000 for VVAW. Often accompanied by Mark Lane, Fonda devoted herself passionately to her newfound political agenda. At the close of her lecture tour speeches, she raised a clinched fist in the air and shouted, "All power to the people!"[29] She also pitched VVAW on her many visits to the *Dick Cavett Show*.[30] Conservatives detested the outspoken performer. While raising funds for the VVAW, her militant speeches drove some students away, and she received "innumerable bomb threats."[31]

Authorities carefully scrutinized Fonda's movements. Agents with the FBI's Counterintelligence Program (COINTELPRO) increased their surveillance of the actress after she attended a benefit for the Black Panther Party during the summer. On November 3, Fonda flew to Cleveland from Canada to raise money for the Winter Soldier Investigation. At Cleveland's Hopkins Airport, customs officials arrested and detained Fonda, alleging that her shoulder bag contained amphetamines and tranquilizers and that the contents of her suitcase included 105 plastic vials of capsules. She claimed the capsules were "organic vitamins I brought on the advice of my father."[32] The following day, Lane arrived in Cleveland to defend Fonda in court. "She was my most militant client, too militant for me," he recounted. "We got into the courtroom before a federal magistrate, and there are certain rules, you're trying to win the case. . . . She turned her chair with her back to the court, to show her contempt for the court. I told her I didn't think it was a good idea, but she did it."[33] Fonda later learned that she was on a government list of radicals to be searched by customs officers. Her arrest amounted to nothing more than harassment, and the charges were eventually dismissed.[34]

In the meantime, Winter Soldier Investigation organizers faced their own obstacles. Some witnesses were intimidated by authorities. After the pilot Dave Bressem appeared at a CCI event to discuss "turkey shoots," in which helicopter personnel shot fleeing Vietnamese peasants from the air, investigators claiming to be from the Pentagon visited his house seeking the names of those involved in the incident. Their purpose, Ensign remembered, was to frighten Bressem into naming names so that they could "prosecute low-ranking G.I.s."[35] Bressem also received a telephone call from his commanding officer, who warned him that publicly discussing atrocities might jeopardize his military career.[36]

In addition to the threat of persecution, many participants were troubled by their recent experiences in Vietnam. Their accounts transformed the abstract issue of war crimes into the very real terror of routine torture and murder. But such stories were not easy to tell. "While we did befriend a number of the veterans with whom we worked," remembered Ensign, "I don't think we understood that some of them were suffering from posttraumatic stress disorder. I'm afraid our concern for uncovering and presenting powerful testimony of war crimes policies sometimes blocked our awareness of the anguish many vets felt about their role as soldiers."[37]

In other instances, attention seekers embellished or lied about their experiences. Because the strength of a witness depended on his credibility, organizers carefully weeded out hoaxers. "You had to find somebody else to back up what they've got to say," recalled Barry. "You've got to double-check their credentials. If they claim they were in Special Forces, they goddamned well better have been in Special Forces."[38]

But the worst setback to the Winter Soldier Investigation occurred in early November, when a bitter schism developed between VVAW and CCI. Like most sectarian divisions that fractured antiwar and New Left groups throughout the sixties and early seventies, the split made the most sense to those directly involved. Different factions offered conflicting explanations.

For their part, CCI organizers distrusted Mark Lane. They found him too arrogant and authoritarian. "The disharmony . . . was between CCI and Lane," explained Michael Uhl.[39] In October, Uhl and other veterans returned to New York from a war crimes inquiry in Stockholm, Sweden. At the Stockholm gathering, the veterans had had a negative encounter with Lane. Uhl reported to Ensign that Lane had acted belligerently, attacking one witness as a racist and dismissing the veterans' testimony as unimpressive. Moreover, Lane's recently published *Conversations with Americans* was criticized by CCI staffers as sensationalistic, "sleazy exploitation."[40] "The book had . . . shoddy reporting in it, some really questionable accounts," Ensign remembered, such as "people using terms that anyone who was in Vietnam would know were not accurate, unit designations that were inaccurate, that would raise your eyebrows about the people and their credibility. But Lane didn't care. The more bodies, the better."[41]

In early November, Ensign and Rifkin proposed that the Winter Soldier Investigation steering committee expel Mark Lane. But Jane Fonda was fiercely loyal to him. For months, the two had been inseparable, traveling to college campuses and parties, raising funds, rallying support. He had defended her when she was arrested in Cleveland on trumped-up drug charges. Now a group of impetuous antiwar organizers were demanding that she jettison her close friend. "Fonda, Lane, and the VVAW came as a package," wrote James Simon Kunen.[42] When Fonda "threatened to withdraw her cash," Ensign recounted, "the VVAW stuck with them and we split."[43]

VVAWers had their own version of events. They were skeptical about CCI's goal of aiming testimony at policymakers and the media. Many

VVAW activists felt that "everything's been directed at Congress for years, and what have those fuddy-duddies ever done?"[44] The place to start making change, they reasoned, was in the heartland, not in the centers of power. "One camp [CCI] wanted to go to [Washington,] D.C., because the idea was to influence the politicians," remembered Joe Urgo. "The other camp [VVAW] wanted to go to a place like Detroit . . . because of its working-class history and the auto plants. And it was an attempt to reach out to . . . middle America."[45]

To other organizers, the split made little sense, and neither side offered cogent justifications. Tim Butz believed the rift was the result of personality clashes, not genuine political differences:

> In retrospect, my overriding impression was the two efforts really held much in common, but there was a lot of personality and ego involved in how the information was going to be presented. And there were these fine points that divided people that served probably as the window dressing to make the split seem political rather than personal.[46]

Jan Barry, who had desperately tried to keep VVAW and CCI together, had grown disillusioned with the organization he had helped to create in 1967. "I attempted to bridge the two groups and almost got torn apart," Barry recalled.[47] Barry could not understand why "people on the same side of the same issue" felt such "bad vibes" toward one another.[48] His inability to prevent the split was indicative of his weakening influence over VVAW. Since its revival in the fall of 1969, the very essence of the VVAW had changed. It had become an angrier, more militant organization, and the easygoing leader could do little to temper its members. The internecine struggles that characterized the parting of ways between CCI and VVAW bewildered Barry. Such behavior seemed to him to be symptomatic of the left's failure to put aside differences and coalesce around significant matters.[49]

In early December, a frustrated Barry wrote an open letter of resignation to CCI and VVAW activists. He had had enough, he said, of being VVAW's president and a member of the Winter Soldier Investigation steering committee. "I believe in poetry, not politics," Barry wrote. "The ripoffs and power plays of the past month—both within and outside Winter Soldier and VVAW—are disgusting. . . . We war criminals, even retired, should not shout again at each other of 'purity'—we lost that right, and innocence, when we went to war."[50] After distributing the letter, Barry quietly withdrew for a short time, to reassess his role in VVAW. The infighting had demoralized him, and his friends knew that he disliked strife of any kind. "Jan, of course, was a very intelligent man, a poet and a writer," Madelyn Moore remembered. "He added some smoothness to this whole affair, as opposed to . . . the rawness of some of the vets."[51] Other observers believed Barry could not understand the rage and combativeness of newcomers. "He was not a happy camper," recalled Michael Uhl, who remained on good terms with Barry after the split. "As a 'peace person,' Jan hated conflict and 'politics.' His brand of moral witness was completely out of sync with the gritty, blue-collar temper of the antiwar veteran culture."[52]

With some misgivings, Barry returned to the position of VVAW president. But recent events had soured him. He would remain the organization's leader through the end of April 1971.

By mid-November, CCI was busily planning its National Veterans' Inquiry, scheduled to occur in Washington, D.C., on December 1–3. VVAW had relocated its Winter Soldier Investigation headquarters to a small, rented house at 967 Emerson Street, in the industrial east side of Detroit. Six full-time staffers, Tim Butz, Bill Crandell, Art Flesch, Al Hubbard, Scott Moore, and Michael Oliver, worked day and night, making telephone calls, crossing the country, searching for new witnesses. The often gruesome testimony jarred them. Mark Lane, who frequently stayed at the house, heard veterans screaming in the middle of the night. So troubled was Jane Fonda by the nocturnal yelling and moans that she moved out of her room at Emerson Street after a few days. "It gave everybody who worked on the project bad dreams, obviously," recalled Robert Hanson, who occasionally visited the Detroit headquarters.[53]

At the same time, regional organizers canvassed veterans in their area. In Philadelphia, Joe Bangert and Ken Campbell, two former marines who planned to participate in the Detroit hearings, founded a local VVAW chapter. "Whenever anybody called to ask about joining the chapter, who we were, what we were about, I would also ask them about the war crimes atrocity angle," Campbell remembered. He and Bangert built a "sizable" Philadelphia-area contingent. "We were well represented in Detroit," he said.[54]

The Winter Soldier Investigation introduced many veterans to the VVAW for the first time. Jon Floyd, a fighter pilot from Dallas, Texas, said it was his first "overt" protest against the war. VVAW had asked Floyd to discuss the effects of the air war in Vietnam. Before going to Detroit, the twenty-four-year-old marine captain felt a sense of "great disappointment and real alienation" as a result of his experiences in Vietnam. "But there was no place to put it until Vietnam Vets Against the War came along," he explained. Providing information at the hearings was "the right channel, it was the right thing to do."[55] Rusty Sachs, another newcomer to the antiwar movement, "begged, borrowed, and ingratiated myself to others, borrowing ten bucks here, five bucks there," to raise the money for a one-hundred-dollar roundtrip airline ticket from Boston to Detroit. He discovered VVAW after John Kerry called him to discuss one of his antiwar letters to the editor. "John came over for dessert, he discussed VVAW the entire time," Sachs remembered.[56] Kerry persuaded the young veteran to attend the upcoming war crimes inquiry. Scott Camil "had never been to an antiwar demonstration. I didn't even consider this to be an antiwar demonstration. I just considered it to be patriotic duty. The public has the right to know the . . . truth."[57] Mark Lane interviewed prospective witnesses and encountered some active-duty soldiers who were eager to testify. "We had no right to say, 'you can't speak,'" he recounted. "But we had an obligation to say, 'this could be dangerous for you.'" Few were dissuaded by Lane's warnings.[58]

To the organizers of the Winter Soldier Investigation, it seemed that the worst crisis had passed. VVAW had emerged from its split with CCI with determination and vigor. New participants came forward daily. But with one month left until the hearings, VVAW suffered another difficult blow. On December 27, Neil Sheehan, a reporter who had spent three years in Vietnam, wrote a scathing review of Mark Lane's *Conversations With Americans* in the *New York Times Book Review*. "This book is so irresponsible," the review began, "that it may help provoke a responsible inquiry into the question of war crimes and atrocities in Vietnam."[59]

After checking Pentagon and military records, Sheehan discovered that several of Lane's interviewees had fabricated accounts of atrocities in Vietnam. One ex-marine, Chuck Onan, told Lane he had been in a long-range patrol unit and received parachute, frogman, and jungle-survival training. In the latter course, Onan claimed, he learned how "to torture prisoners."[60] Marine records, however, indicated that Onan never received such training, and he had deserted his job as a stockroom clerk in 1968.[61] Sheehan found three other individuals in the book who had provided Lane with false information. "'Conversations with Americans' is a lesson in what happens when a society shuns the examination of a pressing, emotional issue and leaves the answers to a Mark Lane," Sheehan concluded.[62]

For VVAW, the controversial review could not have appeared at a worse time. The book's publisher, Simon & Schuster, canceled all further printings of the book and demanded Lane return his advance.[63] Not only was Lane's reputation severely undermined; the very credibility of the Detroit hearings was at stake. Sheehan's exposé had placed VVAW leaders in a difficult position. Lane's involvement with the planning of the Winter Soldier Investigation had been extensive. His legal and financial assistance had proven invaluable. Few VVAWers doubted his sincerity or devotion to the effort. Yet they feared that associating with Lane could tarnish months of difficult work. "Then the question became, 'How do we protect our integrity?'" recalled Joe Urgo, "'How do we separate ourselves from this guy?'"[64]

Organizers hoped Lane would maintain a low profile. Their wishes were fulfilled. In the weeks that followed Sheehan's review, Lane spent much of his time trying to refute what he believed was a Pentagon disinformation campaign against him. "I went around the country and got statements from everybody [in the book] to prove that they existed, all kinds of proof," Lane remembered. "I got these documents, and sent them over, at which point Simon & Schuster apologized profusely, for having been used by the Pentagon and the *New York Times*."[65] Still, the damage had been done. Sheehan's review had weakened Lane's believability.[66]

VVAW escaped from the imbroglio unharmed. With the inquiry fast approaching, funds continued to pour in from antiwar celebrities. Before the event, Jane Fonda organized a show, "Acting in Concert for Peace," which featured performances by Fonda, Donald Sutherland, and Dick Gregory, as well as the singers Barbara Dane, Graham Nash, David Crosby, and Phil Ochs. Two Detroit attorneys, Dean Robb and Ernest Goodman, rallied support from local lawyers. United Auto Workers Secretary-Treasurer Emil Mazey and Michigan's secretary of state, Richard Austin, endorsed the program. Protestant, Jewish, and Catholic clergy in Detroit arranged lodging for the witnesses. "[It] is important that the public realize that American atrocities in Vietnam are an everyday occurrence," announced one supporter, Dr. John B. Forsyth, director of missions for the Detroit Metropolitan Council of Churches.[67]

The biggest boost to VVAW, however, came from *Playboy* magazine. During the last week in December, subscribers and newsstands received the February issue. The periodical contained a stark, full-page advertisement for VVAW, featuring a lone coffin with an American flag draped over it. "In the last ten years, over 335,000 of our buddies have been killed or wounded in Vietnam," a bold headline announced, "And more are being killed and wounded every day. We don't think it's worth it."[68] A coupon in the lower left side invited Vietnam veterans to join VVAW. "[*Playboy* editor] Hugh [Hefner] decided he was going to give us a full page of advertising," recalled Madelyn Moore, "and my husband convinced our advertising agency to do the ad." By the middle of January, Moore said, the national office began receiving "mail not to be believed. I mean, sacks and sacks and sacks of this mail came in. Finally, we had to call for volunteers to help."[69]

Hundreds of letters arrived daily, many from Vietnam. Joe Urgo, who handled the mail, was overwhelmed. He estimated the advertisement drew more than five thousand new members to VVAW. The number of names on the membership rolls rapidly surpassed 8,500 and continued to rise.[70] Robert Hanson helped sort the correspondence. He noticed that Urgo seemed troubled. "He would get letters from . . . people who became members in Vietnam, courtesy of the *Playboy* ad, that would come back 'person deceased,' and that happened a lot," Hanson recalled. "And that started to make him crazy, because from his point of view, he could see the whole organization. People were not numbers, but names."[71]

The sizable influx of joiners expedited activists' efforts to restructure VVAW. The small bureaucracy that Jan Barry and other veterans had created in 1967 no longer sufficed for the growing numbers. VVAW would become, in Bill Crandell's words, "a national organization run by a steering committee composed of twenty-six regional coordinators."[72] The coordinators agreed to meet in New York City, after the Detroit event, to ratify a new constitution. VVAW was moving beyond the confines of New York City and transforming itself into a mass movement. Its leaders hoped the Winter Soldier Investigation would nurture that growth even more.[73]

VVAW reserved two ballrooms in the Howard Johnson's New Center Motor Lodge at West Grand Boulevard and Third Avenue in Detroit for the Winter Soldier Investigation. The order of the testimonies had been meticulously structured, well in advance of the hearings. Witnesses included veterans from each branch of the armed services and from virtually every combat unit. They represented different periods of the war;

some had served as early as 1962. The goal of the inquiry, Joe Urgo explained, was to demonstrate that war crimes in Vietnam—massacres, torture of prisoners, and employment of chemical and biological weapons outlawed by international treaties—were the inevitable outcome of American military policies in Southeast Asia. He described the framework for the hearings:

> When you . . . divide it up by units, with the earlier years and the later years, a pattern develops. From all of the units in Vietnam, from all of the years in Vietnam, for all of the different sections of Vietnam, the policies are the same. GIs can't be individually responsible for wiping out this village if what they're doing is what's being taught, encouraged, inculcated, all the way from top to bottom.[74]

But organizers would encounter another obstacle. Days before the hearings, the Canadian government denied visas to Vietnamese refugees who planned to present accounts of atrocities via closed-circuit television from neighboring Windsor, Canada. The witnesses included a fourteen-year-old girl and her father, who had bicycled to North Vietnam from their village in South Vietnam. Without the closed-circuit testimonies, the inquiry lost the crucial Vietnamese perspective.[75]

The absence of the refugees fixed the resolve of VVAWers. On Sunday morning, January 31, before the 1st Marine Division panel convened, Bill Crandell read the stirring opening statement of the Winter Soldier Investigation:

> "Like the winter soldiers of 1776, who stayed after they had served their time, we veterans of Vietnam know that America is in grave danger," he said. "What threatens our country is not Redcoats or even Reds; it is our crimes that are destroying our national unity, by separating those of our countrymen who deplore these acts from those of our countrymen who refuse to examine what is being done in America's name."[76]

Then, one by one, witnesses came forward and related their experiences in Vietnam, often in unsettling detail. Veterans testified that they had been conditioned in basic training to commit atrocities. Joe Bangert referred to an officer at Camp Pendleton who used a rabbit to teach Marines about survival tactics. "He has this rabbit, and then in a couple of seconds after just about everyone falls in love with it, . . . he cracks the neck, skins it, disembowels it. . . . That's the last lesson you catch in the United States before you leave for Vietnam," Bangert said.[77] From his first day in boot camp, John Gerryman was told, "'You've gotta go to Vietnam, you've gotta kill gooks. They're no good. . . .' And this thing is built into you, it's thrust into your head. . . . You're not to question, you're not to ask why."[78]

Several witnesses discussed torture methods. Former interrogator Nathan Hale, a Specialist 5th Class with the Americal Division, was told by his captain in Vietnam to use any means necessary to elicit information from prisoners. "I personally used clubs, rifle butts, pistols, knives," Hale explained.[79] Kenneth Ruth, a former E-4 in the 1st Air Cavalry Division, showed slides of torture methods in Vietnam, including one prisoner who was strapped to a tree while an interrogator yanked on a rope tied to his testicles. "This is the general attitude, you know, Vietnamese aren't humans," he concluded.[80]

Accounts of rape were also numerous. "Our platoon sergeant . . . said, 'If there's a woman in a hootch, lift up her dress, you know, and tell by her sex; if it's a male, kill him; and if it's a female, rape her,'" testified Michael Farrell.[81] While outside Hue following the Tet Offensive, Michael Hunter, a sergeant in the Air Cavalry Regiment, watched a squad round up women in the area and threaten to kill them unless they submitted to sexual intercourse with the G.I.s. Joe Galbally of the Americal Division remembered when a "young girl" was "taken out, raped by six or seven people in front of her family, in front of us and the villagers." He claimed that he knew of "10 or 15 such incidents, at least."[82]

But the unifying theme that laced together most of the testimonies was the daily, random horror that characterized combat in Vietnam. Witnesses related story after story of unrelenting carnage: marine officers seeing how far they could throw a prisoner tied in the fetal position out of a helicopter; jets dropping napalm on heavily populated civilian areas; G.I.s torching occupied houses; soldiers shooting fleeing civilians in "free-fire zones." "Its power lay in its very boredom," noted a *New Republic* commentator, "for one kept being jolted by the recognition that multiplied accounts of murder and bestiality were boring. But as the accounts slogged on, the very commonness, the quotidian character of atrocity, identified itself as the core of dehumanization that accounts for war crimes."[83]

With stark eloquence, Scott Camil recounted "the burning of villages, the cutting off of ears, cutting off of heads, torturing of prisoners, calling in of artillery on villages for games, corpsmen killing wounded prisoners, napalm dropped on villages, women being raped, women and children being massacred."[84] He remembered an incident in which a lieutenant tore the clothes off of a peasant who requested water, and the soldiers "stabbed her in both breasts, they spread-eagled her and shoved an E-tool up her vagina, an entrenching tool, and she was still asking for water. And then they took that out and used a tree limb and then she was shot."[85] Special Forces Sp/4 Steve Noetzel watched sixteen prisoners loaded aboard two helicopters. When the helicopters returned to base, only four prisoners were left. He discovered "flesh from the hands of the prisoners when they were pushed out of the door jambs" and "blood on the floor where they had been beaten and pushed out of the helicopters." One of the pilots claimed the prisoners "tried to escape over the Mekong Delta."[86]

While accounts of atrocities dominated the event, special panels also convened to discuss the cultural and ecological destruction of Vietnam, racism in the military, the impact of different types of weaponry, and the treatment of prisoners of war. Conspicuously absent from the inquiry, however, was a session on women and the war. A number of women had served as nurses or in noncombat roles in Vietnam. Moreover, the mothers, sisters, and companions of veterans understood well the war's toll on soldiers.

Nevertheless, only four of the more than one hundred veterans and sixteen civilians who presented testimony were women. The mother and the sister of prisoner-of-war James Warner appeared. Dr. Marjorie Nelson, a medical doctor who volunteered at a child day care and civilian rehabilitation center in Quang Ngai, discussed an incident in which she was kidnapped by NLF and NVA forces during the Tet Offensive. Mary Emeny of the American Friends Service Committee recounted her experiences at a Buddhist orphanage in Da Nang in 1968. Yet the Winter Soldier Investigation failed to address crucial gender issues related to the Vietnam War. So noticeable was the shortage of women witnesses that, at one point, an audience member charged the hearings' organizers with sexism. A panel moderator condescendingly replied, "Well, madam, the fact is that there's very few women, and this is a credit to them, that have picked up guns and bombs and killed Vietnamese and that's mainly who has testified today."[87]

This was not the first or last time that allegations of male chauvinism were levied against VVAW. The organization repeatedly endured criticism from feminists, and debate would later stir within its ranks. While some veterans thoughtfully grappled with matters of gender inequity, many others failed to confront their machismo.

The winter soldier investigation concluded on Tuesday evening, January 2, 1971. Veterans went home, and organizers lamented the event's sparse media coverage. In fact, the inquiry instantly became a case study for its failure to attract television and newspaper attention. There was much that was newsworthy about the hearings. On the first day, panels on the 1st and 3rd Marine Divisions offered the first public evidence that American troops were conducting combat operations in Laos early in 1969, a fact not widely known at the time. Other veterans recounted an incident during the Christmas truce of 1969 in which American soldiers ambushed unarmed Vietnamese, killing as many as thirty-one villagers. During a session on weapons, Dr. Bert Pfeiffer, a biologist from the University of Montana, presented the first public testimony on the toxic effects of Agent Orange.[88]

Daily, the *Detroit Free Press* allocated generous space to the investigation.[89] The *Chicago Sun Times* extensively reported allegations, often including lengthy excerpts of testimony.[90] But most newspapers either downplayed or ignored the Winter Soldier Investigation. "The news was not going out beyond the Midwest," Barry recalled. "The Detroit papers, the Chicago papers, a few other Midwestern cities. That was it."[91] On February 7, a week after the hearings began, the *New York Times* ran a terse story, dismissing the hearings by insisting that "much of what they said had been reported or televised before, even from Vietnam."[92] The veterans anticipated poor coverage from the *Times* when Jerry Flint, the correspondent who covered the event, declared that "this stuff happens in all wars."[93] Though the Associated Press regularly sent updated reports over the wire, most newspapers remained uninterested. Even the then-liberal *New Republic* waited a month to report the highlights of Winter Soldier. With the exception of CBS, which mentioned it, the networks neglected the inquiry entirely. But CBS News "refused . . . to broadcast film that it had already shot of the Winter Soldier Investigation," wrote Todd Gitlin.[94]

The media's indifference demoralized organizers. Speculation about the inquiry's poor exposure was rife. Some veterans believed the American public simply did not want to hear that atrocities were commonplace in Vietnam. Others thought "mainstream" journalists were too terrified to touch the Winter Soldier Investigation.[95] But location also diminished the impact of the inquiry. Early in the its planning stages, the CCI leader Jeremy Rifkin repeatedly warned organizers that the selection of Detroit as a venue would significantly decrease the event's media coverage. "The problem Jeremy had was that VVAW wanted to have it in Detroit, not in

Washington," Tod Ensign recalled. "He thought that was stupid. . . . Jeremy always focused on the power and on the real media centers."[96] VVAW organizers dismissed Rifkin's warnings, emphasizing instead the importance of reaching out to "the heartland" and "the working class."[97] Yet Rifkin's advice proved prophetic. CCI's smaller National Veterans' Inquiry, conducted December 1–3 at the Dupont Plaza Hotel in Washington, D.C., drew far more national newspaper attention than the Winter Soldier Investigation. "[Detroit] may not have been the wisest place in the world to have it, in hindsight. It should've been in Washington," VVAW organizer Ed Damato concluded.[98]

Nevertheless, authorities were alarmed about VVAW's potential to influence public opinion. A White House official, Charles Colson, began to investigate the organization. "The men that participated in the pseudo-atrocity hearings in Detroit will be checked out to ascertain if they are genuine Viet Nam combat veterans," read a confidential memo titled, "Plan to Counteract Viet Nam Veterans Against the War," in Colson's White House files.[99] After the hearings, the FBI and the Nixon administration stepped up surveillance of VVAW.[100]

Despite poor publicity, the Winter Soldier Investigation was successful in other respects. On a personal level, the hearings became a therapeutic event for many veterans. One former army sergeant, who was "shaking and half in tears," later recalled that it was "the first time I ever got up in front of a group of people and told them anything about myself."[101] Other witnesses confronted their past for the first time in Detroit. "I came here for a lot of reasons," one explained. "I have bad dreams. I have nightmares. I have guilt feelings."[102] William Bezanson traveled to Detroit to present his testimony and "find out how many of my brothers felt the same way I did." For Bezanson, speaking out about his personal experiences diminished some of his anguish and remorse. He hoped his recollections would "stop . . . my younger brother or some of your younger brothers or sisters, or your children, from going over there and having to come home and live with these same nightmares."[103]

In broader terms, VVAW matured as a result of the hearings. In addition to the hundred witnesses who testified, as many as five hundred Vietnam veterans met in the hallways and rooms of the motel to discuss VVAW's future. Ed Damato remembered a feeling of excitement in the air in Detroit. He marveled at "how that drew people together, people from around the country. Out of that, the groundwork was laid to build a national organization."[104] Veterans swapped telephone numbers and addresses. Many returned to their hometowns feeling empowered and politicized by the event.[105]

It also inspired congressional doves in Washington, D.C. The inquiry was endorsed by Representatives John Conyers of Michigan, Ron Dellums of California, Bella Abzug of New York, Robert Drinan of Massachusetts, and others. "The atrocities and war crimes that these men—all honorably discharged and many decorated veterans of the Southeast Asian conflict—alleged were committed in Vietnam are of so serious a nature that they must be heard," Representative Michael J. Harrington (D-Mass.) announced at a VVAW press conference on February 5.[106] While veterans presented testimonies, Senator George McGovern of South Dakota and Representative Conyers called for a congressional investigation into the charges made at the Winter Soldier Investigation. "These are serious facts that require immediate and intensive review," McGovern announced. "The American people must know all the facts about our military policy in Indochina."[107] In April, Senator Mark Hatfield, the antiwar Republican from Oregon, read the entire transcript of the inquiry into *The Congressional Record*.[108]

But VVAW leaders were disappointed with the event, largely because of the scant media coverage. Their morale dropped even more during the hearings when, on February 1, Senator George Aiken, a Republican from Vermont, announced that troops from the South Vietnamese army (ARVN) and U.S. forces were massing near the border of Laos and Vietnam. Pentagon officials and American planners in Saigon hoped an invasion of the Laotian panhandle would sever the portion of the Ho Chi Minh Trail that ran through the region. But a cautious President Nixon wanted to keep the incursion a secret through a press blackout. In the wake of the Cambodian operation the previous year, Congress had passed an amendment barring American ground troops from entering Laos and Cambodia. Therefore, the invasion, code-named Operation Dewey Canyon II by Americans ("Dewey Canyon I" refers to the 1969 American incursion into Laos), would be carried out by South Vietnamese infantry. On February 8, following several days of unrelenting B-52 air strikes inside Laos, ARVN troops penetrated the Laotian countryside.

The poorly trained and outnumbered ARVN forces quickly retreated. Yet, in the United States, a mood of resignation and despair prevailed within the antiwar movement, particularly VVAW. Once again, President Nixon had broadened the scope of the war, and many activists began to doubt the effectiveness of peaceful protest. "We wanted fast results, we had friends in Vietnam. . . . . We were terribly impatient," Bill Crandell explained. "And I don't fault us for that. But it was unrealistic. If you had said to us that the major result of Winter Soldier would be that it would organize for the long run, we'd have been terribly disappointed. But that's what happened."[109]

Few Americans braved the bitter cold on February 10 to protest the invasion of Laos. An "angry and sullen" crowd of four thousand attended the nation's largest demonstration in Boston.[110] The antiwar movement was sluggish, and a vacuum existed within its leadership. Gone were organizations such as the Mobe and SDS, which had provided decisive guidance and leadership. Many militants decided to follow Timothy Leary's advice and "drop out," abandoning the streets in favor of New Age religions and Eastern gurus. The student uprisings of the previous year had ebbed. Burnout was rampant. "Activism never recovered from the summer vacation of 1970," Todd Gitlin later wrote.[111]

The movement had little direction or inspiration during the early months of 1971. In the VVAW national office, organizers realized that the time was right for Vietnam veterans to position themselves at the forefront of the struggle. As a result of the *Playboy* ad, membership had climbed closer to ten thousand, and veterans from all over the United States had mailed dues and requested chapter materials. But the Winter Soldier Investigation, while fostering significant structural changes, did little to enhance VVAW's prominence. On February 18, leaders met in New York to discuss VVAW's next action. They hoped to maintain the momentum from the previous months. The meeting was tense, and tempers ran high. "People were hollering and screaming," Barry recalled, "and at one point, somebody said, 'I'm going to tell you right now, I was in army intelligence and there's an army intelligence agent from my former unit in this room.' It was a really ugly mood. . . . And John Kerry got up and said, 'I propose that we march on Washington and take this whole thing to Congress.'"[112] Mike McKusker suggested they call the demonstration "Dewey Canyon III," or "a limited incursion into the country of Congress," a sardonic reference to the invasion of Laos.[113] The march would occur in April, they decided, giving them two months to rally fellow veterans.

Scott Camil journeyed back to Florida after the Winter Soldier Investigation with a deeper understanding of "the broad scope of what had happened" in Vietnam.[114] "For the first time, I realized for sure that we were wrong and what we had done to the people of Vietnam was bad," Camil later wrote.[115] He spoke against the war at schools, churches, synagogues, and protests. Under the close scrutiny of FBI agents, Camil recruited other antiwar veterans and performed guerrilla theater in the streets. VVAW "somehow got me motivated to do something," Camil explained.[116] In the middle of February 1971, Camil traveled to New York City to participate in the ratification of VVAW's new constitution. There, he was selected to be the regional coordinator for Florida, Alabama, Georgia, and South Carolina. "I'm telling you that I don't believe the founding fathers could've felt any different or better than I felt about what we were doing. I felt extremely patriotic," he recounted.[117]

Like Scott Camil, VVAW was an organization in transition. As a result of the persistent efforts of its New York City-based cadre and its highly visible *Playboy* advertisement, VVAW had experienced sudden and meteoric growth. For years, the antiwar movement had ignored the small network of Vietnam veterans. But Operation RAW had demonstrated that VVAW was a force to be reckoned with, and the Winter Soldier Investigation, in spite of paltry publicity, had fostered its flowering.

Meanwhile, the antiwar movement, also in a state of flux, had little energy by the winter of 1971. The liberals who had dominated it in 1967, the student militants who had taken over by 1970, and the numerous teachers, homemakers, laborers, and clergy who had kept it going on a day-to-day basis, were running out of ideas and patience. VVAW activists were aware that it was their time to infuse vitality and relevance into the movement. Most of them had only recently turned against the Vietnam War and their own participation in it. The six-year-old struggle to stop the war was new to them. Many had escaped the cynicism and despair so prevalent in the movement. Adding to their sense of urgency were the 334,600 Americans still in Vietnam, fighting a war that even President Nixon conceded had to be halted.

The forthcoming march on Washington was to be the true test of their effectiveness, and they planned accordingly. Two months of round-the-clock preparations went into it. The veterans hoped the American public would finally listen to them. "Demonstrators are easy to put down," remarked one, "But we're vets . . . and they've always had such faith in their vets."[118] If the Winter Soldier Investigation represented a public acknowledgment of what they believed to be the insanity and criminality of the Vietnam War, Dewey Canyon III would symbolize their rejection of the war.

4

Prelude to an Incursion

Government officials watched VVAW closely during and after the Winter Soldier Investigation. Though the hearings resulted in little media coverage, the organization alarmed the FBI and the Nixon administration. Authorities monitored activists, collected dossiers on witnesses who had testified in Detroit, infiltrated meetings, and attempted to rouse prowar veterans. Of particular significance was information that VVAW leaders were planning an event, Dewey Canyon III, in Washington, D.C., five days of marching, lobbying Congress, performing guerrilla theater, and speaking against the war. At the close of the week's activities, VVAW-ers planned to return their combat medals to the government.

With close to ten thousand members and chapters emerging in fifty states and Vietnam, VVAW was seen as a threat to policymakers. President Nixon and his advisers, like their predecessors in the Johnson administration, had long dismissed antiwar protesters as "spoiled children," "bums blowing up the campuses," and "bomb-throwers and window-busters."[1] By tarring demonstrators as misguided, affluent youths pitted against the rational "silent majority," officials sought to discredit the antiwar movement. But they could not dismiss VVAW so easily. These activists had the credentials to make the public listen. Summoning members to attend Dewey Canyon III, VVAW declared: "The President watched football on TV during the last peace march, and American accepted his indifference to students and 'peaceniks.' We know he will notice Vietnam veterans when they surround the capitol. They are the men who fought, the men the President praised and decorated."[2]

VVAW continued to grow and mature before Dewey Canyon III. Activists transformed it into a mass organization; liberals contested with radicals for its soul. Meanwhile, leaders initiated group therapy meetings, in which veterans talked about "the war, American society, and their own lives."[3] Chapters across the country offered counseling and other services that the Veterans Administration lacked.

By the beginning of March 1971, plans were underway for the VVAW's largest offensive against the war, Dewey Canyon III. The organizers believed the protest would prove to be a turning point. "Vietnam Veterans Against the War, the winter soldiers of today, have identified the enemy," Al Hubbard announced, evoking the language of Thomas Paine. "He is us. Armed with this knowledge, we will not in this crisis shrink from the service of our country."[4]

On February 19, 1971, regional coordinators from around the country assembled at 156 Fifth Avenue in New York City for the first VVAW steering committee meeting. At stake was the future of the recently restructured organization. The old-timer Bill Crandell, who had mailed his dues to VVAW after the Tet Offensive, was delighted that his responsibilities had diminished as the organization had grown. Once the sole supervisor of the Midwest region, when he traveled to New York in February 1971, "there were enough strong chapters and talented coordinators to allow me to cut my territory down to Ohio and Indiana, which I shared with Jim Pechin of Terre Haute."[5] Mike McKusker, another early joiner, was relieved that he no longer carried the burden of the western states on his shoulders. His area had been reduced to Oregon.[6]

In the New York offices, recent recruits joined seasoned activists. Many of the regional coordinators, such as Barry Romo (California/Nevada/Hawaii), Jon Floyd (Texas), Scott Camil (Florida/Georgia/Alabama), Brian Adams (Colorado/Utah), and Bill Hatton (Minnesota/Iowa), were new to VVAW, having entered its ranks prior to the Winter Soldier Investigation. Overseeing the February 19 gathering were the VVAW leaders Jan Barry, Al Hubbard, Scott Moore, John Kerry, and Joe Urgo. The organizers planned to ratify an updated constitution and a set of objectives, evaluate the spate of newly formed chapters around the country, and discuss the group's next national protest. Weeks earlier, VVAW's membership rolls had been processed on computer tape, and Urgo provided regional coordinators with an updated list of joiners in their areas. Logistical support had finally caught up with the VVAW's advance units.[7]

The meeting continued through the weekend. Participants unanimously agreed that VVAW should retain a decentralized structure, with autonomous local chapters. However, the veterans represented a broad range of beliefs, and tempers soon flared over the organization's next national protest. John Kerry believed that VVAW should "march on Washington," envisioning an intensive lobbying effort aimed at Congress. Following the Winter Soldier Investigation, Kerry concluded that antiwar veterans should try to influence policymakers. "I saw guys [in Detroit] who couldn't talk about what they'd done in Vietnam without crying. That's when I realized we had to take this thing to the government."[8] Joe Urgo concluded that Kerry and his supporters reflected a segment of the Democratic Party that "understood that the war was lost, and that they've got to now have some impact . . . on this side."[9]

Scott Camil was skeptical about the prospect of lobbying. Despite his distrust of the Left, Camil was furious at officials, and he wanted to take the protest "out to the streets." Recalled Camil: "I came [to VVAW] without any politics, in the sense of having an ideology. All I knew was what was going on in Vietnam, and what the government was saying, and that the public had the right to know the truth so they could make a decision."[10] Other veterans shared Camil's doubts. "We took Kerry's demonstration and turned it into something else," Urgo explained. "We turned it into, 'Let's bring vets in from all over the country, let's camp out, let's take over.' This isn't what Kerry had in mind exactly. He wanted a simple lobbying campaign."[11]

A radical bloc emerged for the first time at the national steering committee meeting. In the past, antiwar Democrats had vied with anarchical militants for control of VVAW. The latter group, while aware of the shortcomings of liberalism, rejected a more ideological approach to politics. But a shift was under way. "Guys were coming in from around the country who were a lot more radical than me. In some cases, they were talking about Marxism, all kinds of stuff that I'd never heard of, that I wasn't really familiar with," Urgo remembered.[12]

Barry Romo, the regional coordinator for California, Nevada, and Hawaii, represented the growing left wing of VVAW. Romo was born and raised in a predominantly African American and Chicano working class neighborhood in San Bernardino, California. With his nephew, Robert Romo, one month his junior, he grew up in a staunch Catholic household. Romo sympathized with the Civil Rights movement and abhorred racism, but he embraced conservatism and supported Barry Goldwater in 1964. In high school, Romo was the president of the local Young Republicans and joined Young Americans for Freedom. Patriotism motivated him to enlist in the army, and in January 1966 he entered Infantry Officer Candidate School at Fort Benning, Georgia. At the age of nineteen, Romo was a first lieutenant, with "forty-year-old World War II sergeants saluting me."[13]

In the fall of 1966, Romo received orders to go to Vietnam. He was troubled by the thought of taking other peoples' lives, but his priest assured him that "it was good to go kill communists." His father tried to talk him out of going. "I said, 'Look, dad, you went off to the Second World War and you didn't have to do it,'" Romo remembered. "And he said, 'Yeah, but that was to fight Nazis. That was to overturn Hitler and free people from concentration camps. You're just going to go fight some poor farmer who doesn't want to hurt anybody. I don't want you to die.' Of course, I didn't listen to him, because I was nineteen years old, and he was sixty-six, and what did he know?" Days later, Romo joined the 196th Light Infantry Brigade in I Corps, the northernmost province of South Vietnam.[14]

By 1968, Romo's unit had been incorporated into the 11th Infantry Brigade in the Americal Division. Action was heavy, and American casualties reached 40 percent. "Only one man was shot," Romo later wrote. "[T]he rest were [victims of] bouncing bettys, foot poppers (anti-personnel mines) and a few anti-tank mines."[15] At night, the brigade was repeatedly mortared. Romo felt himself "really turning brutal," and he "stopped giving a shit about body counts." Following a firefight, "one of my sergeants said, 'Let's go get a body count.' I said, 'Why? If there's a whole bunch of Viet Cong over there, you're going to take some casualties. If they're dead, they're dead. Who cares?' He said, 'What about a body count?' I said, 'I don't care. Keep on moving.'"[16]

During one particularly intense day of combat, a sergeant under Romo was blown apart by a bouncing betty. After a medic stitched the young man together, Romo returned to base, where a battalion chopper awaited his arrival. Under the loud, whirring blades, a major held a sign for Romo to read: "Your nephew Robert was killed along the DMZ; your brother asked that you be a body escort; will you go?"[17] Romo was stunned as he rode in the helicopter to Cam Ranh Bay. Unlike Barry, Robert had been drafted, and he had not been enthusiastic about going to Vietnam. During a patrol near the border of North Vietnam, he had been shot in the neck while trying to help a wounded friend. Robert did not die instantly, but the heavy fire in the area prevented medics from treating him, and, according to Barry, "he drowned in his own blood."[18] Barry accompanied Robert's body back to California.[19]

Romo left the Army in the summer of 1968, declining a promotion to captain. For the next several months, he attended junior college in San Bernardino and worked full-time. At night, he "drank wine, smoked dope, took speed, and stayed awake, like in Vietnam." He seldom picked up a newspaper or turned on the television. "I couldn't talk about Vietnam without crying. I heard [Country Joe and the Fish's] 'Fixin' to Die Rag,' and I started to cry on campus, in broad daylight, in front of people." Supportive professors encouraged him to discuss his feelings. His childhood friends, who had also served in Vietnam, were now marching in antiwar demonstrations. When he heard about the invasion of Cambodia, Romo "discovered the peace movement and went to work with antiwar GIs." His first involvement with VVAW was testifying at the Winter Soldier Investigation.[20]

Romo traveled to the national steering committee meeting in February 1971 with a raised consciousness of his Chicano and Irish heritage. He "backed the Black Panthers, La Raza Unida, and the Brown Berets." He disagreed with John Kerry about the effectiveness of lobbying. "I didn't believe in lobbying. I didn't want to lobby. I didn't feel it would do any good. I thought only demonstrations would do any good," he recalled.[21] Romo and other radicals took the logic of the Winter Soldier Investigation one step further. The Vietnam War was not aberration, they reasoned, but the act of an aggressive nation that sent its poor, disproportionately, to fight and die in wars of conquest. A sign of the left wing's growing clout was the approval of a new VVAW objective at the weekend gathering, which declared that "the membership is not only concerned with ending this war, but changing the domestic social, political, and economic institutions that have caused and permitted the continuance of war."[22]

By the end of the meeting, the exhausted members of the steering committee had agreed to lobby in Washington but had also voted to expand the scope of the demonstration to include marching, guerrilla theater, and other activities.[23] Before adjourning, VVAW leaders decided that Dewey Canyon III would culminate with veterans returning "their combat decorations to the nation."[24] The most effective way to conduct such a ceremony became yet another matter of debate. Since 1966, veterans from various wars, including Vietnam, had been returning medals to the president or other officials to protest the war.[25] Some had done so at demonstrations, while others had opted to mail them to Congress, the White House, or the Pentagon. On Lincoln's Birthday in 1971, a small group of veterans gathered near the White House in a rally that was a precursor to Dewey Canyon III and lobbed their medals and ribbons over the wall.[26]

In almost all cases, such acts of protest had been solemn, low-key events, resulting in little or no media attention. VVAW coordinators discussed different options. John Kerry proposed that demonstrators deposit the objects in a body bag and carry them to Congress. "He decided that . . . it wouldn't be respectful to throw the medals," Romo recalled.[27] Someone else suggested that members pin the decorations to a uniformed mannequin and try to present it to Richard Nixon.[28] They even considered dropping "them into shitcans filled with blood."[29] A more militant segment of the steering committee agreed that the veterans should throw or "drop them on the Capitol steps."[30] At the conclusion of the meeting, the matter of how the medals should be returned was left unresolved.[31]

Dewey Canyon III triggered a nationwide organizing drive. VVAW activists believed that the demonstration was destined to make history. From Maine to California, they built chapters and recruited veterans to attend the April protest. "VVAW's . . . time had come," recounted Ed Damato, who traveled across New York state after the February steering committee meeting. "I had some names and addresses . . . and I went up to Plattsburgh, New York, which is near the Canadian border on the east, next to Vermont, then all the way to Jamestown on the Pennsylvania border, . . . down to Syracuse, Rochester. We met these people, formed a state organization, and everybody was building to go to Washington."[32]

VVAWers in other parts of the country maintained the same pace. John Upton, a medic who had joined VVAW in Vietnam, returned to his hometown of Kansas City to rally support in Kansas and Missouri for Dewey Canyon III. In Wisconsin, John Lindquist, a former sergeant with the 3rd Marine Division at Quang Tri, and his companion, Anne Bailey, planned a carpool to travel from Milwaukee to Washington with seventeen other veterans. Jon Floyd flew back to Texas, canvassed the state, and rented an old school bus to transport members to the demonstration. The Pennsylvanians Jon Birch, Ken Campbell, and Joe Bangert distributed literature about the upcoming event and encountered widespread enthusiasm. Brian Adams and other Colorado VVAWers opened an office in downtown Denver that served as a base for fledgling chapters in the Rocky Mountain area. "In California, the junior college and state college system was our base," recalled Romo. "Tons of people were majoring in the GI bill and using it as a base to do political work. . . . We [eventually] had more than fifty chapters throughout the state."[33]

Coincidentally, the antiwar movement was planning a series of demonstrations in Washington, D.C., scheduled for late April and early May. Divisions were rife, and antiwar leaders argued endlessly about strategies. The Socialist Workers Party–dominated National Peace Action Coalition (NPAC) organized "peaceful and orderly national demonstrations in Washington, D.C., and San Francisco," scheduled for Saturday, April 24.[34] In the meantime, Rennie Davis's youth-oriented May Day Tribe announced plans to engage in massive civil disobedience in the nation's capital on May 1. Because the SWP rejected civil disobedience, NPAC refused to endorse Davis' May Day protests. A third organization, the People's Coalition for Peace and Justice (PCPJ), a network of radical pacifists that included Dave Dellinger and Brad Lyttle, was caught in the middle. Like NPAC, PCPJ was the product of a split within the once-powerful Mobe. PCPJ entered into an uneasy alliance with both NPAC and Davis's followers, backing the April 24 and the May Day actions.[35]

All three groups were headquartered at 1029 Vermont Avenue in Washington, D.C. PCPJ occupied the ninth floor, NPAC the eighth, and Rennie Davis's May Day Collective had an office on the tenth floor. After the Winter Soldier Investigation, Sid Peck of PCPJ hired the VVAWer Tim Butz to work full-time on the spring events. Butz recalled: "They gave me free rein to work around the issue of Dewey Canyon III and getting active duty support for May Day. So even though I was getting paid by PCPJ, I spent most of my time helping to organize for VVAW."[36] Butz was joined by the District of Columbia coordinator Mike Phelan and the VVAW activist Jack Mallory.

VVAW shared an office briefly in the NPAC headquarters, but the veterans moved as soon as new space became available. They found SWPers in NPAC to be too authoritarian and manipulative. NPAC maintained rigid control over all aspects of the April 24 demonstration. At one point, to make sure that no other activists interfered, NPAC installed steel doors at its entrance that could be sealed shut with two-by-fours.[37] Explained Butz: "NPAC was basically the Young Socialist Alliance [the youth wing of the SWP], the SWP, and whoever they could bring in from the Student Mobilization Committee. I hate to play into that old McCarthyistic 'front group' thing, but their people were in positions of leadership in [NPAC] and they pretty much followed the SWP line."[38] On numerous occasions, VVAW members derisively referred to the Trotskyist SWPers as "Trots." Quipped one VVAWer: "A chicken in every pot, an ice pick in every Trot."[39]

Meanwhile, informants from the FBI and other agencies carefully scrutinized activities at 1029 Vermont Avenue. "I'm not sure what floor the FBI was on. They had the whole damned building," remembered Butz.[40] The FBI regularly sent reports on preparations for Dewey Canyon III to the White House. Fearing that the veterans would be able to mount a formidable challenge to the Nixon administration, officials investigated the military records of VVAW members. They believed that the most effective method of discrediting the organization was to raise questions about the credibility of its members. Dick Howard, an aide to White House Counsel Charles Colson, blasted VVAW as "a group that are apparently not veterans and most of which are not combat veterans, who are apparently trying to compensate for some guilt feeling . . . by participation in this organization."[41] The Nixon administration also attempted, with little luck, to rally prowar veterans to counter VVAW's growing influence. Most efforts failed. "What happened to the President's request that we take steps to mobilize veterans?" demanded an angry memo from White House Chief of Staff H. R. Haldeman to Colson late in February.[42] "The President should know that we are continuing the effort to discredit VVAW," Colson assured Haldeman.[43]

Government agents remained busy, receiving constant updates from undercover plants. Many informants attempted to provoke VVAWers to violence. These infiltrators were often easy to spot. Their behavior and rhetoric were wildly exaggerated. They used phrases such as "offing pigs" and were overly insistent about the need to solve all problems with guns and explosives.[44] VVAWers usually ignored the agents provocateurs. Scott Camil remembered several "informers . . . who tried to play upon our Vietnam experiences, to manipulate us into some violent response, some confrontation with authorities."[45] Added Bill Crandell: "We became used to it. People continually approached me with offers to supply weapons or explosives. . . . I gave them a speech on nonviolence."[46]

Not all infiltrators were so obvious. John O'Connor, a former air force medic stationed in Germany, joined the Washington, D.C., police department in November 1970. His superiors immediately asked him to go undercover to investigate antiwar groups. He posed as an activist, but he did not fabricate any information about his background. He simply concealed the fact that he was a police officer. "I was just John O'Connor, from Rochester, New York," he said. His purpose was to report the time and location of protests and the turnout that organizers expected. "Then [the police] knew how much manpower to send, to control things, so it didn't turn into a violent incident," he explained. At first, he disliked the antiwar movement, and he "cheered the hardhats when they smacked them around."[47]

O'Connor went to work for NPAC as the group's office manager. At times, he had to suppress his hostility toward his coworkers. When an NPAC activist applauded a headline that announced the number of Americans killed in Vietnam during one week, O'Connor "wanted to kick his ass."[48] He met a VVAW organizer, Mike Phelan, who was then working at NPAC's headquarters, a few weeks before the Winter Soldier Investigation. O'Connor expressed interest in the VVAW, and Phelan asked him to help recruit prospective members in the area who had replied to the recent advertisement in *Playboy*. In mid-February, they were joined by Tim Butz and Jack Mallory.[49] "I had negative feelings for the antiwar movement," O'Connor recounted, "but these guys were different. They had paid their dues. They earned the right to say what they were saying. And they were good guys. It was interesting to hear their story. I started to have a different outlook on the war."[50]

O'Connor appreciated the VVAWers' irreverent and anarchical style. During tedious NPAC-PCPJ planning meetings, the veterans sneaked out to bars. "We were busy," said Butz, "but not so busy that we didn't have fun."[51] The VVAWers played jokes on agents provocateurs and other activists, and their antics appealed to O'Connor. The friends eventually rented a home together and christened it "the Vets' House." "We just really jelled. . . . That was it, we were the core of [the D.C. VVAW]," O'Connor reminisced. He continued to report to the police, even though "it was difficult . . . to be in that position where I was something that I wasn't."[52] Yet he spent most of his time organizing Dewey Canyon III, and his efforts proved invaluable. Recalled Butz: "Contrary to the image of a police officer as an agent provocateur, John . . . really helped lessen the tension, and did whatever was asked of him. He could've fucked us up good on several occasions, and he didn't do it."[53]

O'Connor was exceptional. VVAW converted few infiltrators to the antiwar cause.[54] Most informers worked effectively, without remorse, funneling information regularly to police or federal agents. But they failed to hinder preparations for the VVAW's April demonstrations. "There was a lot of paranoia around," Ed Damato recalled. "We didn't have great security precautions and . . . there were people we always suspected. . . . But I don't think it ever stopped us from doing anything."[55]

*

With new chapters forming in every state and plans solidifying for Dewey Canyon III, Vietnam Veterans Against the War became the mass movement that Jan Barry, Al Hubbard, Scott Moore, and Joe Urgo had envisioned. As a sign of its growth, organizers in the national office decided, for the first time, to print membership cards identifying those who had paid the annual dues of five dollars. Elsewhere, local branches of VVAW thrived. In March, sixty veterans from the Queens, New York, chapter traveled to Washington, D.C., to enlist the support of congressional doves for Dewey Canyon III. Minneapolis VVAWers, with the help of local churches, created a "half-way" house for veterans that featured psychiatric and legal services. Boston members chartered buses and traveled around New England, lecturing on college campuses. The Wisconsin group lobbied for a bill to make the state's draftees ineligible to serve in Vietnam. Chicago VVAWers organized GIs. New Mexico activists maintained a prominent role in the Chicano rights movement.[56]

Taking its cues from the Citizen's Commission of Inquiry on War Crimes in Vietnam, VVAW conducted local, small-scale Winter Soldier hearings. The inquiries were held in Philadelphia; St. Louis; Denver; South Orange, New Jersey; New Haven, Connecticut; and Gainesville, Florida. VVAW was the focus of an hour-long documentary on NBC, which aired March 16, as well as a *60 Minutes* segment and a number of articles in magazines and newspapers. Chapter organizers across the country requested slides, audiotapes, and documentary films faster than the national office could ship them.[57]

Meanwhile, VVAW's perennial president, Jan Barry, still disgusted with the VVAW-CCI split, assumed a lower profile. "I was fed up with much of this back-and-forth stuff going on. But I also felt that there were so many people who were good leaders that I wasn't necessary at all. And I wanted to do something else with my life. I wanted to go back to being a writer."[58] He accepted a writing job at CBS television news. In his spare time, he collaborated with Basil Paquet and the New Mexico VVAWer Larry Rottman to edit a book of Vietnam War poems called *Winning Hearts and Minds*. But Barry still exerted influence within VVAW. In November 1970, he invited Robert J. Lifton, a noted antiwar psychiatrist, writer, and professor at Yale University, to participate in the Winter Soldier Investigation and to help the national office do something about "the severe psychological problems of many Vietnam veterans because of their experiences."[59]

Lifton and Dr. Chaim Shatan, a psychoanalyst at New York University, began meeting weekly with groups of Vietnam veterans at the VVAW offices at 156 Fifth Avenue in New York late in 1970. Participants called the gatherings "rap groups." "We were drawn to the project by the interest we had in people who had been in the war and were turning against it," Lifton recalled.[60] A VVAWer, Arthur Egendorf, who helped organize rap groups, explained that veterans "talked, argued, made up, hugged, got confused, told stories, asked for advice, gave advice, complained, cried, and occasionally laughed. We followed no special formula or set procedure."[61] Veterans and therapists assembled in the cluttered VVAW offices each Saturday. The sessions were scheduled to last two hours, but they usually went much longer. Some veterans struggled to tell their stories, while others talked easily. All of them opposed the war, and many were articulating their feelings for the first time. "The rap groups became known as the place where you could tell your story, even the most horrible parts, and people would listen," remembered a veteran.[62] Added another: "Here was the first opportunity that I really had to talk with guys who had gone through the same thing. They were having the same doubts about themselves, you know, and digging inside themselves—and you didn't want to do that with just anybody."[63]

The New York gatherings spawned similar dialogues around the country. "I was called in to help set up rap groups in various parts of the country," recalled the San Francisco VVAWer Jack McCloskey, a combat veteran and therapist. "Again, under the auspices of VVAW, we started doing the self-help groups, but it was a natural offshoot of one of the directions that VVAW would go to take care of its own, as well as trying to stop the war."[64] Psychiatrists and veterans assembled regularly in the San Francisco VVAW offices, and McCloskey enlisted the aid of the psychologist Steven Tunnington to visit disturbed and suicidal veterans in the middle of the night. Said McCloskey: "You've got to understand the anger, the frustration, the alienation, that a lot of Vietnam veterans came home with. How else are you going to come from that situation not feeling these things? But you need to be able to work through these things. A lot of guys did things they were ashamed of, a lot of guys felt the peace movement didn't understand them."[65]

The political significance of rap groups went beyond providing therapy for veterans. "They were initiated by a group that formed to oppose the war. The rap groups were part of VVAW," Lifton explained. The sessions frequently had a "political edge," and participants never lost sight of their antiwar perspective. Nevertheless, the men sought to "render the process as psychological as possible," Lifton remembered. They became increasingly critical of "highly politicized statements which seemed to avoid the personal human involvement" and resisted "any sort of political structuring of [rap groups]."[66] The veterans were even more skeptical of "bullshit and war stories," McCloskey recounted.[67] Those who bragged about their combat experiences in Vietnam were ridiculed. Machismo gave way to open expression as the men confronted their inner feelings. "I felt sorry. I don't know why I felt sorry. John Wayne never felt sorry," said a former infantryman, describing his torment after killing an NLF guerrilla with a knife.[68] Added McCloskey: "It was amazing to see the vets open up. The guys actually . . . became their own therapists. I thought that was beautiful."[69]

In New York and Washington, D.C., activists put the finishing touches on Dewey Canyon III. They worked long hours through late March and early April. Hundreds of veterans, from nearly every state, had committed to attend the protest. Personality conflicts and logistical problems beset planners as the event drew closer. The VVAW's permit to camp at Georgetown University during the week of activities was rescinded after the person who issued it was fired by the school. Organizers relocated the campsite to West Potomac Park, next to the Washington Monument. However, with only a few weeks remaining until the demonstration, Mike Phelan was told by the U.S. Park Service that such a permit would take three months to obtain. When a VVAWer, Jack Mallory, arranged for a permit to protest at the U.S. Capitol, he was told by Vice President Spiro Agnew's aide Alice Lane that he "did not look like a [former U.S. Army] captain."[70]

Tim Butz endured the ordeal of handling media relations. A *Washington Post* staffer told him to try pitching the Dewey Canyon III story to the Style section editor. Exacerbating matters were poor relations between the D.C. group and the national office. "For one thing, the New York guys didn't send us any money. . . . They were sort of like saying, 'We're the big boys.' Jack and Tim and Mike took offense to that," O'Connor recalled.[71]

Tensions mounted between John Kerry and grassroots organizers in VVAW. Ever since Kerry's March 16 news conference with retired Marine Corps commandant General David Shoup in a congressional hearing room, the veteran had become a darling of the media, and the most high-profile VVAW leader. He was well acquainted with many congressional doves, and he had arranged to testify before a televised session of the Senate Foreign Relations Committee during Dewey Canyon III. His comrades knew of his aspirations. "He'll be president of the United States some day. . . . Kerry looks like Abe Lincoln and talks like John Kennedy," one VVAWer remarked.[72] However, many members were suspicious of Kerry. Their distrust was often rooted in petty jealousy: Kerry was in the spotlight, and they were not. There were, however, legitimate political conflicts between Kerry and other VVAWers. Some veterans emphasized class differences. Barry Romo remembered: "He had servants. . . . He went to the best schools, schools that we can only dream about. He came back and he didn't have to get a job in a plant or a post office. . . . The gulf was just too great."[73]

Dedicated activists questioned Kerry's refusal to perform the menial tasks often referred to as "shit work": stuffing envelopes, photocopying documents, obtaining permits. The Washington organizers Mike Phelan, Jack Mallory, and Tim Butz jokingly telephoned the national office, demanding that Kerry come in and "do Xeroxing," and they considered putting him in charge of Port-o-Potties for Dewey Canyon III.[74] Robert Hanson, a regular staffer in New York, saw Kerry infrequently. "He was around the office, but I had no feeling for who he was or what he was about."[75]

From the outset, Kerry felt uneasy with the militants in VVAW. He thought the fastest way to end the war was for antiwar activists to engage in a reasoned dialogue with policymakers. Confrontations with authorities, particularly in the form of violent protests, would alienate potential allies in high places, he believed. "I am determined to work within the system. We are totally nonviolent and nonaggressive."[76] However, a growing number of VVAWers lacked Kerry's faith in "the system." Tension was palpable when Kerry asked Jack Mallory to fill in for him as speaker at a Common Cause meeting. Mallory agreed. At the end of his talk, he concluded: "I ask you people, liberal Democrats and administrative lackeys one and all: How can you sit on this cushion of self-congratulation that you call service in the public interest, when Vietnam veterans, the Vietnamese people, and people servile to our oppressive, imperialistic policies live with the horrors of the aggression you profit from?" The following day, Kerry stormed into the Washington VVAW offices and yelled at Mallory. "When I'm out sticking my neck out for this organization, you're blasting away at everyone's politics and espousing revolution," he complained.[77] At another meeting of Dewey Canyon III organizers, a radical, Indiana-based collective known as the Raintree Tribe offered to provide meals to camping veterans. Kerry opposed the Tribe's offer because he wanted to keep the event "mainstream." The other VVAWers at the meeting overruled him.[78]

Meanwhile, government officials targeted Kerry and other VVAW leaders in an effort to disparage the group. Colson assisted a *Detroit News* reporter who wrote an article attacking Kerry, which was syndicated to more than one hundred newspapers and disseminated to "veterans organizations and military groups in plain envelopes with no cover letter."[79] The Nixon administration created Vietnam Veterans for a Just Peace to oppose VVAW. The group consisted of nothing more than a desk in the White House and one prowar veteran, John O'Neill. Nixon touted the group as "the other side."[80] Said Urgo: "We told these guys again and again, 'Fine, come on out, debate us! We'll go on any show you want.' On *The Dick Cavett Show*, [VVAWer] Bobby Muller in his wheelchair just devastated them. Basically, they couldn't mount an offensive against us."[81] Nevertheless, Colson persisted. At a press conference he coordinated before Dewey Canyon III, Herbert R. "Chief" Rainwater, president of the VFW, assailed VVAW as communistic. "I think our boys are getting a little better," Colson chimed, in response to the press conference's widespread coverage in the media.[82]

Such coups were rare, and the Nixon administration quickly recognized its impotence in the propaganda war against VVAW. Officials shifted tactics and moved the battleground to the courtroom. On April 16, two days before the first groups of veterans were scheduled to arrive in Washington for Dewey Canyon III, attorneys from the Interior Department obtained an injunction from Federal District Court Judge George L. Hart Jr., prohibiting the veterans from camping at West Potomac Park. Former Attorney General Ramsey Clark, appearing as counsel for the veterans, declared, "We do not lightly enjoin people from conduct, particularly when that conduct is so clearly associated with the right of free speech." When Clark argued that many of the veterans could not afford to pay for sleeping accommodations, Judge Hart replied: "Washington is a city noted for its hospitality. I don't believe you'll have any difficulty with housing here."[83] Hart's directive against sleeping in West Potomac Park was a setback for VVAW. Ramsey Clark prepared to take the case before the U.S. Court of Appeals the following Monday. In the meantime, VVAWers openly talked about violating the injunction, and John Kerry lamented the judge's decision: "We can dance and sing and even have a rock concert if we like, as long as we don't do anything quiet like lay down and sleep."[84]

The conflict escalated when the Justice Department requested that Judge Hart prohibit veterans from holding a planned march near the White House. Government attorneys charged that the route selected by VVAW would present security problems. But the Nixon administration was singling out the organization. The day before the hearing, the Justice Department had granted NPAC permission to conduct its much larger mass march on April 24 through downtown Washington, and Vice President Spiro Agnew's office had granted the organization a permit to rally on the West Lawn of the Capitol. Judge Hart rejected the injunction against VVAW's march, claiming that the government was "making a mountain out of a molehill."[85]

VVAWers understood that if they planned to disobey the government by camping at West Potomac Park, they ought to work closely with the District of Columbia to avoid violent clashes. The veterans were in a special position to deal with the police. "The Pentagon had established a program that allowed troops serving in Vietnam to muster out early if they became law enforcement officers. The D.C. police had a heavy contingent of Vietnam vets in their ranks," recalled Bill Crandell.[86] The VVAWers Mike Oliver, Jack Mallory, and Mike Phelan wrote an open letter to the police department outlining VVAW's opposition to "pig-baiting." The leaflet declared: "If a confrontation does occur during our stay, we must insure that it is clear to everyone—the press, the public, the government—that any violent acts were initiated by others than ourselves. We are here to educate the people of America. We are here to show them that we want peace and not another war."[87] Even before the demonstration, VVAW had won widespread support within the District of Columbia police force.[88]

In the final days before Dewey Canyon III, VVAWers settled all last-minute details. The Philadelphia chapter sent Joe Bangert, a highly effective yet offbeat organizer, to assist with final preparations. Bangert drove all over Washington in an old Army Jeep, collecting cans of food for the demonstration, stopping frequently along the way to shout at confused by-standers: "Guess what's coming down? Your town!"[89] Despite his decidedly unconventional style and haggard appearance, Bangert leafleted area grocery stores and collected thousands of dollars' worth of donated canned food in a few days.[90] In New York City, Al Hubbard, Scott Moore, Joe Urgo, and Jan Barry attended one fundraiser after another, mingling with sympathetic celebrities and businesspeople. Urgo remembered: "Thousands and thousands of dollars were coming in. . . . When Dewey

Canyon III came around, and there were vets sitting in trucks and cars all around the country that had to get [to D.C.] . . . in one day, I wired $23,000 in cash through Western Union to everybody who needed it."[91]

On the morning of Sunday, April 18, downtown Washington was still. The march organizers—Tim Butz, Mike Phelan, Jack Mallory, and John O'Connor—played a quiet game of hearts and waited for the first VVAW-ers to arrive at Potomac Park. Veterans from around the country had packed their medals, sleeping bags, old uniforms, and discharge papers and boarded trucks, cars, planes, and trains headed for the capital.[92]

The interlude between the Winter Soldier Investigation and Dewey Canyon III had been a time of expansion and restructuring for VVAW. The new constitution and bylaws, ratified in February 1971, facilitated its growth. The revamped bureaucracy, with a steering committee that consisted of national leaders and regional coordinators, democratized decision-making processes. VVAW had been transformed into a nationwide organization with chapters in fifty states and in Vietnam. Activists predicted that the April protests would be the ultimate test of VVAW's strength.

VVAW had challenged the Nixon administration more than any other antiwar or New Left organization. It fed into declining morale at home and in Vietnam, where active duty soldiers openly responded to the *Playboy* advertisement. Charles Colson, who was coordinating the White House's efforts against VVAW, knew that a successful event in April would energize the antiwar movement, which had been ailing since the aftermath of the invasion of Cambodia and Kent State. He sought to do everything possible to undermine Dewey Canyon III, right down to having "no one of real stature" collect the medals that veterans planned to return, "just as any other package or piece of mail would be received."[93] Still, Colson knew that, despite his efforts, VVAW was a formidable foe.

On the eve of Dewey Canyon III, VVAW was, in the words of Al Hubbard, poised to "press on with the winter soldier offensive . . . [and] bring the war home."[94] Americans had largely ignored the Winter Soldier Investigation, but VVAWers predicted that the country would pay attention to Dewey Canyon III. They believed the "limited incursion into the country of Congress" would summon "America to be true to its deepest beliefs."[95] "This demonstration by the men who have fought the war will be the most significant in the history of the peace movement. You have a chance to effect [*sic*] the course of history," the Connecticut VVAW newsletter told its readers.[96] Hopes were high. Leaders expected five thousand veterans to show up in Washington "wearing jungle fatigues."[97] Tim Butz remembered that "a sense of euphoria" prevailed in the days leading up to the protest.[98] Yet, in the face of mounting tensions, organizers never lost their sense of humor. "Support forces will be provided by eight hundred Nam vets in Indochina who signed our *Playboy* ad, eighty-nine members of the 101st Airborne Division—and the U.S.S. *Hancock*, all VVAW members or supporters. . . . Two full regiments of ex-troops should suffice to cut off this branch of the Nixon-Agnew Trail," the national office declared, mocking Nixonian rhetoric.[99] During the early afternoon of Sunday, April 19, veterans began trickling into Potomac Park under the watchful eye of government agents.

5

The Turning

The Winter Soldier Investigation was a critical juncture for VVAW. Entering its fifth year, the organization had come a long way since its early existence as a New York–based speakers' clearinghouse headquartered in a cramped office shared with other peace groups. It had metamorphosed into a nationwide, multi-issue organization, with chapters in all fifty states. By 1971, it had emerged as the sixth largest veterans' order in the country, and members talked about VVAW as a radical alternative to the more conservative Veterans of Foreign Wars (VFW) and the American Legion. They hoped one day it would be able to provide extensive psychiatric counseling, physical therapy, drug rehabilitation, and other services to meet the needs of the growing population of Vietnam veterans. As former soldiers, these activists believed that G.I.s returning home from Southeast Asia felt a greater sense of anger and betrayal than combatants of earlier wars and therefore were more likely to embrace antiwar beliefs. They wanted to offer alienated youths coming back from the jungles of Vietnam, Laos, and Cambodia a haven of kindred spirits, free from the hawkish politics of other veterans' organizations.

Whatever differences existed among them, VVAWers believed the Vietnam War was a morally reprehensible and indefensible conflict. But they knew it would not last forever. Therefore, a growing number of members sought to fashion a VVAW that would outlast the war. Such an organization, they hoped, would help Vietnam veterans adjust to the postwar world and serve as a check against similar acts of American aggression in the future.

Nevertheless, their immediate concern remained ending the war quickly. Several joiners still had buddies in Vietnam, and they felt no sense of comfort when President Nixon spoke about "Vietnamization." Beginning late in the summer of 1970, the veterans planned and participated in a series of remarkable events. The gritty style of protest that had emerged during Operation RAW, characterized by a mixture of counter-cultural fashions and military attire, became the prototype for future VVAW demonstrations. Operation RAW impressed the antiwar movement and energized the veterans. But the Winter Soldier Investigation four months later left the young activists feeling dispirited. Despite the event's remarkable qualities, it failed to convey the brutality and senselessness of the Vietnam War to a broad segment of the population. The media and the public, for the most part, ignored the hours of testimony presented in Detroit.

For the next two and a half months, VVAW invested all of its labor and money in Dewey Canyon III. Organizers no longer talked about appealing to the heartland, as they had before the Winter Soldier Investigation. Everybody agreed that Washington, D.C., was the ideal target. Steering committee members, regional coordinators, and chapter presidents lined up in lockstep behind the planning. Their status as veterans added a sense of urgency to the undertaking. With a vacuum in the antiwar movement's leadership, there was no better time to take center stage. The demonstration would be the best opportunity to transmit the message of VVAW to America. If done right, they believed, it could potentially expedite the Vietnam War's conclusion.

Four hundred veterans had arrived at Potomac Park by five P.M., on Sunday, April 18, 1971. The number escalated to nine hundred before the end of the evening. Protesters pitched tents, erected banners, and unpacked their belongings. "The park now is looking like a campground. VVAW regional state flags are blowing in the breeze above the tents," noted an observer.[1] Organizers feared that Dewey Canyon III had failed to attract "enough participants to accomplish our several missions," but their anxiety would turn out to be groundless.[2]

A steady flow of veterans continued to arrive at the park until dawn. Reinforcements came from all parts of the country. A convoy of cars carried sixty-five men from the Colorado VVAW. Scores of Ohio VVAWers, nicknamed the Buckeye Liberation Army, entered the park Sunday night. A huge contingent from southern California arrived by airplane. Reminiscent of novelist Ken Kesey's irreverent LSD-tripping Merry Pranksters, the proto-hippies who traveled America's highways in their psychedelic bus during the mid-sixties, one member from Texas, Jon Floyd, drove a ramshackle school bus filled with singing veterans. New Englanders reached the capital on a chartered train. Mike McKusker led a ragtag brigade from the Northwest. A moving van from Wisconsin deposited its contents at the park: a column of men in fatigues, equipped with ponchos and sleeping bags. Signs indicated support from other parts of the country: New Mexico, Missouri, Wyoming, Florida, Alabama, Minnesota, Illinois, Pennsylvania, Idaho, Hawaii, Oklahoma.[3]

On the morning of Monday, April 19, the camp was 1,200 men strong, and the event was under way. Eventually, the total number of veterans at Dewey Canyon III rose to twenty-three hundred. The average veteran at Potomac Park was between twenty-one and twenty-five years old. Most had graduated from high school and attended college when they could afford it. They came from all parts of the country, but, predictably, 54 percent arrived from the Northeast. The overwhelming majority (83 percent) were single. Half were raised in blue-collar households. Almost two-thirds had changed their "views about U.S. involvement in Vietnam" while serving in Vietnam. About 70 percent considered themselves "radical" or "extremely radical" "in relation to the current social, economic, and political thinking in the U.S."[4]

Traditional varieties of opposition dominated the first two days of Dewey Canyon III. Veterans marched, rallied, and lobbied. A handful of them performed guerrilla theater, the cornerstone of Operation RAW. Few, if any, participants came to Washington with the intention of taking part in civil disobedience. Even the most radical members agreed that activities must remain orderly and legal. Almost all of the campers at Potomac Park frowned on the sort of disruptive behavior advocated by more aggressive segments of the antiwar movement.

Dewey Canyon III began with a march. On Monday morning, a column of eleven hundred veterans, some in wheelchairs, others with crutches, left the camp and marched across the Lincoln Memorial Bridge to Arlington National Cemetery. They were joined by Representative Paul McCloskey, an antiwar Republican from California. A small group of widows and Gold Star Mothers whose sons were killed in Vietnam led the procession. The march was Anne Pine's first antiwar protest. Pine, a homemaker from Trenton, New Jersey, had lost her son in the jungles of Vietnam. She carried a newspaper clipping headlined: "A Birthday Not to Be: Medals, Memories Enshrine Trenton GI Who Died a Hero."[5]

At the cemetery, Arlington officials barred a small delegation of widows, Gold Star Mothers, and veterans from entering to lay two memorial wreaths in a ceremony. The superintendent of Arlington announced that no group could use the grounds for political purposes.[6] The veterans were outraged. Al Hubbard took a megaphone and condemned "the insensitivity of the government and the military."[7] His words stirred an already agitated throng. Scott Camil, Jack Mallory, and other leaders attempted to calm the marchers. "I had to keep saying to people, 'If we fight here, we're going to be the bad guys. We've started a fight at the national cemetery, we'll be the bad guys.' I kept saying, 'Save it for the Capitol, save it for the Capitol,'" Camil remembered.[8] The Gold Star mothers placed the two wreaths at the gate of Arlington. The procession turned and marched toward the Capitol. Solemnness gave way to outrage as the veterans waved clenched fists and chanted, "One, two, three, four, We don't want your fucking war!"[9] Veterans waved middle fingers at a helicopter hovering above their heads. Little did they know that one of the passengers in the helicopter was President Nixon.[10]

The column approached the Capitol to hear statements by Representatives McCloskey and Bella Abzug of New York.[11] Along the way, marchers passed a crowd of predominantly elderly women, members of the Daughters of the American Revolution, which was conducting its annual convention in Washington. Robert Hanson recalled: "Here we are, coming down the street, and . . . they're looking at us like we're from Pluto. There was one guy with this Marine Corps dress-blue jacket on, with his sergeant stripes, and on the back of his jacket he had a picture of [cartoon character] Beanie from 'Beanie and Cecil.'"[12] A Daughter of the American Revolution approached one of the VVAWers and said, "Son, I don't think what you're doing is good for the troops." Replied the VVAWer: "Lady, we are the troops."[13]

The experience of being turned away at Arlington National Cemetery undermined morale in VVAW's tent city. The next day, a smaller group of veterans, about two hundred strong, repeated the march. While they were fewer in number, their mood was decidedly more combative than that of their comrades the day before. When the line reached the entrance to Arlington, Al Hubbard talked with Superintendent John Metzler. A few minutes later, guards opened the gates and allowed the marchers inside. Said Metzler afterward: "I had no idea they wanted to do this yesterday. I didn't know they were angered or upset until one man threw his toy cannon against the gate."[14] In the distance, a rifle salute shattered the stillness, followed by bugle taps for a funeral service. The contingent laid wreaths under a tree, one marked "Allied," the other "Indochina." Then they filed silently out of Arlington with clenched fists raised above their heads.[15]

98 | The Turning

Guerrilla theater activities occurred during the first few days. Like marching, guerrilla theater brought veterans into the streets, making them more visible. Against the backdrop of Capitol Hill, members staged search-and-destroy missions for audiences that consisted primarily of tourists and journalists. Remembered Bill Crandell: "Having led the guerrilla theater during Operation RAW, I was asked to do the same thing in the streets of D.C. again with the Buckeye Recon and the Philadelphia Quaker Troupe."[16] Veterans rounded up actors portraying Vietnamese civilians as part of mock combat scenes. "It's disgusting. It's horrible," commented a middle-aged woman, as soldiers fired simulated rounds at actresses wearing straw coolie hats.[17] At the end of the reenactments, in an action reminiscent of Operation RAW, veterans lined up on the steps of the Capitol and smashed their toy M-16 rifles.[18]

The marches to Arlington National Cemetery and the guerrilla theater in downtown Washington, D.C., drew only modest media coverage. The Tuesday morning march was much smaller than its Monday counterpart, and the street performances attracted few veterans. The "limited incursion into the country of Congress" commenced sluggishly. VVAWers would not hit their stride until the middle of the week, when events beyond their control led them down an unexpected path.

If VVAW's street resistance had been of limited success, its lobbying efforts were more disappointing. The idea of trying to influence policymakers originated with John Kerry and other VVAW moderates. Indeed, without the input of VVAW's militant members, Dewey Canyon III would have amounted to little more than a week-long series of meetings between veterans and politicians. The majority of VVAWers traveled to Washington believing that their credentials would enable them to persuade even the most hawkish of senators and representatives of the folly of Vietnam. But even for these ex-soldiers, the hurdles were numerous. Many conservatives who supported Nixon's policies in Southeast Asia refused to meet with antiwar activists, even those who had served in Vietnam. Those who decided to make a special exception for VVAWers were unaccustomed to such encounters and were visibly uncomfortable.

For their part, the veterans were not versed in the protocol of lobbying. They distrusted all types of authority, and they exhibited little or no deference to their elected representatives. To stand and shout in the middle of a conference with a senator seemed like an appropriate gesture to the angry young men. Legislators found such conduct unseemly, and none of the war's supporters on Capitol Hill publicly acknowledged having second thoughts about their positions as a result of their exchanges with VVAW members.

The lobbying began after the opening rally on Monday, when veterans assembled with others from their region to meet with delegations of representatives and senators. Conflicts surfaced immediately. Uncooperative staffers turned away numerous veterans. Some politicians returned home during the week, citing "urgent business."[19] Several representatives refused to meet with veterans who were not from their district. Congressman John Rooney of Brooklyn asked each veteran where he lived and eventually gerrymandered "as many vets as he could out of his office." With only a handful of veterans remaining, Rooney announced, "I'm going to shoot straight from the shoulder with you guys. I know where you stand and you know where I stand. We're on opposite sides." Rooney indicated the direction of the exit.[20]

Other representatives assumed a patronizing tone with the veterans. A Florida congressman told a group of VVAWers from his state, "I just returned from a four-day stint in Vietnam and you don't know what you're talking about."[21] Samuel Stratton, a Democrat from upstate New York, lectured about his visits to Vietnam, never hesitating long enough to allow the veterans to speak. When one of the veterans pleaded with him to "shut up . . . and listen," the congressman stopped only briefly, then resumed talking until the veterans departed. Barry, who was one of the veterans in Stratton's office, later recalled: "This was all being filmed by a television station in Albany, and I heard later that he came across as such a jerk in lecturing these veterans. . . ."[22]

Most encounters left the lobbyists feeling frustrated and powerless. Said one VVAWer of his experiences on Capitol Hill: "Those who have tended to be liberal on the war talked to us. Those who were more hawkish were 'out.'"[23] Some senators and representatives criticized VVAWers for their unkempt appearance. One Massachusetts activist, Rusty Sachs, believed the fashion styles reflected the alienation and anger shared by the young men. Added another activist: "The way we dressed was largely the way we dressed in Nam."[24] The scruffy veterans irritated lawmakers, and tempers occasionally flared. A Danish film crew that "wanted to see how the American system worked" filmed an Iowa VVAWer as he was being berated by an angry congressman. "You're a disgrace to the uniform! Get out of this office!" the representative shouted, slamming the door on his constituent.[25] Sixty-five members of the Colorado VVAW met with Senator Gordon Allott Monday afternoon. When informed of the decrepit conditions in VA hospitals, Allot responded, "The Denver VA hospital has taken the national lead in kidney and liver transplants." In reference to high unemployment rates among Vietnam veterans, Allot asked, "Are you really having a tough time finding jobs?"[26] The Colorado veterans had an equally exasperating discussion with Representative Mike McKevitt of Denver, and they were barred from the offices of two Colorado congressmen.[27]

While not lobbying, large numbers of VVAWers also attended various hearings on Capitol Hill. About 150 veterans greeted Senator George McGovern in the Senate Foreign Relations Committee hearings with cries of "Hi there, Senator Dove!" and "Right on!"[28] They stood and applauded Senator McGovern when he accused the American military of committing war crimes in Vietnam. "I have never been prouder of a group of Americans than I am of these combat veterans," McGovern declared, gesturing to the VVAWers in attendance.[29]

Approximately fifty members of VVAW entered a meeting of Representative Clement Zablocki's Foreign Affairs Subcommittee. The veterans requested an opportunity to present testimony about war crimes. Zablocki yielded, allowing VVAWer Larry Rottman, of Corrales, New Mexico, to take the stand and speak for the group. Eventually, twenty-four other VVAWers recounted atrocities they had personally witnessed in Vietnam. Rottmann asked Zablocki to continue the hearings on Wednesday, and Zablocki said he would explore such a possibility.[30] Another contingent of VVAWers protested at a Senate subcommittee meeting as the chief of the United States "pacification program" in Vietnam, Ambassador William Colby, testified about civilian casualties.[31]

Lobbying continued until Thursday. However, many veterans wondered about its effectiveness. They knew their efforts had support among Congressional doves. Senators and representatives from both parties frequently visited the camp and offered their unqualified support. Senator Eugene McCarthy shipped cases of beer, soda, and cigarettes to grateful VVAWers and allowed them to use the shower in his apartment during the day.[32]

But the veterans had not traveled to Washington to preach to the converted, and their impact on congressional hawks was negligible. At many offices, VVAWers faced a barrage of insensitive comments or, worse, closed doors. One veteran, Gary Battles, of Chesterland, Ohio, wept as he left a meeting with Ohio Senator Robert Taft Jr., referring to the senator as "a sheep."[33] New Hampshire VVAWers were astonished when Representative James Cleveland declared: "My position is substantially the same as President Nixon's. I am not a supporter of the war."[34]

Antiwar politicians likewise incurred the wrath of the protesters. Representatives Paul McCloskey and Bella Abzug expected deafening applause at the opening rally when they announced their plans to try to terminate the war by the end of 1971. Instead, they were greeted with boos, hisses, and chants of "End it now!"[35] The veterans who testified before Representative Zablocki's Foreign Affairs Subcommittee were disappointed to learn that the congressman had canceled the hearings in response to pressures from within the committee.[36] In the meantime, lawmakers tried to explain the slowness of the legislative process, but impatient VVAWers refused to listen. Senator Edward Brooke, an antiwar Republican from Massachusetts, told a small crowd that ending the war would be a complicated and lengthy process. One veteran said, "Then what you're telling me is that your system can't deliver. Seventy-five percent of the American people want the war ended now, and you say there is a lag of seven to eight months."[37]

Some demonstrators simply wanted the congressional doves to admit the complicity of liberals in initiating and conducting the war. One group of angry veterans demanded that Senator Edward Kennedy, a repeat visitor to the VVAW campsite, acknowledge the role of his brother, President John Kennedy, in escalating the American involvement in Vietnam. Kennedy ignored them.[38] At a Tuesday night fundraiser hosted by Senator Philip Hart, a heated exchange occurred between Scott Camil and Arkansas Senator J. William Fulbright. Camil recounted: "Here he was, bragging about how much he was against the war, so I just went up to him and said, 'Look, the Gulf of Tonkin [resolution] gave the President the power to do what he did. You voted for it. Why did you vote for that?'"[39]

By the middle of the week, even the moderates at the Potomac Park campsite had developed misgivings about lobbying. The terrible treatment veterans endured in the offices of elected policymakers prompted many VVAWers to shun the practice entirely. Explained Joe Urgo: "Every time the vets confronted the government, they found out that these guys didn't care. . . . Essentially, they're not going to be moved. So that made the vets more radical."[40] Those who had rejected lobbying from the outset felt vindicated by the discouraging experiences of members on Capitol Hill. Since he had arrived in Washington, Barry Romo had avoided the process, and he counseled his comrades to do likewise. "If [senators and representatives] thought the war was wrong, then just stop voting it money and it would end. It wasn't a very hard thing to do," reasoned Romo.[41] VVAWers departed Washington, D.C., at the end of the week with a strong distaste for partisan politics. "The politicians sent us to Vietnam. Now they don't want to hear us," concluded one ex-Marine, Mike Milligan.[42]

Had officials been more receptive to the veterans, they might have been able to diminish the impact of Dewey Canyon III. But their dispiriting response, at virtually every turn, reinforced the antiauthoritarian politics of the campers in Potomac Park. First, the Justice Department pursued an injunction against the protesters before the event even began. Then officials at Arlington National Cemetery arbitrarily prohibited a memorial service on the first day. Next, frustrations mounted as lobbying failed. President Nixon exacerbated tensions when he speculated on Monday evening that "only 30 percent of the people" who marched to Arlington and the Capitol "are Vietnam veterans."[43] The VVAWers at Potomac Park responded to his accusation by collecting twelve hundred DD-214s (discharge papers) from the veterans at the camp and showing them to the press. Retorted one member: "Only 30 percent of us believe Nixon is President."[44]

Events took a positive turn for VVAW on Monday when the U.S. Court of Appeals reversed Judge George L. Hart's injunction against protesters sleeping at Potomac Park. Veterans in the small tent city cheered and embraced one another. But the triumph was short-lived. The next day, Chief Justice Warren Burger, acting in his capacity as circuit judge for the District of Columbia, reinstated Hart's injunction. Burger announced that the camp would "set a precedent for further demonstrations" and gave the veterans until four-thirty Wednesday afternoon to vacate the Mall.[45]

Burger feared that allowing VVAWers to sleep in Potomac Park would encourage May Day protesters arriving in the city the following week to do likewise. Former attorney general Ramsey Clark, once a supporter of the war, now a dove representing the veterans, informed his clients that he would seek a decision by the entire Supreme Court on Wednesday to overrule Chief Justice Burger's order.[46]

Intensifying the activists' distrust of government were the numerous encounters with agents provocateurs, particularly in the evening, when all participants were present. Veterans patrolled the camp's perimeters each night. A checkpoint at the entrance weeded out suspicious individuals. "There were all kinds of infiltrators coming in, and we knew what was happening. Of all the people to try to do this to, they were doing this to the people who have been taught to do this," said Joe Urgo.[47] Bill Crandell encountered new members who appeared questionable. Crandell and other leaders performed background checks by asking with what unit a newcomer had served, then finding another VVAWer who had been in the same unit at the same time and asking him to confirm a joiner's claim. "Among those with phony stories who were recognized by men who had met them in Vietnam were a CIA agent and a Special Forces type who claimed to have served only in a regular infantry outfit."[48] Tim Butz, who drew guard duty at the camp, recalled several puzzling visitors, including man with a counterfeit badge who announced he was "sheriff of Washington, D.C.," and a Bureau of Alcohol, Tobacco, and Firearms agent who regularly circled the area in a Jeep.[49] Infiltrators were often easy to detect and repel. VVAWers would face a more significant challenge the following day from the chambers of the Supreme Court.

The tone of the protest changed after Chief Justice Burger reinstated the injunction. A spirit of nonviolent resistance quickly replaced more passive displays of dissent. The veterans felt cornered. In the armed forces, they had been taught to believe that retreating without a fight was the ultimate form of cowardice. Yet they feared that the alternative here in Washington would be a clash. The veterans never intended to defy authorities or trigger mass arrests, yet they were prepared to do so if the government offered them no other options. One of the participants, the Colorado native John Mitchell (no relation to the then-U.S. attorney general of the same name), echoed the prevailing sentiment at the camp when he declared his intention to remain at Potomac Park despite the injunction. "It's against my grain to take part in something like this, but the morality of this week of protest overpowered my reservations. . . . It may be illegal to spend the night here. But it's a lot more illegal to continue the war in Vietnam, to commit the atrocities we've committed."[50]

On Wednesday morning, veterans unanimously agreed to defy Chief Justice Burger's four-thirty deadline and wait to find out whether the Supreme Court would act. Then state delegations filed back up to Capitol Hill to resume lobbying. A smaller contingent, numbering about seventy-five, decided to try something more venturesome. With discharge papers pinned to their chests, the column of men marched to the Pentagon to surrender themselves to the Defense Department as war criminals. Before they departed, an organizer spoke into a public-address system: "Will all the war criminals please assemble across the street."[51] "We all want to be arrested along with Lieutenant Calley," explained twenty-three-year-old Sam Schorr of Los Angeles.[52] At the Pentagon, three representatives of the group met with Air Force Brigadier General Daniel James, deputy secretary of defense for public affairs. The officer rejected their request to speak with General William Westmoreland. "I'm sorry, but we don't accept American prisoners of war here," James told the men. "Why don't you try the Justice Department?"[53]

The small, yet dramatic incident at the Pentagon aroused the other veterans. Protesters applauded the plucky and impulsive quality of the marchers, and all of the state delegations decided to return to the camp before four-thirty and risk arrest for violating the injunction. While crowds accumulated in the campsite early Wednesday afternoon, VVAW staff assembled a stage and tested sound equipment for an afternoon rally. Ominous gray clouds hovered over the city, promising rain. At four P.M., organizers asked everyone who was not a veteran, member of the press, or support personnel to leave the camp. A delegation of senators and representatives, including Senator Jacob Javits of New York, arrived to provide encouragement. Sixteen House Democrats offered to let members sleep in their offices. The venerable journalist I. F. Stone assured his audience that Nixon would make "the biggest mistake" of his career if he tried to destroy the encampment.[54]

Representative Don Edwards of California approached the microphone with a ticking clock in his hand. The alarm bell rang at four-thirty. The veterans roared in approval. "If you get evicted from this land," declared Edwards amid the cheers, "you can sleep in our offices tonight!"[55] An hour later, Ramsey Clark informed the crowd that a compromise had been reached with the Supreme Court. If the veterans remained awake, they would not be arrested. "You cannot sleep, lie in or under bedrolls, make fires, erect any shelter other than a medical tent, break any earth or carry on any cooking activities. As the attorney who has pursued this, I would urge you to comply."[56]

Initially, the majority of VVAWers supported a plan that allowed half the demonstrators to remain awake at the Mall and the other half to sleep in congressional offices or at the National Cathedral. Following some discussion, a "long-haired, bearded young man" from California walked onto the stage and proposed that protesters remain on the Mall and risk arrest. He suggested that if a bust occurred, the veterans should nonviolently resist and imitate prisoners of war, with their hands raised over their heads, when they were hauled off to jail. Listeners applauded the speaker, and the matter was left to the participants to decide.[57]

Veterans caucused into state delegations to vote on the proposals. Many delegations voted unanimously to sleep. Even the usually reserved John Kerry lashed out at a "government more worried by the legality of where we sleep than by the legality of where we drop bombs."[58] For nearly two hours, the animated crowd argued and exchanged ideas. "Discussions were going on among informal groups sitting in circles," remembered the antiwar activist Fred Halstead, who visited the camp that night. "At one spot, where a flatbed truck was parked, a continuous camp meeting was in progress, with speakers mounting the truck to say words of encouragement to the vets or to express defiance of the authorities."[59]

Shortly after seven P.M., John Kerry, sweating under the glare of television camera lights, announced the outcome. "New Mexico votes seven to sleep [on the mall] and twenty-five to stay awake." The crowd groaned. "Wisconsin votes thirty-three to sleep." Applause. "Virginia votes forty-nine to stay awake. Maryland votes forty-four to sleep and one to stay awake."[60] Jan Barry used a portable field telephone, wired to a nearby telephone pole, to keep Madelyn Moore informed of the activities in the park. Moore remained on standby, prepared to rally support from activists and wealthy sympathizers who could provide bail money if the police arrived.[61]

In the end, four hundred veterans voted to stay awake; 480 voted to sleep. The narrow victory indicated the reluctance of members to engage in an act of passive resistance. Nevertheless, the minority agreed to accede to the will of the larger group and risk a confrontation with the police. "This group has logged a thousand years in Vietnam. We think it's worth five days of a piece of grass here in Washington," proclaimed one protester.[62] Following the vote, participants wrote "POW" on their shirts, anticipating arrests.[63] A light rain fell on the nervous men while they ate dinner. Missing from the camp was the singing and revelry of previous nights. Men in combat dress walked along the edge of the camp, waiting for the police.[64]

Yet the protesters had allies in high places. "The night we were supposed to be arrested, we had congressmen and congresswomen, congressional aides, and senators that were there that were going to get arrested also. We really felt our power," explained Ed Damato.[65] Representative Ron Dellums, an African American and a Korean War veteran from Oakland, came to the California contingent and informed them of his intention to get arrested with them. "He didn't get up on stage, didn't go make a big deal about it. He stayed and sat there with us, and he said, 'They're going to arrest you, they're going to bust me too,'" remembered Barry Romo.[66] The VVAWers also enjoyed strong support from active-duty GIs stationed nearby.[67] The honor guard from the Tomb of the Unknown Soldier visited the campsite. "If they try to call the troops out against you, there'll be hell to pay!" one of them affirmed.[68] A group of soldiers from Fort Bragg entered the camp and assured organizers that troops would not be used to disperse the veterans. "You know we're on alert to put you down. We've already sanded all the gas tanks. Trucks will never move from Bragg," reported a GI.[69]

VVAW leaders met with police, and they agreed that if a bust occurred, veterans would walk out of the park peacefully, by state delegation, in alphabetical order.[70] Yet the police never had any intention of arresting the veterans. John O'Connor had the unique perspective of being a VVAW organizer and a police officer. He recalled that most police officers wanted to avoid a confrontation. The VVAW's strategy of rejecting "pig-baiting" and appealing to Vietnam veterans in the police force had worked. Opposition to a bust was widespread within the department. Most officers had no desire to be used as pawns in a conflict between the Nixon administration and the protesters. A crisis in police leadership exacerbated matters. "Jerry Wilson, who was the chief of police at the time wouldn't arrest them. . . . He was gone, nobody could get a hold of him," O'Connor remembered.[71] Park police patrolling the Mall ignored the veterans. "Camping? I don't see any camping," quipped one officer.[72] Later that evening, Police Lieutenant William R. Kinsey angrily declared, "We are not going in there at one in the morning and pick up some wounded veteran and throw him into the street. We don't treat people like that."[73]

Orders not to arrest the veterans came from President Nixon. Behind White House doors, officials reacted to events with alarm. President Nixon publicly feigned a lack of concern for Dewey Canyon III. Privately, however, he maintained an "intense" interest in the VVAW's activities. Various security agencies provided him with hourly updates on the protest. White House Counsel John Dean "became the White House collecting point for antiwar intelligence reports," and he directed information to President Nixon.[74] When the Supreme Court ruled against protesters' sleeping in the park, Dean advised White House Chief of Staff H. R. Haldeman and White House assistant for domestic affairs John

Ehrlichman that arresting VVAWers would be devastating politically. "The policy—which the VVAW are totally unaware of—is that there will be no arrests made of VVAW who violate the [court] order and it has been clearly and unequivocally given to the appropriate authorities," Dean wrote.[75] Patrick Buchanan, Nixon's speechwriter, agreed with Dean. In a memo to Haldeman, Buchanan counseled the administration to save the fight for the "crazies" who would be "coming Friday." He concluded: "If we want a confrontation, let's have it with them—not with the new Bonus Army [a reference to protesting World War I veterans who marched on Washington, D.C., in the summer of 1932, only to be routed by orders of President Hoover]. This is not a recommendation that we not be tough—but that we pick the most advantageous enemy from our point of view."[76] On Wednesday morning, President Nixon, fearing a clash with the veterans might be "rather nasty," privately ordered officials, "Don't bust the Viet Nam veterans on the Mall—avoid confrontation."[77]

At ten P.M., a radio newscaster announced that police would not arrest the veterans at Potomac Park. The protesters rejoiced. Tensions eased. The cast from the Broadway show *Hair*, on tour in Washington, D.C., arrived at the site and performed numbers from the countercultural musical. Veterans joined the ensemble in singing "Age of Aquarius" and two songs by John Lennon, "Power to the People" and "Give Peace a Chance." Noted a *Washington Post* journalist: "The scene now evoked was less that of a firebase than, perhaps, an Aquarian version of the American Legion."[78] Exhaustion quickly displaced jubilance. Many of the campers had settled into their sleeping bags and bedrolls by midnight. Hundreds of veterans eventually sought sleeping accommodations elsewhere. By two A.M. Thursday morning, the site held only six hundred people, many of whom slept in the rain. Those who stayed away sought to avoid bad weather or arrest.[79]

Despite the flight of hundreds of veterans from Potomac Park that morning, VVAW enjoyed a stunning victory. A headline in bold across the front page of *The Washington Daily News* the following day declared, "VETS OVERRULE SUPREME COURT."[80] The action also demonstrated the reluctance of government officials to restrain veterans in the same manner as other antiwar demonstrators. For the most part, the campers were not proponents of civil disobedience, but once they committed to such a course of action, there was little the government could do to repel them. President Nixon and his staff had "a long session" Thursday morning to discuss "the fact that the veterans are in violation of the Supreme

Court order by staying on the mall." They hoped to "negotiate the issue to death."[81]

Attorney General John Mitchell, acting under pressure from Chief Justice Burger and the Supreme Court, asked U.S. District Court Judge George L. Hart to dissolve the original injunction. Hart was outraged. "This court feels that one equal and coordinate branch of the government, the judiciary, has been dangerously and improperly used by another, the executive," he declared. He scolded the Nixon administration for putting "the veterans in the position of openly defying the laws and courts of this country" and concluded that the matter could not "have been handled worse."[82] Judge Hart's decision gave the May Day protesters the green light to camp in the city. In an effort to save face, Justice Department attorneys issued a statement proclaiming that the VVAWers had "served their country honorably" and "their activities in the camp area have proved to be peaceful."[83] Later that day, a weary H. R. Haldeman expressed regrets in his diary about obtaining the injunction:

> We asked for it to begin with, and then we didn't enforce it after we got it, which put the veterans in the position of violating the law and us in the position of not enforcing it. Fortunately, I don't think this point has come through very clearly, and it probably won't. We did move a little too fast on getting the order to begin with, though.[84]

The veterans' decision to sleep at Potomac Park discredited the Nixon administration and the Supreme Court, while enhancing VVAW's reputation. It emboldened the campers at the makeshift firebase. Thanks to their credentials as former soldiers, as well as the enduring tragedy of the Bonus Marchers (the two thousand protesting, unemployed World War I veterans forcefully routed out of their ramshackle tent city in Washington, D.C., by the U.S. Army in the summer of 1932), VVAW members had successfully faced down the federal government in a way that no other antiwar activists could. The experience reinforced the veterans' militance. After their Wednesday evening triumph, many of them began to favor the more defiant approach of throwing their medals at the Capitol Building instead of returning them in a body bag.

Thursday morning saw another daring act of resistance. Shortly before nine A.M., 170 veterans gathered on the steps of the Supreme Court to demand that the Court "rule on the constitutionality of the Vietnam War."[85] Two of them, James Dehlin, from Flushing, Michigan, and Bill Weiman, of Boston, Massachusetts, arrived in wheelchairs. A few demonstrators attempted to enter the building but found the doors had been locked. The veterans, still "a bit tired and cranky" from the night before, sat on the steps and began singing "God Bless America."[86]

The police arrived an hour later, sans riot gear, and peacefully escorted the fatigue-clad protesters into buses with iron bars over the windows. Two women and 108 male veterans pressed their hands atop their heads, POW-style, and chanted "Chou Hoi" (Vietnamese for "I surrender") as they boarded the buses.[87] Bill Weiman, who lost both his legs after stepping on a land mine in August 1970, told the officers, "I want to go with my brothers. If you're going to take them, take me."[88] Police Chief Wilson ordered his men to avoid Weiman. "I just won't do it. I just won't arrest him," he said.[89] Police charged demonstrators with obstructing and impeding justice, charges that carried a maximum penalty of five thousand dollars and one year's imprisonment. Later in the day, a judge reduced the charges to disorderly conduct and released each veteran on a ten-dollar bond.[90]

While police arrested protesters on the Supreme Court steps, John Kerry prepared his testimony for the Senate Foreign Relations Committee. Accompanied by 150 of his VVAW comrades, Kerry entered the committee room in the early afternoon, dressed in fatigues and with a Silver Star, three Purple hearts, and three citation clusters on his chest.[91] The senators were polite as he sat under the glare of television lights. He spoke "in very general terms" about the war and its impact on the people who fought. His persuasiveness and eloquence put a human face on the week's events. His clean-cut appearance appealed to even the most prowar Americans. "How do you ask a man to be the last man to die for a mistake?" Kerry asked. He discussed "men who have returned with a sense of anger and a sense of betrayal which no one has yet grasped." He told stories about atrocities that soldiers committed in Vietnam and recounted the terrible conditions in VA hospitals at home. He condemned leaders such as Robert McNamarra who "have deserted their troops." He attacked the Nixon administration for attempting to "disown us and the sacrifices we made for this country." He concluded his testimony with a stirring passage:

> We wish that a merciful God could wipe away our memories of [our] service as easily as this Administration has wiped away their memories of us. But all they have done and all that they can do by this denial is to make more clear than ever our own determination to undertake one last mission—to search out and destroy the last vestige of this barbaric war, to

pacify our own hearts, to conquer the hate and the fear that have driven this country these last ten years and more, so when thirty years from now our brothers go down the street without a leg, without an arm, or a face, and small boys ask why, we will be able to say 'Vietnam' and not mean a desert, not a filthy obscene memory, but mean instead a place where America finally turned and where soldiers like us helped it in the turning.[92]

Kerry's speech impressed the senators, as well as millions of viewers who watched it on television. The address proved to be a masterstroke for Kerry and VVAW, and one of the highlights of Dewey Canyon III. After testifying before the committee, Kerry "ended up being the spokesman for VVAW and did a brilliant, brilliant job," recalled his friend Madelyn Moore.[93] Jan Barry agreed with Moore. "It was an absolutely incredible speech that he gave. He really distilled what most of us wanted to say."[94] The antiwar leader Fred Halstead called Kerry's performance "memorable" and "impassioned."[95]

Kerry's speech transformed him into the symbol of the antiwar veterans' protest in Washington, D.C. But the attention he received stirred jealousies and anger among other VVAWers that had been fermenting since he joined the organization's Executive Committee in late 1970. Some of his harshest detractors were in VVAW. His radical critics often emphasized the class differences between Kerry and most of the other protesters. One zealous veteran scrawled "PIG" across a "personality poster" that displayed Kerry's picture. While he "was delivering his talk, a different VVAW faction strenuously demanded a spokesman who more closely represented their views," recalled Halstead.[96]

Despite the widespread favorable publicity that followed Kerry's address, antagonism festered. Other veterans presented equally compelling testimony on Capitol Hill and did not understand why they were largely ignored by the media.[97] Joe Urgo, who strove to maintain unity between moderates and radicals, conceded that most VVAWers believed Kerry "was a rich guy, . . . a politician, who was in it to use us."[98] The internal struggle that developed following Kerry's testimony bewildered centrists such as Jan Barry. "There were these constant tensions if somebody was slightly different in some way. I welcomed this diversity." But even Barry admitted that divisions in VVAW based on the former military status of members exacerbated the anger some veterans felt toward Kerry. "There was always resentment between enlisted men and officers, unless people became friends with each other; then it became irrelevant."[99]

While John Kerry testified before the Senate Foreign Relations Committee, authorities erected an enormous makeshift fence around the Capitol to protect the building from incoming May Day protesters, who were expected to arrive over the weekend. Many VVAWers regarded the barrier as a tangible symbol of the shabby treatment they had encountered in the offices of various senators and representatives. Veterans met early in the evening to decide on the nature of the medal-returning ceremony the next morning. Explained Ed Damato: "I remember there was a big debate about whether we should throw the medals away at the Capitol Building or put them in a body bag. The people who wanted to throw them away won out, correctly."[100]

That night, Mike Milligan, an ex-Marine from Pennsylvania, led a silent march of five thousand veterans and supporters. A group of veterans carried an American flag upside down, an international symbol of distress. The flag had been used to cover the coffin of a buddy who had died in Vietnam.[101] The veterans returned to the camp for their last night in Washington. They were relieved that their small tent city was no longer illegal, but they went to bed cold and exhausted. The chill created by strong wind gusts that blew through the Mall brought the temperature down to thirty-five degrees. Hundreds of passersby brought bedding to the shivering protesters. "I don't agree with what you guys are doing politically, but it's cold tonight," said a sixty-year-old man who deposited a load of blankets at the campsite.[102]

The eleven P.M. broadcast of the *NBC Nightly News* on Thursday temporarily interrupted the momentum of Dewey Canyon III. Pentagon sources had tipped Frank Jordan, Washington Bureau chief for NBC, that the VVAW's executive director, Al Hubbard, had been not an air force captain, as he claimed, but an air force staff sergeant E-5. NBC confronted Hubbard in a telephone call to his hotel room that night, and he admitted he had lied about his rank. The following morning, on the *Today Show*, Hubbard insisted that he had served in Vietnam as a sergeant and a flight engineer. "We came to Washington to tell the truth, and I've allowed this lie to continue because I recognize in this country that it's very important that one has an image."[103] To be certain, Hubbard's fraudulent credentials probably enhanced his credibility in the media before his lie was exposed. On the Sunday before Dewey Canyon III, he had appeared on *Meet the Press* with John Kerry. Next to Kerry, Hubbard was the most visible spokesperson for VVAW.

Publicly, his comrades reacted nonchalantly to the news. After Dewey Canyon III, John Kerry praised Hubbard for his honesty. "He thought it was time to tell the truth and he did it because he thought it would be best for the organization."[104] Added Scott Moore: "I really don't care whether Al was in Vietnam or not. He's a good man. That's all that counts."[105] However, even before NBC revealed Hubbard's lie, VVAW leaders had learned about the forthcoming report and "confronted him in a trailer." They considered censuring him. Jan Barry spoke against such a move, arguing that "there's no punishment that we can lay on Al Hubbard stronger than what has already happened to him. He's been humiliated on national television."[106]

The damage to VVAW proved minimal. A story that could have been injurious to the organization was either ignored or scarcely reported. But the revelation had a long-term impact that went beyond adding drama to the week's events. After Dewey Canyon III, Hubbard assumed a decidedly lower profile in VVAW. His tight control over the national office waned, permitting the process of decentralization to continue in the organization. Once widely respected for his unassuming modesty and astute leadership skills, he saw his reputation deteriorate, and he became more elusive and withdrawn.

On Friday morning, a line formed near the west front of the United States Capitol that stretched back to the VVAW campsite. Estimates of the number of participants in the demonstration varied between six hundred and three thousand.[107] Thousands of spectators jammed the lower west terrace of the Capitol. The sizable press contingent, enhanced by the presence of the three networks, signified that the event would be reported extensively. The ceremony began at ten A.M. "It almost seemed . . . spontaneous, even though it was planned," described an eyewitness.[108] Neil Russell, a fifty-five-year-old World War II veteran, walked to the front of the line, accompanied by two Gold Star mothers. He wore the fatigue jacket that had once belonged to his son Bill, who was killed in Vietnam in January 1969. The teary-eyed music teacher blew taps to begin the proceedings. Following the bugle call, a Gold Star mother declared, "I am here to join all of these men. In each one of them, I see my son."[109]

Most of the veterans who lined up to throw their medals away had ambivalent feelings about what they were doing. In the military culture, citations, ribbons, and decorations assumed a significance that most civilians did not understand. Like other soldiers, VVAW members had been conditioned to accept the sanctity of such objects. Scott Camil kept his medals inside a glass container on his fireplace mantle. "That was my thanks for Vietnam. That was my recognition. That was all the fuck I had for my sacrifices," he recalled. Camil received one of his Purple Hearts after he was blown to the ground by an explosion during a combat mission. "When I opened my eyes, I was laying on the ground, and the people around me were calling for help, and I tried to stand up and I couldn't. And the first thing that came to my mind was, 'I'm going to have a Purple Heart.'"[110] Over time, Camil saw his medals as "tokens for something I wasn't proud of anymore."[111]

Ron Ferrizzi came to Dewey Canyon III from Philadelphia to cast away his Silver Star and his Purple Heart, against the objections of his wife and family. "My parents told me that if I really did come down here and turn in my medals, that they never wanted anything more to do with me. That's not an easy thing to take. I still love my parents. My wife doesn't understand what happened to me when I came home from Nam. She said she would divorce me if I came down here because she wanted my medals for our son to see when he grew up."[112] Some of the ex-soldiers could not bring themselves to throw away their medals. Igor Brovosky of New York City discarded most of his decorations but kept "two Purple Hearts in memory of friends."[113] For many of the people in line that morning, the memories of friends in Vietnam, not the military pomp and grandeur, gave the medals significance.[114]

The first veteran in line was Jack Smith, a twenty-seven-year-old former Marine sergeant from West Hartford, Connecticut. "We now strip ourselves of the medals of courage and heroism . . . those citations for gallantry and exemplary service. . . . We cast these away as symbols of shame, dishonor, and inhumanity," he announced.[115] One by one, veterans inched forward, hurling their awards over the chicken wire and wood fence surrounding the Capitol. Gradually, a "garbage heap of honor," as *Newsday* described the discarded objects, accumulated at the base of a statue of Supreme Court Chief Justice John Marshall. Hundreds of veterans made statements as they passed the microphone. "My name is Peter Branagan. I got a Purple Heart, and I hope I get another one fighting these motherfuckers."[116] "I pray that time will forgive me and my brothers for what we did," declared an African American ex-serviceman.[117]

A number of men cast medals for other veterans who could not attend Dewey Canyon III. Paul Wither tossed nine Purple Hearts, a Distinguished Service Cross, a Bronze Star, a Silver Star, "and a lot of other shit

. . . for my brothers."[118] Ed Damato brought "some medals people had sent me to throw away."[119] John Upton carried a bucket of medals from his friends in Kansas.[120] In addition to medals, veterans rid themselves of other belongings. A flurry of discharge papers covered the ground near the statue of John Marshall. Bill Crandell remembered "a vet [who] tossed the artificial leg he had been issued."[121] A Marine sergeant with a missing arm chucked a blue-and-red dress coat over the fence. Another participant tossed a black Viet Cong pajama suit into the pile. Some threw nothing at all. The sister of a soldier missing in action filed past the microphone and said, "I don't have any medals to throw. Nixon took his life and that's enough."[122]

The column moved slowly. "I was at the front of the line, so it seems like most of the famous comments and dramatic stuff I saw firsthand," recounted Robert Hanson. Like other African Americans, Hanson stood near the front of the line. "There weren't that many African Americans in the organization, and there were not a fair number in the line up of guys . . . so I guess visuals of me were deemed educational to the other guys. Here's a black guy who's saying, 'This is all fucked,' and he's throwing his medals."[123]

Rusty Sachs found himself in a dilemma. The former marine captain had privately submitted his decorations to the government before Dewey Canyon III. He waited empty-handed when an organizer approached him and gave him a Silver Star and a Distinguished Flying Cross. "At first, I didn't know whether to throw medals that weren't really mine. I wondered if that would be potentially harmful to the organization. But then I remembered that I had two friends who had been killed recently. One had received a Silver Star, and the other one a Distinguished Flying Cross. So I threw the medals in their memory." Afterward, Sachs "felt spiritually close to the guys who had died."[124]

During the first hour of the ceremony, only a few hundred veterans passed the microphone. To expedite the process, scores of protesters silently discarded their medals. Bill Weiman navigated his wheelchair toward the fence and deposited his decorations without saying a word. But comments continued to flow out of the loudspeaker. "The line was huge, and some of these guys were making statements that were several minutes long, so some of the vets started getting pissed off," remembered Bill Branson, a Southern California VVAWer.[125]

When Barry Romo reached the front of the line at Dewey Canyon III, painful memories of the men in his platoon who were killed in Vietnam returned to him. "All I could manage [to say] was, 'These ain't shit.'"[126] Another veteran pointed toward the Capitol and said: "We don't want to fight anymore, but if we have to fight again, it'll be to take these steps."[127] Alex Munzell, a seventy-five-year-old World War I veteran, threw his victory medal from the French Campaign of 1918. "I don't need it anymore. It's no good."[128] Congressman Ron Dellums turned in his medals from the Korean War. "They can have them back."[129] A veteran yelled: "Here are my merit badges for murder . . . from the country I betrayed by enlisting in the U.S. Army."[130] Before volleying his medals, one man said, "I earned a Good Conduct Medal in Vietnam. In the words of another son of Massachusetts, Henry Thoreau, my only regret is my good conduct."[131]

The last of the veterans had thrown his medals around noon. By the end of the event, fourteen Navy and Distinguished Service Crosses, one hundred Silver Stars, and more than a thousand Purple Hearts lay on the ground. For many of the VVAWers who had come to Washington, the ceremony assumed a significance that rivaled their service in Vietnam. "Dewey Canyon III was the defining moment of my life," recalled the Kansas VVAW organizer John Upton.[132] "It was a cathartic experience," concluded VVAW's founding vice president, Carl Rogers.[133] Ed Damato still remembers "every millisecond" of "the act of turning around and facing the Capitol building and throwing the medals and my discharge papers. . . . We were giving a finger to Congress."[134] For Barry Romo, the event was a combination of "energy and comradeship and anarchy and discipline and release. We weren't responsible anymore. And we thought we were going to end the war."[135] Added Bill Crandell: "Guys walked away from that feeling healed. . . . There was an incredible sense of freedom."[136] After discarding their medals, Rusty Sachs and Ron Ferrizzi embraced one another and wept for two hours. When the ceremony was over, Ferrizzi proclaimed, "I feel fantastic. I feel like I'm clean, that I'm completely cleansed."[137]

Movement activists who watched the proceedings were awestruck. The antiwar leader Sid Peck later claimed that Dewey Canyon III "set the whole tone" for the demonstrations that followed it.[138] The war resister David Harris broke down and cried on the freeway while he listened to a radio report about the climax of Dewey Canyon III.[139] Fred Halstead had observed the ceremony with "a white-haired, gentle old man, a survivor of Hiroshima." When the event ended, the elderly visitor turned to Halstead and said, "Perhaps humanity shall yet save itself from the nuclear holocaust."[140]

The veterans returned to Potomac Park and broke camp. They dismantled their tents, rinsed their pots and pans, packed their luggage. In the early afternoon, a small group of them gathered with representatives from the Parks Department and planted a tree near the campsite. During the quiet, moving act, a group of veterans, along with their companions and children, surrounded the tree and lowered its roots into the earth.[141]

Dewey Canyon III was over.

On Saturday, April 24, 1971, half a million people marched through the streets of Washington, D.C. It was the largest antiwar demonstration in the history of the United States. An estimated 250,000 participated in a similar event in San Francisco. Despite the enormous turnout, the marches lacked the spark of Dewey Canyon III. Editorialized a Pennsylvania newspaper: "It is to be doubted that this great outpouring of conscientious men and women will influence the thinking of the nation even nearly as much as the appearance of 900 warriors for peace dressed in their battle attire."[142] VVAW organizers had modestly assumed their "limited incursion into the country of Congress" would prove little more than a minor prelude to the April 24 marches and the May Day activities thereafter. But Dewey Canyon III overshadowed the remainder of the Spring Offensive. The week's activities thrust VVAW into the center of the antiwar movement. No prior demonstrations had exerted such an emotional impact on the American public.

The success of Dewey Canyon III owed much to widespread and largely sympathetic media exposure. "The press was listening, and in that sense, America was listening," recalled Bill Crandell.[143] The nightly network news broadcasts often began with footage of the veterans' protests. The *Boston Globe* compared the veterans at Potomac Park to the "local militiamen gathered in their white britches and three-cornered hats . . . [at] the Battles of Lexington and Concord."[144] The *Christian Science Monitor* advised the Nixon administration to "overindulge them, and smother them with kindness."[145] The participation of "2,000 grim combat veterans" in antiwar demonstrations "was deeply impressive," stated an editorial in *The Cleveland Plain Dealer*.[146] Many newspapers emphasized the veterans' credentials. "Certainly the opinions of those who have fought [in the Vietnam War] should carry special weight," insisted the *Philadelphia Daily News*.[147] An editorial in the *Akron Beacon Journal* asserted, "Their testimony must inevitably carry more weight than the protests or endorsements of those who have never seen this war firsthand."[148]

Adding to VVAW's victory was President Nixon's inability to respond decisively to the veterans. John Kerry's testimony before the Senate Foreign Relations Committee and the medal-throwing ceremony resulted in a coup that the Nixon administration, despite its best efforts, could not counter. Judge George Hart worsened matters for the president with his decision to overturn the injunction. After emerging from a hectic meeting with President Nixon, a frustrated H. R. Haldeman recorded in his diary: "We got into quite a discussion of the media problem; they're really killing us because they run the veterans' demonstration every night in great detail, and we have no way to fight back. . . . We're getting pretty well chopped up."[149]

VVAW withstood attacks from conservatives and other veterans' organizations.[150] But the public ignored the critics, and the antiwar veterans basked in the aftermath of Dewey Canyon III. Reflecting on the week's events, Rusty Sachs said, "We wouldn't have been surprised if somebody said, 'Hey, Nixon just announced that all the troops will be out of Nam and back by suppertime.' We would have believed it at that instant."[151]

Once Dewey Canyon III began, it assumed a life of its own. A quarter of a century after the protest, many of its organizers described the week's activities as "spontaneous." But that word belies the extensive planning that went into the occasion. Days before veterans arrived at Potomac Park, the national office compiled itineraries that, in the event, bore little resemblance to what would later occur. Few of the week's incidents were anticipated in the advance planning phase. Nobody predicted the Justice Department would so rigorously and swiftly pursue an injunction against the camping veterans or that, with unprecedented speed, the case would appear before the Supreme Court while the action was still in progress. Moreover, the demonstration's architects did not anticipate the harsh treatment of the lobbyists by prowar senators and representatives, which alienated and radicalized the activists.

As they attempted to piece together a strategy, the only reference point the VVAWers had was the experience of the Bonus Army nearly four decades earlier. The spirited, ragtag collection of World War I veterans who marched on Washington to collect their war bonuses in the spring and summer of 1932 had been routed out of their camps by U.S. Army troops under the direction of General Douglas MacArthur. The government's Pyrrhic victory did irreparable damage to President Herbert Hoover, and the Vietnam veterans understood that a similar move by President Nixon would prove equally costly.

The significance of Dewey Canyon III can be understood only by exploring the event and its aftermath in detail. The televised testimony presented by John Kerry before the Senate Foreign Relations Committee on April 22 and the medal-throwing ceremony the next day turned America's attention to VVAW and placed the protesters in the forefront of the antiwar movement. The anarchical spontaneity of the week became the group's trademark. Such a trait proved a mixed blessing. Veterans who probably would not have paid their dues to a more centralized, formal organization joined VVAW afterward in large numbers. Yet they made an unruly rank and file. VVAW's mailing lists would continue to be in a constant state of flux due to its transient constituency.

But it is a mistake to assume that too much of Dewey Canyon III occurred randomly or was the product of a chaotic environment. Unforeseen struggles shaped the gathering. The evolution of Dewey Canyon III paralleled that of VVAW. Veterans initially participated in conventional forms of resistance. However, disillusionment set in quickly, and most of the VVAWers camping at Potomac Park consciously chose to adopt more confrontational tactics. In the middle of the week, the Supreme Court ordered the veterans to abandon their campsite at the park, but VVAWers voted, by a slim margin, to disobey the ruling and face the consequences. On Friday, April 23, veterans returned their combat medals and ribbons by throwing them on the steps of the Capitol, using a method that was decidedly bolder than John Kerry's proposal to put them in a body bag and deliver it to government officials. Such overt defiance thrust VVAW into the national spotlight, as the image of men hurling medals was etched into the national conscience. Dewey Canyon III ultimately became the turning point that VVAW leaders predicted, but only after the veterans, through trial and error, discovered a means of protesting the war that assuaged their rage and purified their souls.

Unlike the Winter Soldier Investigation, Dewey Canyon III drew the attention of the American public. The medal-throwing ceremony may have symbolized VVAW's internal leftward drift, but it simultaneously facilitated mainstream acceptance of the antiwar movement. Never before had such a widespread segment of the population looked so favorably upon protest as in the weeks following Dewey Canyon III. Commentators speculated that the veterans' actions in Washington played a significant role in shifting public opinion. A June poll indicated that a record 61 percent said the war was a mistake; the following month, by a margin of 65 to 20 percent, Americans believed that the United States should continue to withdraw "even if the government of South Vietnam collapsed."[152]

Previously ignored or ostracized by the antiwar movement, the veterans became the idols of activists everywhere. They replaced earlier icons of resistance such as Abbie Hoffman and assumed an almost mythic status. After Dewey Canyon III, VVAW experienced another meteoric growth spurt. Membership doubled to nearly twenty thousand during the summer of 1971, and there were two thousand joiners in Vietnam.[153] The week's activities tapped into new avenues of support and reinforced fledgling local chapters across the country. It promoted opposition to the war and broadened the antiwar critique beyond the simple demand to withdraw troops. The veterans taught Americans that the Vietnam War was inflicting a devastating human toll and that its soldiers required a chance to heal and come to terms with their past.

New challenges confronted VVAW throughout the remainder of the year. Growing pains plagued the organization. Many of its prominent leaders either departed after Dewey Canyon III or assumed lower profiles. The locus of power would eventually shift from New York City into the hands of a Marxist leadership in Chicago. The process of decentralization accelerated rapidly after the April event, resulting in a VVAW that was larger, yet more challenging to govern.

6

The Spirit of '71

Dewey Canyon III had been one of the most successful demonstrations against the Vietnam War. It thrust VVAW to the forefront of the antiwar movement and quickly doubled its membership rolls. The medal throwers had left an imprint on the popular imagination, and they were subsequently mythologized by their antiwar veteran "brothers" who had not been able to attend the week's events. After the demonstration, participants traveled home, fortified their chapters, and initiated local actions. They borrowed old tactics and devised new ones. The spirited veterans regarded themselves as reinforcements for weary troops on the home front. "We became the darling of the peace movement. It was always, 'You gotta have a VVAW speaker.' It was always, 'Put the vets up front.' They were always deferring to us," recalled Barry Romo.[1] The organization reached its zenith at the end of 1971 and the beginning of 1972.

The Nixon administration regarded VVAW as a threat, but one that had to be dealt with carefully. That its members comprised Vietnam veterans, mostly white men ruled out the violent methods FBI agents had employed to suppress the Black Panthers. The president and his aides realized that zealous persecution of the veterans could have dire consequences, especially with an election year approaching. For the time being, scrutiny by federal agents and infiltration by informers would have to suffice. VVAW was thus able to prosper for several months without facing the same degree of harassment as other radical groups.

Naturally, growth brought transformation. A shakeup at the highest levels led to an even more decentralized structure. The departure of some key figures spurred reorganization. Executive committee positions, such as president and vice president, gave way to the more egalitarian title of "national coordinator." Adhering to the political trend of the time, the New York office relinquished more power to regional leaders; the increased autonomy, it was hoped, would strengthen the local chapters.

Within VVAW, distinct subgroups emerged. Marxist ideologues read Mao Zedong and grappled with the history of capitalism and war. Writers contributed war poems to a highly successful collection of published verse. In Washington, D.C., and in state capitals across the country, lobbyists pressed for improved veterans benefits. Filmmakers edited VVAW documentaries. Rank-and-file activists beamed radio shows into military bases, designed newsletters, leafleted G.I. coffeehouses, planned marches. Women and minorities raised issues unique to their experiences. Differences led to discord, but peaceful coexistence, if not harmony, prevailed temporarily.

A sizable majority of Americans opposed the Vietnam War by the summer of 1971. "I don't think you could find a hawk around here if you combed the place and set traps," observed the editor of small-town Kansas newspaper.[2] Never before in American history had antiwar sentiment been so widespread. A Gallup poll in August showed that 61 percent of those polled favored a pullout. A majority thought the war was "immoral," according to a Harris poll. President Nixon's policy of "Vietnamization" seemed to be an acknowledgment at the highest levels of government that the war was ultimately unwinnable and futile. The crisis deepened in June when the *New York Times* began to publish the Pentagon Papers, the Defense Department's detailed secret history of American involvement in Vietnam prior to 1967. The Pentagon Papers showed that "the predominant American objective was not victory over the enemy but merely the avoidance of defeat and humiliation," wrote Max Frankel in the *New York Times* edition of the Pentagon Papers. President Johnson and his advisers had "an arrogant disregard for the Congress, for the public and for the inherent obligation of the responsibilities and leadership in a democratic society," Frankel concluded.[3] Daniel Ellsberg, the Pentagon analyst who leaked the study, became a hero in the antiwar movement and a villain to the frustrated Nixon administration.[4]

Ironically, at a time when antiwar sentiment was more widespread than ever, the antiwar movement was in a state of disarray. The enormous April 24 mobilization masked deep divisions, rampant burnout, and poor planning. The chaotic May Day protests in Washington, D.C., the following week fueled further splits. "We stand in the antechamber of a dying antiwar movement," declared the pacifist Gordon Zahn.[5] Gone were flagship organizations such as SDS and the Mobe, and membership was dropping in SANE (Committee for a Sane Nuclear Policy), the Women's

International League for Peace and Freedom, and Clergy and Laity Concerned about Vietnam.[6]

The collapse of many key groups did not necessarily lead to an overall decline in resistance. Protests occurred more frequently than ever. Dissent was rife, particularly in the military. By the spring and summer of 1971, the G.I. movement reached its peak in the United States and Vietnam.[7] During 1971, the number of dishonorable discharges climbed to twenty-five thousand, while desertions increased to a record seven out of every one hundred soldiers. One U.S. Army survey found that more than half of troops engaged in illegal drug use, antiwar activities, or some form of disobedience. Three weeks after Dewey Canyon III, hundreds of soldiers marched at nearly twenty bases on "Armed Farces Day." More than a thousand G.I.s at Chu Lai in Vietnam held a peace a rally on July 4. A thousand sailors petitioned the USS *Coral Sea* to halt its cruise to Vietnam. Sailors on half a dozen other ships sabotaged efforts and initiated "Stop Our Ship" (SOS) campaigns. A revolt at Travis Air Force Base in May suspended base operations for four days. More and more pilots, including Captain Michael Heck, who had flown 175 missions over Vietnam, refused to continue bombing.[8]

So acute was the crisis in the military that in the June 1971 issue of *Armed Forces Journal*, retired Marine Corps Colonel Robert D. Heinl Jr. asserted, "The morale, discipline, and battle-worthiness of the U.S. armed forces are, with a few salient exceptions, lower and worse than at any time in this century and possibly in the history of the United States."[9] Added the commanding general at Fort Bragg: "The Army's prestige is at the lowest ebb in memory. There's never been a more unpopular war, and it's had its effect."[10]

VVAW was a direct beneficiary of the breakdown in the American military. In Vietnam, some one thousand soldiers signed a VVAW antiwar petition. Many of those people were drawn to the organization, as were G.I.s returning to the United States. The national office in New York processed dozens of new membership applications daily. Joe Urgo, who once sorted singlehandedly through sacks of mail, now enjoyed the help of a growing volunteer staff.[11] Shortly before he was killed in Vietnam in June 1971, Private First Class Michael Street wrote to the national office about his plans to join VVAW: "The guys over here really appreciate what you are trying to do. . . . You have a lot of support coming home soon. So keep fighting the pigs. And maybe we will end this damn war."[12]

Returning soldiers swelled VVAW's ranks. A series of well-publicized protests that followed Dewey Canyon III enhanced the organization's reputation among antiwar G.I.s and other veterans. After the April protest, some VVAWers remained in Washington, D.C., to participate in the May Day civil disobedience. The Oregon coordinator Mike McKusker obtained one hundred pounds of chicken excrement from a Maryland farmer. On May 3, McKusker, along with a group of VVAWers, including Al Hubbard, dumped it on the steps of the Pentagon, resulting in more than twenty arrests (and prompting McKusker to refer to the arrestees as "the Chickenshit Twenty"). John Kerry condemned the May Day activities as "horrible," declaring that the destruction of private property "should be punished." While not as quick to condemn passive resistance as he was before Dewey Canon III, Kerry still preferred milder, less confrontational forms of protest.[13]

He accompanied nearly two hundred veterans on a Memorial Day weekend march from Concord, Massachusetts, to Boston. The participants, who followed Paul Revere's famous route, dubbed the action "Operation POW." On the night of Saturday, May 29, the marchers camped at Lexington Green, site of the opening battle of the American Revolution, despite warnings from law enforcement officials that camping would result in arrests. Throughout the evening, four hundred local residents joined the veterans. In the early hours of the morning, police arrested five hundred resisters, the largest mass arrest in Massachusetts history. Veterans who had rejected civil disobedience a month earlier were now willingly engaging in it.[14]

Most VVAW protests that happened on the heels of Dewey Canyon III, including Operation POW (a hybrid of Dewey Canyon III and Operation RAW), were little more than repetitions of earlier VVAW events. The national office encouraged such activity by distributing "Guidelines to Marches and Guerrilla Theater" to local leaders.[15] In the fall, chapters in the Boston area staged a second march, similar to Operation POW, from Concord to Charlestown. At the opening of the Lyndon Baines Johnson Library on May 21 in Austin, Texas, demonstrators assembled and threw their medals. Veterans conducted Winter Soldier Investigations in Colorado, Georgia, and Massachusetts. While these activities received media coverage, particularly in area newspapers, organizers were clearly running out of ideas. Some coordinators, such as Bill Crandell, believed the Washington protest represented both VVAW's pinnacle and its last hurrah. He felt the organization "had spent much of its energy" by the summer of 1971.[16]

But Crandell also recognized that VVAW was undergoing a process of decentralization. "A lot of what we did became more local and more diverse. We became involved in a lot more things," he acknowledged.[17] The transfer of power in VVAW from the national office to state chapters reflected a trend in the antiwar movement that had been occurring since 1970. The historian Terry Anderson referred to the early seventies as a "second wave" of activism, characterized by "actions . . . often addressing local concerns."[18] Throughout the sixties, antiwar coalitions, usually based in Washington, D.C., New York City, or San Francisco, planned demonstrations in those cities and invited supporters across the country to attend. In the seventies, a shift toward more regionalized organizing resulted in a proliferation of various types of resistance in smaller cities and towns. This transformation was the result of a growing perception that the war was, in the words of Todd Gitlin, "impervious to protest" and that massive antiwar mobilizations were not having the desired impact.[19]

Changing tactics also grew out of the radicalization and democratization of the antiwar movement. The peace coalition was fragmented by 1971, and many key organizations floundered, in part because leaders had lost touch with the needs of constituents in different parts of the country. Fewer and fewer activists cared whether the National Peace Action Coalition or the People's Coalition for Peace and Justice had the correct line on the war. Like the civil rights and women's liberation struggles, the antiwar movement's most significant achievement was empowering people at the grassroots level. The upsurge of nationwide dissent brought a growing awareness of community problems. Previously disfranchised citizens—women, Chicanos, African Americans, Asian Americans, and so forth—began building viable local groups that addressed immediate grievances.

Like other leftist groups of the early seventies, VVAW advocated multi-issue community organizing. This had not always been the case. Since its revival late in 1969, the scope of VVAW's agenda had expanded beyond its original goal of ending the war. Coordinators directed their energies to a variety of other problems. Still, nearly every VVAW-sponsored action had something to do with some facet of the Vietnam War and its consequences. However, Dewey Canyon III raised the consciousness of participants. Many of the veterans fashioned broader critiques of capitalism and concluded that the Vietnam War was intertwined with larger issues related to gender, race, class, and the economy.

VVAW provided liberal and radical veterans the only viable means of resisting the war and collectively pursuing their demands for improved treatment. Thus, VVAW not only fought to extend Veterans Administration benefits but also provided services the VA did not. The organization initiated an action group and legislative liaison in Washington, D.C., to lobby policymakers on behalf of Vietnam veterans. Group therapy sessions met weekly in San Francisco, New York City, Philadelphia, and Detroit. Members pooled their resources and opened rehabilitation farms in New Mexico and Virginia and halfway houses in Milwaukee and Minneapolis. VVAW thrived in a number of states, with particularly strong chapters in the Northeast, Midwest, and Western regions.[20]

VVAW's ambitious "Lifeline to Cairo," launched in April, signified a change in the organization's focus and direction. Cairo was an economically depressed town in southern Illinois, near the confluence of the Mississippi and Ohio rivers. In the summer of 1969, a civil rights coalition called the United Front, representing African Americans in the area, started a boycott of white-owned businesses to protest repression and poor conditions in black neighborhoods. An alliance of police and white supremacists retaliated by randomly terrorizing citizens at night. Over a period of more than two years, snipers fired an estimated 174 bullets into different parts of the African American community, killing at least four people. Bobby Morgan, a representative of the United Front, traveled to Washington, D.C., in April 1971 and invited veterans at Dewey Canyon III to assist civil rights activists in Cairo. Morgan hoped the veterans would steer attention to the plight of Cairo residents. At a VVAW steering committee meeting in New York City in May, members agreed to join forces with the United Front in Cairo.[21]

While seemingly unrelated to the Vietnam War, conditions in Cairo aroused VVAW organizers. "The government of this country has . . . [said] that we are fighting for freedom and equality and self-determination of the Vietnamese," wrote the executive committee member Scott Moore, "and yet here in our own country people are denied that right and are involved in a struggle to obtain that right."[22] Moore, Al Hubbard, and the Philadelphia coordinator Jon Birch assumed leadership of the "Lifeline to Cairo," which consisted of sending truckloads of food, books, clothing, and medical supplies to the African American community there. Chapters around the country collected canned food and supplies and sent them to Cairo. United Front leaders hoped the veterans' presence in the town would generate press coverage. For VVAW, the project provided an opportunity to move beyond the antiwar movement, strengthen ties with civil rights groups, and assist people "suffering the same indignities as the Vietnamese."[23]

In the summer of 1971, Scott Moore drove by car across America to assess the state of VVAW. He visited chapter coordinators, met new members, and evaluated various activities. He reported his findings to the executive committee on his return to New York City. Those expecting a glowing report of a flourishing VVAW were sorely disappointed. Moore discovered that VVAW's Cairo campaign lacked support in the community and was "not enthusiastically received by the [VVAW] coordinators" in the town. "The time and energy for another operation of this type is too much for the organization to handle," he wrote.[24] In other parts of the country, coordinators were overworked and discouraged. The Colorado coordinator, Brian Adams, told Moore the national office was "hung up to a large degree in New York politics and often does not understand the problems in the field." Adams felt that Colorado members were "apathetic and generally relate only to large actions." "It is his opinion VVAW can only survive if another national action—like DC III—is initiated," Moore noted.[25]

Elsewhere, Moore found the picture just as bleak. "It is my feeling that VVAW is basically a paper organization with a few hard-core leaders who are keeping it alive. General membership participation is lower than ever. Many regions are inadequately covered. People don't know and generally don't care what is happening," he concluded. He recommended a second protest in Washington, D.C., similar to Dewey Canyon III. The next action, he argued, should include "at least one thousand members" assembling to demand a congressional hearing to establish a concrete timetable for withdrawal of U.S. troops from Vietnam. If Congress refused to conduct such a hearing, the veterans should engage in "massive civil disobedience." An alternative, he counseled, would be for veterans in each state to perform passive resistance and fasts. At the close of his report, Moore announced his plans to resign as treasurer and as a member of the executive committee of VVAW in September so that he could return to New York University.[26]

Moore's account ignored VVAW's many success stories. His pessimistic appraisal grew out of his exhaustion. Since 1969, his attempts to turn VVAW into a nationwide organization had been invaluable. But two years of working full-time in the national office had taken their toll, especially for Moore, who had been willing to do the drudgery that other leaders avoided. "I was just burned out," Moore recalled.[27] His departure was a significant loss, but it was part of a transformation in VVAW's leadership after Dewey Canyon III. Jan Barry had resigned as president a few months earlier to edit a book of poetry by Vietnam veterans and to assist Dr. Robert Jay Lifton with rap groups.[28]

John Kerry was already beginning to distance himself from VVAW. He had an eye on an upcoming House race in Massachusetts's Fifth District, and he was aware of the growing hostility toward him in the organization. He appeared in the national office less frequently and skipped the national steering committee meeting in St. Louis in August. "Sailor" John McGarraty, a VVAW activist from the Northwest, wrote about the anti-Kerry sentiment at the gathering: "John Kerry did get kicked around a bit. Larry Rottman put up a sign saying 'Free John Kerry's Maid.' John is in Europe for the summer. I don't think he'll be around VVAW long."[29] One VVAWer, Rod Kane, who was also present at the St. Louis meeting, remembered a "power struggle among the chapters to unseat John Kerry as head spokesman of the organization. It has been implied that he is using the organization to further his political career. I think that being the leader of an organization of disgruntled veterans is political suicide to begin with."[30]

John Kerry remained in the organization for several more weeks after the St. Louis meeting. On August 29, he spoke to wealthy supporters at a VVAW fundraiser in East Hampton, Long Island. He resigned his position as national coordinator prior to the November 12 steering committee meeting in Kansas City because of "personality conflicts and differences in political philosophy."[31] Kerry's downfall in the organization promised him a bright political future. Ironically, no other individual had done more to advance VVAW's cause in the public mind. Others followed his example and left about the same time. Rusty Sachs, whose image throwing medals at Dewey Canyon III appeared in numerous magazines and newspapers, distanced himself from VVAW in the summer. He was "wary of extremists" and believed VVAW had "turned into an organization of radicals." Their increasingly combative behavior alienated Sachs and other veterans. "We were just regular Democrats," he recalled.[32]

Most moderates continued paying dues in the hope of influencing policies. Those who abandoned VVAW feared that they were losing control of the group's direction. Pete Zastrow, a VVAW activist from

Kentucky, remembered: "The basis of the organization had by then changed from a kind of radical liberalism to something much more akin to real political radicalism." A split occurred between members who wanted to work "within the system" (e.g., political campaigning, Democratic Party activism) and those who chose to work "outside it," Zastrow concluded.[33]

Despite John Kerry's high-profile exit, VVAW continued to grow, reaching twenty thousand members by the summer. In August, the national office began publishing the official VVAW newspaper, *First Casualty* (derived from a quotation from Aeschylus: "In war, truth is the first casualty"). Originally a crude-looking photocopy with a hand-drawn masthead, *First Casualty* soon evolved into a slick, tabloid-sized newspaper. Local chapters produced their own publications, which varied in quality from the gritty *Minnesota Homefront Sniper*, consisting of pen drawings and typewritten articles, to Southern California's handsome monthly, *Favorite Sons*, and Colorado's elaborate *Hóa Bính*. These periodicals served the important function of mobilizing members and addressing relevant concerns. Articles also reflected the heightened consciousness of members. Unlike articles that had appeared in earlier veterans' and G.I. newspapers, which tended to focus exclusively on Vietnam and military issues, contributions to *First Casualty* addressed racism and sexism in American society.[34]

Such subjects were often sensitive for VVAW members. Growth brought diversity to the organization, but membership continued to consist primarily of "white working- [and] middle-class" men.[35] Still, many VVAWers strongly empathized with women's liberation and with the struggles of Black Americans. In its premier issue, *First Casualty* editorialized: "The danger facing VVAW, as a predominantly male organization, is that it might start to emulate the very thing it is fighting against—the arrogant chauvinism of the military, which encourages all . . . forms of male dominance that exist in society as a whole."[36] The Texas VVAW newsletter condemned the numerous "VVAW communications" that contained references "to our sisters as 'our chicks' and 'their own women' . . . as if they are a piece of chattel property."[37]

Nevertheless, VVAW never mounted an effective campaign to recruit minorities and women. Individual organizers sought to diversify VVAW, but their task was a difficult one. The politics of identity, so prevalent in the early seventies, often drove minorities and women to join "power" groups, such as the Brown Berets, the Black Panthers, and various radical feminist collectives. Even the prospects for attracting white male antiwar veterans were not always promising. An activist noted the difficulty of mobilizing Vietnam veterans: "The idea of organizing around a past status is a very questionable tactic. These guys aren't 'vets.' They're students. They're workers. . . . They're not in the Army anymore. The reason that all these vets groupings are so weak is that they're trying to create a nexus to something that most guys would rather forget about or at least minimize in their daily lives."[38]

Women and minorities joined VVAW in small numbers, and they were usually welcomed. Yet women, particularly those who had been nurses in Vietnam, encountered enormous hurdles in VVAW. Lynda Van Devanter's ordeal illustrates the alienation that many nurses felt when they gravitated toward the organization. Van Devanter had been an army nurse at the 71st Evac Hospital at Pleiku. She entered the army's nursing program for the same reason many young men enlisted in the military. She was moved by President Kennedy's stirring inaugural speech and felt a deep sense of commitment to her country. "Nursing was the way I was going to make my contribution to society. I was part of a generation of Americans who were 'chosen' to change the world. We were sure of that. It was only a matter of waiting until we all grew up."[39] She went to Vietnam in 1968 with high ideals. But her first "Mas-Cal" (short for "mass casualty situation") quickly revealed the savagery of the war. "The emergency room was practically covered with blood. Dozens of gurneys were tightly packed into the ER, with barely enough space for medical people to move between them. And the helicopters were still bringing in more."[40]

Van Devanter returned to the United States in 1970. Her parents "had said good-bye a year earlier to a happy-go-lucky all-American girl who thought she could grab the world by the tail. Now in that girl's place they had a very sad and bitter young woman who did little but brood."[41] Van Devanter dealt with many of the same problems that combat veterans faced. She struggled with depression, nightmares, alcoholism, and a lack of self-esteem. "I was as popular as a disease and as untouchable as a piece of shit," she recalled.[42]

The army ordered her to report to Walter Reed Army Hospital, near Washington, D.C. One day, while walking through Washington, she received a VVAW handbill announcing a march on the White House. She later attended a VVAW planning meeting in the basement of a local church, wearing her fatigue shirt, army hat and jeans. "I listened to the things the other vets were saying about the war and how we should be out of Vietnam immediately. I was in total agreement."[43] But a VVAWer approached Van Devanter and told her that she could not participate in the march because she did not look like a vet. When she told him that she had been a nurse with the 71st Evac and wanted to march with her fellow veterans, the VVAWer repeated the organization's policy. "If we have women marching," he reasoned, "Nixon and the network news reporters might think we're swelling the ranks with nonvets." Lynda Van Devanter left the meeting disappointed, and VVAW lost a prospective member. "If they didn't want me, why bother?"[44]

Other nurses had a difficult time fitting in with the VVAW. "Don't tell me women don't know anything about war because we weren't out on the 'front lines,'" wrote an antiwar nurse, Judy Marron, in a VVAW newspaper. "I had battle fatigue, too. From those grueling years in surgery; it was a war zone there, believe me. There were days when the stress and strain and blood and guts almost had to equal what you experienced."[45] Nurses such as Van Devanter and Marron confronted their doubts about the war in private. Few felt comfortable within the ranks of VVAW, and the organization did not always allow them to join. Recalled a female VVAW activist: "The nurses who served and who were antiwar were really sort of forgotten. The VVAW allowed a lot of guys to heal after they came back, but there was nothing of that sort for women. There was a lot pain there for the nurses . . . and there was no camaraderie for these women. They were not encouraged to join VVAW."[46]

Despite widespread sexism within its ranks, VVAW was less chauvinistic than many other civil rights, New Left, and antiwar organizations. Since the mid-1960s, women activists had challenged their status within various social movements. Two members of the Student Nonviolent Coordinating Committee (SNCC), Casey Hayden and Mary King, addressed the problem early in a paper that criticized SNCC for not offering women "jobs commensurate with their abilities."[47] When women in SNCC and SDS questioned their subordinate roles, they were verbally abused. "The only position for women in SNCC is prone," announced the civil rights activist Stokely Carmichael.[48] Women in SDS and SNCC grew tired of running errands and cleaning offices. By the late 1960s, while the VVAW was still in its infancy, more women were embracing the radical feminist movement. They protested at the Pentagon in 1967, started underground newspapers such as *Rat*, and created their own consciousness-raising groups.[49]

The women's liberation movement was a few years old when VVAW began to blossom in early 1971. As a result of the growing influence of feminist thought, many VVAWers consciously sought to distance themselves from the pervasive and blatant sexism in SNCC and SDS. Women were also playing a more critical role in VVAW. Ever since Madelyn Moore had brought her talents as a full-time organizer to the national office in the fall of 1969, the veterans grew to depend on the contributions and energy of women activists. In certain chapters, such as the Detroit office, women were as numerous as men. But VVAW was caught in a dilemma. Beginning with the Winter Soldier Investigation, Nixon administration officials believed that the best way of neutralizing the group was to discredit its members. Officials searched for evidence that joiners either were not veterans or had lied about their service and experiences in Vietnam. VVAWers were aware of such efforts, and they limited membership to Vietnam veterans. Nurses and servicewomen were occasionally allowed to join as full members, but nonveterans could sign up only as honorary members, which meant they had no voting rights and could not hold office.[50]

Women protested such treatment. The Milwaukee activist Anne Bailey tried to join in December 1970 with her companion, John Lindquist, but she was told that she could not become a full member. She wrote an indignant letter to the national office:

> I am this guy's soul mate. We're not married yet, we're probably not going to. But this is my man, I've stood against the war since I was a freshman in high school and I lost my friend over there, and I agree with all the objectives that you have. And now you're going to tell me that you're going to treat me like the VFW and the American Legion and all these traditional vets groups treat their women? Put them in an auxiliary position, no voting rights, and you can contribute as long as you're in the kitchen or doing day care. Forget it![51]

After a long struggle with the national office, Bailey received a "conciliatory" letter, which contained a button and a membership card. But she found that "rank-and-file guys who were against the war were all very supportive of any woman who was willing to put up with them and help them along in the struggle to end the war."[52]

Other women experienced different degrees of sexism. Linda Alband, a native of Portland, Oregon, became a liaison between chapters in the

Northwest and the national office in 1971. She was neither a nurse nor a veteran's companion. A newcomer to the antiwar movement, Alband thought VVAW was "an important group politically," and the veterans appreciated her organizing skills. Yet she was troubled that many members regarded women as "mindless cadres who do shit work." "There was this whole thing about, 'Well, you weren't there, you don't understand it,'" she recalled.[53] Jeannie Friedman, a professor at the University of Redlands, worked extensively with VVAW in Southern California. She encountered "very little" sexism and felt comfortable working with the predominantly male chapters in the region. "It wouldn't be true to say that feelings of 'she's not a veteran' weren't there," recalled Friedman, "but it didn't interfere with my good relations with VVAW."[54]

Conflicts between the sexes occurred most noticeably in rap groups. Women, most of whom were companions of the veterans, wanted to participate in the therapy sessions. When the men rejected their pleas, women initiated their own rap groups. In the meantime, men in rap groups continued to grapple with their relationships with women. Their fears of women were often rooted in low self-esteem, and they expressed their anxieties to their "brothers." Some "didn't believe anyone could love a man who had killed as easily as they had," remembered one participant.[55] Another proclaimed, "If I'm fucking, and a girl says I love you, then I want to kill her . . . [because] if you get close you get hurt."[56] Arthur Egendorf summed up the frustration and anger that many of his fellow VVAWers were unable to articulate: "Often it felt as if we had to atone not only for the war in Vietnam but for the wrongs done by the males of all time in the battle of the sexes."[57]

There were no pat answers to the gender conflicts in VVAW, but the status of women would continue to improve in the organization. Eventually, they would be able to join as full members, vote, and hold office. Combating sexism later became a significant objective in the VVAW's statement of purpose. Until then, women would have put up a fight with the aid of sympathetic male allies.

The organization invited African Americans into its ranks more enthusiastically than it accepted women. As early as August 1970, VVAW attempted to make inroads among African American veterans when it sponsored a vigil at Fort Pierce, Florida, to protest the refusal of an all-white cemetery to bury the body of a black soldier killed in Vietnam. Yet race, like sex, had an impact on the status of VVAW members. That Al Hubbard, VVAW's most prominent African American, felt he had to lie about his past because he was "convinced no one would listen to a black man who was also an enlisted man" showed that he feared that a double standard existed in the organization.[58] Indeed, VVAW had no other African American leaders on a national level, and few rank-and-file African American members. Robert Hanson encouraged antiwar African Americans to join VVAW, yet he understood why many opted against such a decision. "The Black Panther Party had lots of Vietnam veterans at the time. . . . So that was the focus for lots of guys, especially those who came from the ghettos of America."[59]

Ironically, among soldiers serving in Vietnam, antiwar sentiments were more widespread among blacks than among whites. A survey of 392 African American enlisted men, conducted in 1970 by *Time* magazine and the *Washington Post* correspondent Wallace Terry, indicated that 64 percent believed their "fight is in the U.S.," not Vietnam. One-third believed withdrawal should come immediately, compared to 11 percent of whites. Only 3 percent of African Americans approved of President Nixon's order to invade Cambodia, compared to 8 percent of whites. Fewer than a third of the men thought their efforts were helping to stem the spread of communism, in contrast with 54 percent of whites. The overwhelming majority of those polled, 83 percent, felt that America "is in for more race violence," and 50 percent vowed to use weapons "in the struggle for their rights in the U.S."[60] Nearly 60 percent of black GIs, as well as many black officers, used a clenched fist—the Black Power sign— as a form of greeting.[61]

African American soldiers created their own subculture in Vietnam. Clarence Fitch, a marine who later joined VVAW, observed that attitudes among African Americans changed after the assassination of Martin Luther King Jr. in April 1968. King's death sparked riots on bases in the United States, Europe, and Vietnam. The rise of black militance radicalized Fitch and other African Americans serving in Vietnam. Recalled Fitch: "There was a whole Black Power thing. There was Black Power salutes and handshakes and Afros and beads. It was a whole atmosphere. All that was a way of showing our camaraderie, like brothers really hanging together. When a new brother came into the unit, we used to really reach out for the guy, show him the ropes and tell him what's happening."[62]

Fitch and other African American soldiers discovered ways of promoting black pride and consciousness in their daily lives, such as listening to music together, carrying "power sticks" (African walking sticks with a carved fist on top), and mixing African clothing and jewelry with military attire. David Cortright, author of *Soldiers in Revolt*, the first history of dissent in the military during the Vietnam War, noted: "African-Americans comprised the most militant and politically active group of soldier-resisters during the Vietnam era."[63]

Lieutenant Colonel Frank Peterson, an African American marine pilot who led a squadron of Phantom jets at Chu Lai, warned that "angry blacks who are here who are going to go back" to the United States would, "if they encounter the right set of conditions, . . . become urban guerrillas."[64] When Wallace Terry polled African American soldiers, he discovered that their heroes were primarily black militants. The Black Panther leader Eldridge Cleaver received the highest approval rating, 72 percent, followed by Malcolm X (70 percent) and Muhammad Ali (69 percent). "A significantly high percentage promised to carry home the lessons they learned in self-defense and black unity to . . . the Black Panthers," Terry concluded.[65]

Some African Americans thought VVAW ignored racial issues. During the Winter Soldier Investigation in Detroit, a lively argument occurred between a black veteran and a group of white veterans in the lobby of the hotel where the hearings were conducted. The debate was captured by Winterfilm, a collective that was producing a documentary about the event. The African American veteran, dressed in a black sweater and sunglasses, scolded a group of testifiers for their lack of concern about racism. The single session that addressed the topic was insufficient, he charged. "That's how come you ain't got no black people behind you, because you forgot about racism, man. . . . The brothers look at that and they say, 'Why? Why I wanna go down there and get involved in this shit? It ain't for me.'" Poor and working-class African Americans, he argued, had fewer options than whites. "The only way a brother can live when he gets out of school if he ain't got no smarts is to go into the army. We only have one or two outlets to go, man; you have three or four."[66]

The VVAWers listened to the veteran without challenging his criticisms. Some even nodded in agreement. They appeared resigned to the idea that becoming a moral witness was a luxury that few African American veterans could afford. One organizer speculated that African American veterans "just don't have the same faith . . . that when people see how bad it is they'll oppose it."[67] But African Americans trickled into VVAW, and the organization even shared some members with the Black Panther Party. Robert Hanson estimated that VVAW appealed to African Americans who did not care "what the composition of the organization was, . . . so long as we made an impact and helped end this thing."[68]

Like African Americans, few Latinos affiliated with VVAW. Their influence, however, was greater than their numbers. Militant Latino veterans spearheaded the first protests in New York VA hospitals. In 1970, Cruz Sonabria, a Puerto Rican from East Harlem, joined VVAW and became a leader in the VA hospital protests. Two years earlier, as a "gung-ho" seventeen-year-old, Sonabria had enlisted in the Marine Corps. He served with the 3rd Battalion of the Third Marine Division, operating near the demilitarized zone (DMZ) between North and South Vietnam. While patrolling the area in May 1969, he was wounded seriously. He miraculously survived and was sent to Manhattan's notorious VA hospital. Sonabria was radicalized amid the squalor of the hospital's poor facilities, and he helped other Latino veterans circulate petitions calling for better treatment for disabled veterans. One year later, Sonabria threw his medals away at Dewey Canyon III.[69]

Latinos, particularly Chicanos,* should have provided fertile recruiting ground for VVAW. The emergence of "brown pride" in the late 1960s and early 1970s absorbed the energy of countless young Chicanos, including many Vietnam veterans. By 1970, after a five-year strike against powerful growers in California, Cesar Chavez's United Farm Workers' Union (UFW) had prevailed.

The strike, known to farm workers and supporters as *la causa*, triggered a nationwide awakening in Chicano communities. "Brown power" groups, such as La Raza Unida and the Brown Berets, were highly successful in the Southwest and the Midwest. In Vietnam, Chicano soldiers often formed tight bonds with one another, as well as with other Latinos. Some units consisted entirely of Chicanos. A soldier who was part of an all-Chicano platoon remembered that his fellow GIs "had to protect each other 'cause no one was going to protect us. . . . Everybody was a big family."[70]

Chicano veterans confronted their own unique issues. Before the war, numerous Chicanos had grappled with their status as "aliens" in their own land. Serving in Vietnam provided many with an opportunity to prove their loyalty and manhood. Once in Vietnam, however, they encountered the worst of the war. "Vietnam, to Chicanos, was the most questionable and dangerous undertaking of their lives," observed the

---

*Latinos are U.S. residents of Latin American descent. Chicanos are, more specifically, U.S. residents of Mexican descent.

writer and poet Victor Martinez. "When drafted, they served. When [they] 'volunteered,' they did so because of the scarcity of jobs and unequal opportunity of hope. Once there, they populated for the most part the trenches, and they were often maimed and killed."[71]

The Chicano presence in VVAW was "not that strong," recalled Barry Romo, because "there was a lot more pull toward working with the farm workers [in California] or working with [Chicano rights groups such as] the Brown Berets." Chicanos made up approximately 2 percent of VVAW's national membership, slightly lower than the percentage of African Americans, Romo estimated.[72] Some chapters attracted a larger Chicano membership. Not surprisingly, the Texas and California units enjoyed the strongest support in Chicano communities, largely because local VVAW chapters sponsored several Chicano-oriented events. VVAW activists also recruited joiners among farm workers in rural areas and targeted antiwar Chicano moratorium participants in cities such as Los Angeles.[73]

Two Chicanos, Barry Romo and Del Rosario, became VVAW national coordinators at the national steering committee meeting in Kansas City in November. Rosario, an organizer from Seattle, had been the leader of the Washington state chapter.[74] Romo, who had testified about Latino soldiers at the Winter Soldier Investigation, actively encouraged other Chicano veterans to join. The results were mixed. Chicanos who had lived in the United States for a few generations, as well as Puerto Ricans, were more inclined to join VVAW than were recent immigrants. "There was a feeling of safety in terms of citizenship."[75]

The groundswell of liberation struggles in the early seventies, especially among Chicanos, African Americans, and women, made VVAW a more diverse organization than it had been a year earlier. By the summer of 1971, even gay VVAWers were more open about their sexual orientation. One New Yorker, Vince Muscari, led a contingent of gay VVAW members to the National Gay Conference in Madison, Wisconsin, in the fall. "Gay veterans served side by side with our brothers, but had to endure a special form of psychological oppression," the delegation declared.[76] Despite an increasingly varied rank and file, the composition of VVAW never mirrored the diversity that characterized the American soldiers in Vietnam. The participation of nonwhites and females reached its highest level in 1971, but their numbers were still sparse. As was the case at the time of its founding in 1967, VVAW remained thoroughly dominated by white males, possibly more than any other mass movement at the time. The contributions of gays, women, African Americans, Chicanos, and other racial and ethnic groups were invaluable, but the pull of identity politics elsewhere ensured that such individuals would constitute a small percentage of the organization. VVAW would never become heterogeneous. To their credit, however, most members rejected the insensitivity of many of their New Left predecessors.

Before he resigned as national coordinator, Scott Moore had written a pessimistic evaluation of the state of VVAW. In reality, however, VVAW chapters throughout the land were stronger than ever during the summer and fall months. Organizing had never abated. The veterans, still energized by Dewey Canyon III, pressed on with plans for an ambitious fall offensive. Of utmost importance were the upcoming Veterans Day protests and a series of nationwide demonstrations during the Christmas holidays known as Operation Peace on Earth. "The Veterans Day Parade will be very big this year. All chapters . . . should apply for a permit to march in the local parades," advised the national office.[77] The Christmas protests "will test our determination to help end this war" and "rededicate ourselves to the goals and beliefs that led us to join VVAW," wrote the New York coordinator Ed Damato.[78]

Activists had plenty of work to do. Some began to spread VVAW's message abroad. In July, a total of six veterans from VVAW and the Citizens Commission of Inquiry traveled to Europe for a month-long series of speaking engagements, which took them to the Soviet Union, Finland, Norway, England, France, and Italy. The veterans gathered with representatives of the South Vietnamese Provisional Revolutionary Government (PRG) in Paris on July 17 to show their support for the PRG's peace plan. The following month, Joe Urgo became the first Vietnam veteran ever to visit Hanoi when he traveled with a delegation of antiwar leaders to North Vietnam. Recalled Urgo: "I felt this incredible responsibility. . . . I'm there in the land of the people we're killing. So I'm carrying this tremendous weight, and I walked off the plane and they put their arms around me." Urgo met with Prime Minister Pham Van Dong, toured North Vietnamese factories hidden inside caves, and learned about the country's "culture of resistance."[79] Before Urgo left Hanoi, Pham Van Dong embraced him and said, "I understand who you vets are, and the Vietnamese people love you as a brother."[80]

Back at home, VVAW blossomed amid an antiwar movement that was winding down. John Upton and other VVAW organizers in the Midwest initiated a successful three-day protest in Kansas City known as Operation Heart of America in July. It began with a demonstration at the World War I Liberty Memorial and spread from there. "We did actions throughout the Kansas City area," Upton recalled. "We went down to the exclusive shopping area here called the Plaza. We did guerrilla theater inside the restaurants, where all the high rollers were eating. . . . We took mini-convoys out to various areas, doing things here, there."[81] Operation Heart of America drew scores of VVAWers into the streets of Kansas City and inspired other chapter coordinators. Similar large-scale actions occurred in Texas the following month with Operation Turning the Guns Around and in Philadelphia in September with Operation Keystone. VVAWers in the South participated in their own Operation RAW march in Arkansas on October 30–31, 1971.[82]

Adding to VVAW's prestige were the widespread and well-attended Veterans Day protests on October 25. Approximately 150 VVAWers were arrested in San Francisco when they attempted to enter the Presidio to join a memorial for the dead of all wars. Authorities in New York City also refused to admit VVAWers into a memorial, sparking seven arrests. In Denver, eighty members were arrested when they tried to participate in a Veterans Day parade. Police arrested more than one hundred in Killeen, Texas, and thirty-five in New Orleans, for marching without a permit. But most events failed to trigger confrontations. A paraplegic veteran led a column of five hundred VVAWers in Chicago, while three hundred prostesters turned out in New York City, one hundred at Fort Bliss, Texas, one hundred in Anniston, Alabama, seventy in Tuscon, and two dozen in Albuquerque. Teach-ins, rallies, memorials, and lobbying took place in a number of cities.[83]

Some VVAWers pursued quieter endeavors away from the streets. Jan Barry, Larry Rottman, and Basil Paquet collected poems from Vietnam veterans for their upcoming book, *Winning Hearts and Minds*. "We were going to do a book on the G.I.'s perspective on the Vietnam War. Obviously, some other group of G.I.s would have another perspective. I became focused on doing that and getting it accomplished," Barry recalled. The editors ran a query requesting poems from Vietnam veterans in the *New York Times Book Review* in early 1971 and received responses from around the country.[84]

One of the replies came from a twenty-three-year-old Swarthmore College student named W. D. Ehrhart. "When I was a sophomore in college, one of my professors saw a notice in the *New York Times* asking for poetry about Vietnam for an anthology," Ehrhart recounted. Ehrhart, a heavily decorated combat marine from Perkasie, Pennsylvania, sent seven poems. The editors reacted enthusiastically and offered to print Ehrhart's work. "So I wrote back and said, 'Hey, gee, guys, you're not gonna make me look like a Commie crazy, are you?' Man, I can't believe how long it took me to understand what the hell Vietnam really meant."[85]

Ehrhart would have to wait for almost a year to see his poems in print. Rottmann, Paquet, and Barry approached "every major publisher," only to encounter rejection at each turn. Publishers repeatedly said, "These are unknown people, they're not published, the war will be over by the time the book comes out."[86] Finally, the three veterans decided to raise the money themselves. They traveled across the country seeking donations. Barry used his severance pay from a job that he quit at the *CBS Evening News*. Clergy and Laymen Concerned about Vietnam pitched in with financial support and labor. In the summer, Rottmann, Paquet, and Barry created First Casualty Press, a Brooklyn-based operation, to publish the volume and to "create a forum for writings coming out of the Indochina experience."[87] The finished book contained poems by more than thirty Vietnam veterans. They addressed nearly every aspect of the war, from the horror of combat to the suffering of the Vietnamese.

When *Winning Hearts and Minds* finally appeared in early 1972, it was immediately hailed as a major work in the pages of the *New York Times Book Review*, *Newsweek*, the *Chicago Sun-Times*, the *St. Louis Post-Dispatch*, and several other periodicals. Predictably, critics frequently compared the poems to the writings of the British World War I soldier-poet Wilfred Owen. Large publishers vied to produce second editions. McGraw-Hill paid "through the nose" for one-time reprint rights.[88] *Winning Hearts and Minds* turned out to be an unexpected coup for VVAW at a time when the organization's momentum seemed unstoppable. Once again, VVAW had pioneered new forms of expression for Vietnam veterans. W. D. Ehrhart and other poets found that writing was both a healing process and a meaningful way of sharing the experience of war with others. Ehrhart, who "hadn't been able to bring myself to join VVAW," eventually paid his dues and attended antiwar demonstrations. Years later, he edited several influential collections of poems by Vietnam veterans and became a lecturer at the University of Massachusetts at Boston. Contributing to *Winning Hearts and Minds* "touched my life," he later remembered, "leaving me with a permanent fascination in the power of words. It made me want to be a poet—not just a doodler or a hobbyist, but a writer. It opened the way to the life I have lived ever since."[89]

December 26, 1971. Nine A.M. Two VVAW members, Steve Julie and Jim Murphy, entered the Statue of Liberty. For the next several hours, other veterans sneaked inside, until fifteen were hidden within. At five P.M., the monument's personnel locked the doors and left. The takeover was under way. The men barricaded the doors and flew the American flag upside down from Lady Liberty's crown. Eleven years earlier, the National Park Service had barred access to the statue's structurally unsound torch. Nevertheless, the fifteen VVAWers went inside the torch and unfurled the upside down American flag from it. Helicopters carrying journalists and television news cameras whirred overhead. The fifteen veterans originally wanted to "secede from the Union, declare ourselves a sovereign state and recognize North Vietnam."[90] One of the men later offered a more moderate statement to the press:

> The reason we chose the Statue of Liberty is that since we were children, the statue has been analogous in our minds with the freedom and an America we love. Then we went to fight a war in the name of freedom. We saw that freedom is a selective expression allowed only to those who are white and maintain the status quo. Until the symbol again takes on the meaning it was intended to have, we must continue our demonstrations all over the nation of our love of freedom and America.[91]

After a forty-two hour standoff, the fifteen veterans reached a compromise with a federal judge. If they left the statue peacefully, criminal charges would not be pressed. The veterans filed out of the Statue of Liberty, their fists clenched, on December 28, leaving five dollars behind for the coffee and sugar they had used. They had captured America's attention. A week after the incident, *Newsweek* magazine noted: "The White House officially ignored the seizure, but news media carried the story nationwide, and both Armed Forces Radio and *Stars and Stripes* brought it to U.S. troops in Vietnam."[92]

The Statue of Liberty takeover was the highlight of Operation Peace on Earth, a series of protests during the holiday season aimed at bringing home the remaining 140,000 American troops still in Vietnam and ending the war. It began on Christmas Eve. VVAWers carried a defoliated Christmas tree to midnight mass at the Holy Name Cathedral in Chicago, "napalmed" a Christmas tree decorated with war medals in Berkeley, marched through Valley Forge, Pennsylvania, and committed civil disobedience on the steps of St. Patrick's Cathedral in New York. On December 27, twenty-five VVAWers took over the Betsy Ross House in Philadelphia, hanging an American flag upside down in front of the house. The next day 150 protesters broke bags of blood in front of the White House, then occupied the Lincoln Memorial, blocking all entrances and placing a coffin in front of Lincoln's statue. Police arrested eighty-seven people. In San Francisco, members entered the South Vietnamese consulate. They conducted mock arrests of embassy personnel and sent antiwar messages over teletype machines to the South Vietnamese government before police removed them from the premises. Small groups of veterans seized control of Faneuil Hall in Boston, a National Guard office in Hartford, Connecticut, and a hospital ward at Travis Air Force Base in California.[93]

Resistance had subsided by January 1, 1972. On a smaller scale, Operation Peace on Earth had replicated the success of Dewey Canyon III. Veterans had effectively transformed traditional monuments to American patriotism into powerful antiwar symbols. When asked if organizers had accomplished their goals, a stoic Al Hubbard replied, "We got the war back on page one—where it belongs."[94]

As 1972 began, VVAW members from Maine to California had reason to be proud of their achievements. At the beginning of 1971, the outcome of the Winter Soldier Investigation in January and February had left activists feeling dispirited. Nobody believed that, in the span of a few months, VVAW would become one of the largest mass movements in the country.

Then Dewey Canyon III happened. The euphoria that followed it was described by Danny Friedman: "All sorts of things were going on. Demonstrations, marches, . . . live guerrilla theater, speaking engagements, distributing films and buttons. . . . We had a lot of support."[95] Yet even VVAWers, most of whom were newcomers to the antiwar movement, wondered whether their hard work would have an effect. They expected to have more clout than other antiwar activists—and they did—but they did not have enough to end the war by the beginning of 1972, as some had naively hoped at Dewey Canyon III. "Is this the start of another year of terror and destruction for the Indochinese?" asked the Texas coordinator Terry DuBose in December.[96] The mood among the antiwar veterans turned dour after Operation Peace on Earth. Some despairing card carriers dropped out, while others reevaluated the group's strategies. The spring thaw ushered in a sense of renewal and enthusiasm. By the summer of 1972, VVAW would be able to mount a protest at the Republican National Convention in Miami that would rival Dewey Canyon III in scope and intensity.

Meanwhile, the Nixon administration waited for the right moment to strike. If 1971 had been a tranquil year in the relationship between the government and VVAW, 1972 would see an all-out federal offensive against the organization. Harassment, infiltration, thefts, telephone buggings, and arrests became commonplace. In time, VVAW would gravitate to the center of a political conspiracy later known as Watergate.

7

The Last Patrol

VVAW'S evolution in 1971 was rapid, yet far-reaching. At the start of the year, a highly centralized national office oversaw virtually every protest. Local branches, scattered throughout the country, simply recruited antiwar Vietnam veterans. The opposite could be said of VVAW at the end of the year: The national office had diminished in strength, while numerous state and city chapters across the country had assumed responsibility for planning regional actions. The shift in power, it was theorized, would enhance VVAW's numbers and prestige in communities. This transformation occurred when activists began to consider the organization's prospects. The activists knew the war could not last much longer, and they spoke of beginning a different, protracted struggle. Single-issue groups would not survive. Therefore, members sought to reshape VVAW into a veterans' advocacy and anti-imperialist organization—a sort of left-wing Veterans of Foreign Wars.

VVAW's new structure would ensure its survivability amid government harassment, which escalated sharply in 1972. But decentralization had shortcomings. Local, smaller-scale demonstrations were less likely to capture the attention of national newspapers, networks, and the public. Nor did VVAWers feel comfortable resting on their laurels. Dewey Canyon III had made the desired impact, but it was old news. The public's consciousness had to be raised again. In Cincinnati, St. Louis, Dallas, Los Angeles, New York City, Boston, Denver, Kansas City, and Seattle, antiwar veterans continued to march, leaflet, and petition. These endeavors attracted narrow audiences. Thus, national and regional coordinators looked to the summer's Republican National Convention as a catalyst for VVAW's final offensive against the war in Southeast Asia.

VVAW boasted more than twenty thousand members in the early months of 1972. However, apathy, poor communications, a lack of direction, and a general state of disarray hampered the organization's effectiveness.

144 | *The Last Patrol*

Local newsletters appeared sporadically. Dedicated members vanished. Chapter coordinators sent terse notes to the national office wondering what happened to the shipments of books and VVAW buttons they had ordered. The national office shot back: "No one has sent in those project reports which we requested. If you don't tell us what is going on, how the fuck can we do our jobs?"[1] Seasoned resisters knew that winters always brought a lull in activities, and they hoped 1972 would be no exception. "Spring is upon us, and a lot will be happening, . . . so please keep us informed as to your whereabouts," advised the March issue of Philadelphia's VVAW newsletter.[2]

Many struggles simply failed to elicit headlines. Numerous antiwar veterans engaged in behind-the-scenes work not intended to generate publicity. These efforts were often aimed at improving conditions for soldiers and other veterans. In Long Beach, VVAWers spoke at high schools and volunteered two hours a day to work at the local VA hospital. Denver members tried to upgrade dishonorable discharges for antiwar GIs. In Boston and Detroit, VVAW volunteers created programs to assist recently returned veterans coping with drug abuse and "post-Vietnam syndrome." VVAWers in Providence, Rhode Island, started a "Rehabilitation Committee" designed to offer rap sessions, therapy, and drug addiction treatment. The Dayton chapter provided military counseling for GIs at Lockburn and Wright-Patterson Air Force bases.[3] "Nobody did anything for Vietnam veterans until Vietnam Veterans Against the War came along. Nobody. There were no specific government programs until 1979. Yet we . . . started programs in 1971," remembered Jack McCloskey.[4]

Organizers in other parts of the country directed their energy toward the time-consuming and thankless pursuit of freeing political prisoners. They concentrated most of their work on Billy Dean Smith, an African American army private from Watts, and Gary Lawton, an African American civil rights activist in Riverside, California. At the beginning of 1972, Smith languished in solitary confinement at Fort Ord, California. He was accused of "fragging" (assassinating with a fragmentation grenade) two lieutenants and wounding a third in Vietnam in March 1971. Evidence against Smith was flimsy, and he had been openly opposed to the war for several months before the incident. Under equally dubious circumstances, Lawton was arrested for murdering two Riverside police officers on April 2, 1971. Both men became causes célèbres among VVAWers, who thought they had been framed for their beliefs. Members in Southern California participated in defense committees, planned rallies, raised money, and distributed fliers. Photographs of Smith and Lawton appeared in VVAW newsletters across the United States with appeals for help.[5]

While the Smith and Lawton cases dragged on, the spring thaw brought a wave of protests. President Nixon's decision to resume air strikes against North Vietnam on April 6 sparked several actions. On April 19, VVAWers occupied the U.S. Naval Reserve Center in North Hollywood for seven hours. Two days later, fifteen members turned themselves in as "war criminals" at the 11th Naval District Headquarters in San Diego. Four hundred people attended an April 29 VVAW rally at Fort Ord, California, to demand an end to intensified bombing. More demonstrations occurred in May in the wake of the American mining of Haiphong Harbor in North Vietnam. In early May, Seattle VVAWers occupied local Republican headquarters. A VVAW blockade in Boulder, Colorado, resulted in the closure of Highway 36 for twenty-four hours until police dispersed the crowd with tear gas. A group of "brothers" in Denver conducted civil disobedience. In Laramie, thirty-five members took part in a silent vigil. Sixteen San Francisco veterans took over an air force recruiting office. The VVAWer Gary Alexander, carrying an American flag, led a crowd of eight hundred people through Fresno, California, in an action at the Federal Building. The VVAW chapter in Potsdam, New York, spearheaded a takeover of the Federal Building there that involved eight hundred people. In New England, VVAWers seized the captain's quarters on the USS *Constitution*.[6]

The national office strengthened VVAW's presence in the antiwar movement by sponsoring a number of joint activities. In February, a VVAW delegation joined members of other peace groups to attend the World Assembly for Peace and Independence of the People of Indochina in Versailles, France. They met with more than a thousand people from eighty-four countries, including North and South Vietnam, Laos, and Cambodia. In the spring, VVAW endorsed the nationwide April 22 Peace Action Day. One hundred thousand people marched through the streets of New York City, the largest mass protest in that city since 1970. On the same day, marches in Los Angeles and San Francisco each attracted an additional twenty-five thousand people. VVAW was well represented at each demonstration.[7]

Nevertheless, the limitations of local protests and coalition work left VVAW activists frustrated. The war continued. Despite President Nixon's promise to bring seventy thousand soldiers home by May 1—leaving only sixty-five thousand in Vietnam—the veterans regarded "Vietnamization" as a mere shift in tactics. The president stepped up the air war even as he downsized ground forces. Waves of fighter-bombers and B-52s pulverized North Vietnam daily. In South Vietnam, "pacification" programs, which consisted of grouping peasants into tightly controlled government villages, led to numerous human rights abuses. Back at home, however, the president's talk of "Vietnamization" soothed a war-weary public. A May 14 Harris poll found that nearly 60 percent of Americans supported the bombings and mining of North Vietnamese harbors. VVAWers were disheartened to learn what the president and his advisers already knew: The majority of Americans were not necessarily opposed to the war; they simply preferred quick, decisive strikes from the air to protracted military intervention on the ground.[8]

VVAW coordinators decided that another national protest was necessary. During a presidential election year, the most appropriate sites were the cities that were to host the Republican and the Democratic parties' political conventions. At the February VVAW steering committee meeting in Denver, VVAW leaders were already debating various options for summer actions. They reached a consensus: Chapters across the country should try to send as many members as possible to both conventions.

The Democrats chose Miami as the location of their presidential nominating convention; the Republicans selected San Diego. VVAWers knew that the entire tone of protest had changed since the 1968 elections. No longer would clean-cut veterans in suits and ties politely lobby Democratic candidates. Unlike Hubert Humphrey, the Democratic presidential frontrunners in 1972—Senators Edmund Muskie and George McGovern—were doves. Few Democrats in 1972 had to be convinced of the futility of the Vietnam War. While the antiwar veterans felt that a VVAW presence in Miami was essential, they felt it was more urgent to target President Nixon. In its newspaper *Favorite Sons*, the southern California chapter emphasized the need to "confront Nixon" at San Diego: "Veterans bring the reality of imperialism home. We actively participated and our credibility cannot be disavowed. Therefore, if we don't come to San Diego, it will indicate that we believe the war is over and that people of the Third World countries are determining their future."[9]

The Republicans, fearing that San Diego seemed "particularly vulnerable" to "massive demonstrations" from "the thousands of indigenous antiwar activists in southern California," relocated their convention to Miami.[10] VVAW strategists welcomed the move. For the next several months, national coordinators would urge veterans to spend the summer in Miami.

William Walter Lemmer, a twenty-one-year-old ex-army paratrooper, appeared at Dewey Canyon III in April 1971. He approached Don Donner, a New Orleans organizer, and indicated a desire to get involved with VVAW. "Bill Lemmer . . . introduced himself as an active duty brother who would be getting out soon and returning to Arkansas and attending the University of Arkansas. I gave him the name of . . . Arkansas Coordinator Marty Jordan," Donner recalled.[11] Shortly thereafter, Lemmer showed up at Jordan's house in Fayetteville, eager to participate in local VVAW activities. His appearance was similar to that of many of his comrades. He had a moustache, beard, and long hair. He wore combat boots, fatigues, medals, and a ranger beret to demonstrations. He was brash and showy. He was more confrontational than most of his fellow VVAWers.[12]

Lemmer originally came from the Arkansas side of Texarkana, a city straddling the border of northeastern Texas and southwestern Arkansas, south of Red River. He endured a troubled childhood and went on to become a popular class officer and a studious pupil in high school.[13] After he turned eighteen, Lemmer joined the army, went through Special Forces training, and was assigned to the Central Highlands of Vietnam with the 173rd Airborne Brigade.[14] He experienced a severe bronchial asthma attack during his second tour of duty in 1970 and was medivaced to Japan to recuperate. While he was in the hospital, his doubts about the war escalated into open resistance. "I was opposed to . . . the United States presence in Indochina. I was opposed essentially to every policy . . . initiated there by the United States," he recalled.[15]

Lemmer returned to the United States, joined VVAW, testified against the war before Congress, circulated antiwar petitions, and cartooned for an underground newspaper at Fort Benning, Georgia. He moved to Fayetteville, Arkansas, and organized VVAW chapters throughout the state. He served briefly as the state's acting regional coordinator in the early months of 1972 and quickly earned the respect of many activists. "One thing that impressed me about Bill [was his] enthusiasm, his willingness to do something, to be . . . where things are going on. . . . Bill was willing to get in there and do things," recalled Mike Damron, a VVAWer from Fayetteville.[16]

Yet Lemmer also led a clandestine existence. In September 1971, more than four months after joining VVAW, he became an informant for the

Federal Bureau of Investigation. Paranoia drove Lemmer to work with the FBI. Since his hospitalization for asthma, Lemmer had feared that Military Intelligence (MI) was scrutinizing him. He once told a female acquaintance that a hole in his trailer "was made by a bullet shot by MI."[17] Constantly fearing that he was being followed, Lemmer often left his trailer at night so that he could check for spies. The veteran went to the FBI "for self-protection."[18] By the fall of 1971, Lemmer had developed a rapport with his FBI controller, Agent Dick O'Connell. Lemmer's lifestyle and personality began to change. Once burdened with countless debts and unpaid bills, he saw his financial troubles ease. He flew to VVAW meetings in Denver and Washington, D.C., sported an extensive new wardrobe, and traded his old automobile for a flashy sports car. At VVAW meetings, he encouraged his fellow veterans to engage in violent confrontations with police and government officials. Recalled the Arkansas VVAW coordinator Martin Jordan: "He was more radical sometimes than most people I've met who have come out of combat and who were ready to settle down and help get peace back. His attitude was if they didn't go along with it, fuck it, we can kill them."[19]

The FBI carefully monitored VVAW through Lemmer and scores of other informers. Of primary concern to Agent O'Connell was a series of VVAW demonstrations scheduled to occur in Miami at the same time as the national political conventions. He advised Lemmer to collect more information about the protests by attending planning meetings. Ever the provocateur, Lemmer continued to urge the use of force. Ironically, he later tried to justify being an informer by claiming that he was trying to stop violence. "There were people there who had the potential of breaking the law. I could not. . . . I was very, very consistent to my ethic of nonviolence. It was important to me that if there were discrepancies between what was publicly professed and what was privately planned, then it should be made known to a duly constituted authority," Lemmer recalled.[20]

Even as he reported to his FBI contact and helped fatten a number of dossiers, Lemmer had no idea that he was a pawn in an effort, extending to the highest levels of the Nixon administration, to destroy or, at the very least, to severely undermine VVAW. Lemmer would later become the government's key witness in the conspiracy trial of seven VVAW members and one sympathizer accused of plotting to disrupt the 1972 Republican National Convention. The trial would destabilize Southern chapters, halt VVAW's meteoric growth, and hasten its decline.

In the meantime, surveillance teams took photographs of VVAW protests. Informants attended VVAW meetings. The Internal Security Division of the Justice Department sent reports "almost daily" to James W. McCord Jr., the former CIA agent who coordinated security for the Committee to Re-elect the President (CREEP). CREEP staff members sought to link VVAW to George McGovern's presidential campaign. Intelligence documents alleged that George McGovern's presidential campaign "funded a . . . tour of several members of Vietnam Veterans Against the War on the west coast."[21] McCord recalled that he received a report indicating that VVAW "was planning violence at the Republican National Convention involving danger to, threats to life of individuals."[22]

In the eyes of federal agents, the antiwar veterans were dangerous, long-haired riffraff who were mentally unstable as a result of their combat experiences in Vietnam. "The Vietnam Veterans Against the War was one violence-oriented group that was already saying in the spring of 1972 that they were going to cause destruction to life and property at the August Republican convention," McCord later testified.[23] The White House aide Jeb Stuart Magruder echoed many of his colleagues in the Nixon administration when he described VVAW as "the hard-core that have been here in many of the demonstrations, and have actually promulgated violence in each case."[24]

Directives to spy on VVAW came from the highest levels of government. In 1971, Attorney General John Mitchell ordered Robert C. Mardian, director of the Internal Security Division at the Justice Department, to take measures to destabilize the antiwar movement. Mardian placed Guy L. Goodwin, chief of his special litigations section, in charge of collecting information on VVAW.[25] By May 1972, the FBI "already had scores of agents investigating the Viet vets around the country," claimed an issue of *Newsweek* later that year.[26] The Bureau concentrated most of its offensive on VVAW chapters in the South, the epicenter of planning for the Republican national convention protests. In Miami alone, eleven federal and local agencies conducted clandestine undercover operations, regularly reporting information to a national political convention "intelligence center." By early 1972, infiltrators working for the FBI controlled three out of five of VVAW's southern regions. Emerson Poe, an FBI informer, had taken over Scott Camil's position as coordinator for the Florida/Georgia/Alabama section. Bill Lemmer was acting regional coordinator for Arkansas/Oklahoma. Carl Becker, another informant, assumed leadership of Louisiana/Mississippi.[27]

A climate of fear and distrust engulfed many VVAW chapters, particularly in Florida because of the Miami conventions. Scott Camil remembered that federal agents "got people thrown out of school. They went to the employers of ex-GIs in the VVAW and got them fired for being 'communists.' I started getting phone calls: 'Hey man, I can't come to meetings anymore. The FBI went to where my mom works. She almost lost her job.'"[28] The FBI paid close attention to Camil. He had always been one of VVAW's most effective organizers. A December 11, 1971, bulletin from the Jacksonville, Florida, controller to FBI directors in Miami and New York said that agents in the field "will maintain continuous liaison with local, state and federal law enforcement authorities" for the purpose of "neutralizing Camil at the earliest logical date."[29]

FBI agents watched Camil from the home of Mike Carr, head of the local Young Americans for Freedom, who lived across the street from the VVAWer. Neighbors observed plainclothesmen in cars spying on Camil's house. Beginning on Thanksgiving Day 1971, his house was repeatedly burglarized. On January 23, 1972, police arrested Camil, charging him with kidnapping two youths and demanding a ransom of one hundred dollars. The evidence against him consisted of a receipt that one of the kidnap victims claimed the veteran had given him in exchange for the hundred dollars. So outrageous were the allegations that Camil spent only a week in jail. The charges were quickly dropped. The next month, he was arrested for possession of drugs. The charges stuck, but harassment failed to intimidate him. Camil continued as an organizer for the convention protests. He remained philosophical about his experiences. "If we would've been a black group, like the Black Panthers, we'd have people dead all over the place. . . . Murdering veterans is a little harder, so that made it a little easier for us."[30]

Similar episodes occurred in other parts of the country. Busts were common, particularly for drug possession. Thus, the Philadelphia chapter urged members to exercise "revolutionary discipline" by not bringing "booze or dope in the office."[31] VVAWers suspected the federal government was engaged in a campaign to destroy the antiwar movement, but nobody knew the extent of such efforts. "There were all kinds of rumors swirling around. The Man does that purposely," the San Francisco coordinator Jack McCloskey explained.[32] One rumor that alarmed some activists originated during a press conference in Los Angeles in September 1971. Louis Tackwood, an infiltrator who worked for the Los Angeles Police Department (LAPD), read a statement claiming that the Criminal

Conspiracy Section of the LAPD and the FBI had created a special group known as "Squad 19." The purpose of Squad 19 was to use agents provocateurs to incite riots among protesters at the Republican National Convention in San Diego. Meanwhile, Squad 19 members inside the convention hall would detonate explosives, killing scores of delegates. In the aftermath, Tackwood concluded, "Richard Nixon would then arrest all militants and left-wing revolutionaries and cancel the 1972 elections."[33]

At the same time skeptics dismissed Tackwood's allegations as too far-fetched, government officials secretly prepared schemes to undermine demonstrations at the Republican Convention. The main architect of such plans was G. Gordon Liddy, the general counsel for CREEP. In late January and early February 1972, Liddy suggested that government agents kidnap "members of radical groups" who intended to protest at the Republican convention. "Mr. Liddy had a plan where the leaders would be abducted and detained in a place like Mexico and that they would then be returned to this country at the end of the Convention," Jeb Stuart Magruder recalled.[34] Added the president's counsel, John Dean: "Plans [to respond to convention protesters] called for mugging squads, kidnapping teams, prostitutes to compromise the opposition, and electronic surveillance."[35]

The CREEP staff became involved with the offensive against VVAW. During the late spring and early summer, CREEP officers and FBI agents tapped into a shady network of mercenaries, gun runners, Cuban exiles, and ex-CIA agents. At the end of May, Pablo Manuel Fernandez, a Cuban clerk living in Miami, befriended Scott Camil and other VVAW members while working for the FBI and Miami Police. "I convinced them I was a leftist," he recounted.[36] Neither Camil nor his VVAW comrades knew that Fernandez had recently returned from Washington, D.C., where he had been paid to beat up protesters at J. Edgar Hoover's funeral on May 5. Fernandez's cohorts at the funeral included the future Watergate burglars Bernard L. Baker, Frank Sturgis, Virgilio Gonzales, and Eugenio Martinez. In Miami, Fernandez offered to sell hand grenades, mines, submachine guns, and 81-mm and 60-mm mortars to VVAW activists. Suspecting that Fernandez was attempting to entrap them, the antiwar veterans politely declined his offers.[37]

Another informer later testified before the United States Senate that orders to infiltrate VVAW came from the ex-CIA agent and White House consultant E. Howard Hunt, one of the masterminds behind the Watergate burglary. Hunt also offered large sums of money to Vince Hannard, a

Florida detective who had worked as an informer for the CIA and FBI, to "expose the VVAW [as] being pink and Communist and all this stuff."[38] Hannard explained: "It was clear from what they said that I was supposed to incite trouble or riots from the antiwar groups. I was told it would be activity pertaining to the convention."[39] Alfred W. Baldwin, the man in charge of monitoring the bugs inside the Democratic Headquarters at Watergate, was asked by James McCord to "infiltrate the VVAW for the purpose of embarrassing the Democrats" if the veterans protested at the Republican convention.[40]

While CREEP was attempting to subvert VVAW, the FBI's star VVAW infiltrator, Bill Lemmer, was gradually blowing his cover as a result of his increasingly erratic personality. Two former Arkansas/Oklahoma coordinators, Don Donner and Martin Jordan, had long suspected that Lemmer was an agent provocateur. Nevertheless, "family stresses" demanded that both men drop out of leadership positions, thus allowing Lemmer to become a coordinator. Donner and Jordan regretted their decision. "The membership were complaining to Marty and me about Bill urging violence, and we were becoming aware of more arrests of people around Bill Lemmer," Donner recalled.[41] In April 1972, Lemmer participated in a demonstration with a group of VVAWers at Tinker Air Force Base in Oklahoma City. Activists entered the base and were soon arrested. Suspicions were aroused when a U.S. marshall intervened and released only Lemmer. Days later, the son of an official who had arranged Lemmer's release contacted VVAW members and confirmed that Lemmer was an informer.[42]

Word of Lemmer's status spread. Some veterans wanted to expel him immediately. National coordinators opted to wait and see if he would tip his hand. When VVAWers who worked with Lemmer learned of his spying, they began charging pizzas, office supplies, and travel expenses to the FBI-financed credit cards that he freely passed around. Lemmer knew that his "brothers" believed he was an agent provocateur. He became increasingly agitated, and his exhortations grew more violent in content. While driving to a regional coordinators' meeting in Gainesville at the end of May, he reportedly warned an acquaintance to stay away from Miami during the political conventions. He claimed "all of the VVAW leaders were going to be picked up and taken out of circulation."[43]

During the Gainesville meeting, a sweating, glassy-eyed Lemmer advocated bombings and shootings at the Republican National Convention.

His comrades reminded him that the purpose of the meeting was to discuss the Democratic convention. Lemmer left the meeting a nervous wreck. On the way home, he spotted "brand-new Fords all over the road, sitting in exits, driving past me, all the same people . . . all with the uniform sunglasses, all with uniform haircuts. . . . I was observed all the way."[44] Lemmer's wife, Mary, convinced him to meet with VVAWers Don Donner and Martin Jordan to confess his FBI affiliation. He was reluctant at first, but, after much convincing, he finally agreed. Donner and Jordan "isolated him in a safe house with a tape recorder." That day, Lemmer's wife ran away with her lover. "Not very good timing for us, but when Bill found her missing we told him that the FBI probably grabbed her. He bought into it," Donner recalled.[45] For three days, Lemmer told Jordan and Donner everything he knew. The two VVAWers copied the eight hours of tape and sent the copy to Frank Donner (no relation to Don), the director of the American Civil Liberties Union Project on Political Surveillance at Yale Law School.[46]

Soon thereafter, Lemmer disappeared. Unknown to VVAW activists, Lemmer had been sequestered under the federal witness protection program and relocated to Wyoming. He would soon testify before a grand jury in Tallahassee, Florida, about VVAW's alleged plans to disrupt the Republican National Convention. His wife later returned to their abandoned apartment to collect his belongings and discovered macabre drawings and index cards stuck on the walls reading "PVS [post-Vietnam syndrome] Kills."[47]

With the Democratic National Convention a few weeks away, VVAW organizers contacted regional coordinators and asked them to rally veterans in their area to travel to Miami. Leaders expected a low turnout of VVAWers at the convention. By early June, Senator George McGovern, a steadfast opponent of the war in Vietnam, appeared to be a sure winner for the nomination. Members were divided about McGovern. A significant number planned to vote for him, but most did not want their "efforts to be co-opted by the Democrats or the electoral process."[48] When the national steering committee refused to endorse Senator McGovern's candidacy, a group of VVAWers launched "Veterans for McGovern," a group much like the one their predecessors had organized to support Eugene McCarthy four years earlier. Later in the year, the national steering committee met in Palo Alto, California, and drafted a proposal regarding the elections. "We should not endorse McGovern, but rather adopt a campaign to attack Nixon on all the issues for which he is responsible: the continuation of the war, continuing repression at home, manipulation of the economy to benefit a few, etc."[49]

As expected, few antiwar veterans had appeared in Miami by the opening day, July 9. Those who did camped at Miami Beach's Flamingo Park. VVAWers tried to remain separate from the countercultural Zippies (anarchical youths preoccupied with drugs, nudity, and music) and other militants in order to "give us a certain amount of . . . integrity and enable us to have better control over our own people."[50] The marches and guerrilla theater that occurred during the convention lacked the urgency of Dewey Canyon III. The antiwar veterans felt as if they were preaching to the converted. Senators and representatives visited the VVAW camp for photo opportunities. VVAW received official convention representation, and members were allowed to testify before the Democratic Platform Committee. The Democratic Party sent buckets of Kentucky Fried Chicken to the camping veterans. VVAWers rejoiced when they learned that the Democrats' platform demanded "immediate and complete withdrawal" of U.S. forces from Indochina.[51]

FBI agents issued subpoenas to twenty-three VVAW members in five states, ordering them to appear before a federal grand jury in Tallahassee on the morning of July 10. The subpoenaed members, already in Florida for the Democratic convention, refused to testify.[52] FBI agent, Ron Parker, urged Rich Bangert, VVAW's Illinois/Missouri regional coordinator, to testify, telling him that the government was not trying to squelch VVAW but merely attempting to remove the "bad apples in it." Despite Parker's plea, Bangert declined.[53]

On the final day of the convention, July 13, a federal grand jury in Tallahassee indicted six VVAW members on charges of conspiring to cause riots during the Republican National Convention. The six men—Scott Camil, John Kniffin, William J. Patterson, Alton C. Foss, Peter Mahoney, and Donald P. Perdue—were accused of planning to incite unrest by using firebombs, automatic weapons, slingshot-propelled fireworks, wrist rockets, and crossbows. The veterans were also accused of intending to initiate "fire teams" to attack stores, police stations, and automobiles and of attempting to disrupt "communications systems in Miami Beach."[54] Of the six, Mahoney was a national coordinator, and Kniffin and Patterson were regional coordinators from Texas. The grand jury later added two more defendants to the original six, the VVAW member Stan Michelsen and the supporter John Briggs, and switched the venue to nearby Gainesville, Florida, and the men eventually became known as "the Gainesville Eight."

Predictably, the prosecution's key witness against VVAW was Bill Lemmer.[55] The Democratic National Convention adopted a resolution condemning the Nixon administration for its efforts to "deny the veterans their most fundamental constitutional rights to express their dissent and opposition to the war in Southeast Asia."[56] In mid-July, less than a month after the CREEP staff broke into the Democratic National Committee headquarters in the Watergate apartment complex, the six VVAW members were arrested and booked in Tallahassee. The defendants were eventually released on a total of $25,000 bail, paid by the national office.[57] Activists worked with even more vigor to mount a successful offensive against President Nixon. The Dayton VVAW coordinator Gary Staiger warned his comrades: "The government would like nothing better than for us to concentrate all of our energies on this trial, to the exclusion of everything else. This we cannot do."[58]

Everybody in VVAW agreed that dramatic action was necessary. Earlier in the year, two VVAWers from Chicago, Greg Petzel and Bart Savage, proposed that veterans from all parts of the United States travel to Miami for the Republican National Convention in a massive convoy dubbed "the Last Patrol." Plans for the Last Patrol were under way by July, with Petzel and Savage fixing elaborate timetables. Newsletters and posters called on veterans to "confront Nixon at Miami." Regional coordinators recruited veterans in their area to participate in the motorcades. John Lindquist, an ex-marine from Milwaukee who had served as a radioman in an eighty-eight-truck convoy for the 3rd Marine Division in Vietnam, assumed responsibility for the Midwest convoy. "There were three [separate convoys with] starting points in San Francisco, Milwaukee, and Boston," Lindquist recalled.[59]

Days before the Republican convention in August, veterans from across the country assembled in New York City, Boston, Chicago, St. Louis, Los Angeles, Portland, and San Francisco. The eastern branch of the Last Patrol departed August 18 and camped outside Washington, D.C. En route to Miami, they distributed fliers at Fort Bragg, North Carolina, informing soldiers of the 82nd Airborne Division of VVAW's peaceful intentions.[60] Veterans from Los Angeles drove through Texas, while the Portland and San Francisco convoys converged in Salt Lake City. All three of the units linked together in Georgia. Ron Kovic, a paraplegic veteran from southern California, was at the front of the Los Angeles column.

While riding in an Oldsmobile across Texas, he looked back in awe at "the convoy behind me, stretching back like a giant snake so far that I cannot even tell where it ends."[61] A group of "hippy agents" working for the FBI accompanied the VVAWers on the Last Patrol. The infiltrators were impressed with their traveling companions. "It was the unanimous opinion of the four agents who'd traveled with them for many days that the Vietnam vets were deeply committed to ending the war, not to senseless violence," recalled the agent Cril Payne.[62]

John Lindquist led the Milwaukee and Chicago motorcades and met with the St. Louis, Kansas City, and Dayton, Ohio, veterans on route to Miami. Lindquist constantly maintained tight control, using walkie-talkies. He always drove five miles below the speed limit. When one vehicle pulled over, all the others stopped, also.[63] Still, the motorists experienced recurring hassles with the police. In Arizona and Texas, police checked the Los Angeles convoy, delaying it by several hours. A Florida state trooper stopped the Midwest convoy and attempted to ticket the vehicles for driving too slowly. The officer's superiors ordered him to let the veterans pass. The eastern and midwestern convoys eventually met at Fort Pierce, Florida.[64]

On a bright Sunday, August 20, more than a hundred cars, buses, trucks, and Jeeps—several decorated with peace signs, flowers, and upside-down American flags—drove into Miami Beach honking their horns and flashing their lights. Faced with numerous delays, the West Coast convoy arrived hours later. The veterans were greeted by more than thirty-five hundred protesters in Miami Beach's Flamingo Park. A *Newsweek* correspondent described Flamingo Park as a carnival of "peace people, hippies, Yippies, Zippies, Viet vets, trashers, feminists, homosexuals and even a black self-help group incongruously for Richard Nixon."[65] Leaders of the Last Patrol moved quickly to secure a campsite for VVAW, finding a secluded section of the park protected by tall hedges and walls. Guards with walkie-talkies were placed on the edges of the campsite, "just like a perimeter back in Nam," one veteran remembered.[66]

Before the veterans had had a chance to unpack, antiwar activists at Flamingo Park approached them and asked for help. Members of the American Nazi Party had taken over a makeshift platform belonging to antiwar protesters and refused to allow demonstrators to speak. The Nazis yanked the microphone out of the hand of Carol Kitchens, a representative from the Miami Women's Coalition, and pushed her off the stage. Irritable from hours of driving, a group of forty VVAWers confronted the "dozen or so" Nazis. The national coordinator, Del Rosario, mounted the stage and asked the Nazis to leave. One of the toughs hit Rosario in the back with a chair. The infuriated veterans responded by grabbing each Nazi and shoving him through an angry gauntlet of VVAWers. At the end of the line, an enormous, longhaired, bearded veteran named Fred Rosenthal threw each one into the street, some by the scruff of their necks. The leader of the local Nazi Party was seriously injured after being thrown headfirst over a wall. Within minutes, the veterans had routed the offenders. Despite injuries sustained by four veterans and two CBS cameramen, the fight enhanced VVAW's prestige in Miami Beach. The veterans were camped in the heart of a Jewish retirement community, and elderly residents brought pastries, hot meals, cases of beer, and bottles of wine to the campsite. A conservative Jewish alderman, formerly an outspoken critic of VVAW, made sure the veterans had plenty of portable toilets. "I think anybody who was there and who fought the Nazis was invigorated. . . . We kicked their ass really bad," Barry Romo remembered.[67]

Now enjoying widespread community support, the veterans settled into their camp. At night, they bonded with one another, as they had done during Operation RAW and Dewey Canyon III. This time, their "wives, girlfriends, and companions," as well as nurses and female activists, were present.[68] The campers discussed their experiences in Vietnam and in the streets of America. Yet there was an added poignancy to the Last Patrol. The veterans knew that both the war and the movement that was resisting it were in their final throes. On August 12, President Nixon withdrew the last American ground troops from Vietnam. Approximately forty-three thousand air force personnel and support personnel remained. A week after the convention, President Nixon would announce to the nation that only twenty-seven thousand U.S. troops would be in South Vietnam by December.[69] The Miami Beach protests would "be the last of the national jamborees," predicted one activist.[70]

Fewer than ten thousand demonstrators came to the convention, a far lower number than expected. VVAW had one of the strongest showings of any group. The veterans were "tired of marching," but they had witnessed war's devastating toll, and they did not want the public to ignore the daily American bombardment of Southeast Asia. "It is our last patrol together," observed Ron Kovic, "and I know I will remember it as long as I live."[71]

As had been the case at Dewey Canyon III, the veterans created their itinerary spontaneously. The week's activities began with a march on

Monday through eighty-five-degree heat to Miami Beach High School, where a thousand Florida National Guardsmen and advisers from the 82nd Airborne Division were headquartered. To the beat of a drum, marchers waved fists and chanted, "One, two, three, four, we don't want your racist war" and "Hey, hey, ho, ho, Tricky Dick has got to go."[72] National Guard officers ordered the blinds closed inside the high school. A handful of guardsmen watched the protest and the subsequent guerrilla theater outside. Participants returned to camp feeling somewhat disheartened.[73]

The action at Miami Beach High had been a flop, but the next day offered a more memorable event. On Tuesday, an estimated 1,200 to 1,500 veterans lined up in Flamingo Park, forming neat rows of four. They quietly began marching up Collins Avenue, toward the Hotel Fontainebleau, site of the Republican National Convention. Organizers called it the Silent March. There was no chanting, no shouting of slogans. Only the occasional crackle of walkie-talkies or clicking of cameras interrupted the stillness. Platoon leaders provided hand signals for "stop," "start," "fast," "slow," "right," and "left." Leading the march was a group of veterans in wheelchairs. A number of VVAWers walked with crutches. There was a sprinkling of toy M-16 assault rifles in the throng. Hundreds of spectators watched the procession in awe. Republican revelers on yachts docked along Indian Creek stopped what they were doing and gazed at the marchers; sympathetic elderly Jewish residents greeted the silent marchers with cheers and praise. VVAWers responded with clenched-fist salutes.[74] When a reporter inquired about the march, a veteran replied, "There's nothing left to say."[75]

The Silent March had a profound impact on the irreverent "gonzo" journalist Hunter S. Thompson, who covered the Republican National Convention for *Rolling Stone* magazine. Thompson accompanied the marchers for ten blocks, until they reached the Fontainebleau. He had reported on antiwar protests since 1964, but he had never witnessed one with the intensity of the Silent March. "There was an ominous sense of dignity about everything the VVAW did in Miami. They rarely hinted at violence, but their very presence was menacing—on a level that the Yippies, Zippies, and SDS street crazies never even approached, despite their yelling and trashing," Thompson recalled.[76] He was astonished by VVAW's discipline, tactics, and tight control. "The silence of the march was contagious, almost threatening."[77] In front of the Hotel Fontainebleau, five hundred riot police awaited the veterans. Thompson watched as platoon leaders directed marchers into a packed semicircle that blocked the three northbound lanes of Collins Avenue. For several minutes, the veterans stared at the police. Onlookers found the face-off unnerving. A VVAW leader stepped forward with a bullhorn and announced, "We want to come inside."[78]

Tensions eased when Congressman Paul McCloskey appeared in front of the Hotel Fontainebleau. The Republican representative from California had long been one of VVAW's staunchest allies. McCloskey greeted his friends and warned them that an attack on the hotel would be futile. Platoon leaders assured him that they simply wanted network TV cameras to film the Republicans refusing to allow veterans into the Fontainebleau. Unfortunately for the veterans, few journalists were present. Most were inside covering the convention. But those who observed the Silent March would not soon forget the spectacle of twelve hundred angry Vietnam veterans marching quietly in the sun. Theodore H. White, the famed chronicler of presidential elections, could not help noticing the "lean, hard-muscled Vietnam veterans sitting quietly in protest in the sun on the street paving before the Fontainebleau."[79] Added the novelist Kurt Vonnegut Jr.: "The most honorable military reviews in American history took place on the afternoon of August 22, 1972, in front of the Hotel Fontainebleau."[80]

Three VVAWers in wheelchairs were permitted to speak with the Republican liaison to the Hotel Fontainebleau. It was a brief, fruitless encounter. McCloskey and a group of veterans then addressed the marchers with a bullhorn. Most of the speeches were drowned out by two Army helicopters whirring overhead. Only Ron Kovic's speech was heard above the din. "You have lied to us too long, Mr. President. Too many babies have been burned. Too many lives have been lost. You might have taken our bodies, but you have not taken our minds," Kovic shouted amid cheers.[81] Following the speeches, Hunter S. Thompson and other bystanders watched as the veterans, like "golems" who had "come back to haunt us all," turned around and marched quietly back to Flamingo Park. Much of the media missed the march, but Thompson concluded that it "had the same ugly sting" as Dewey Canyon III.[82]

After repelling the Nazis and participating in the Silent March, the veterans were considered vogue among the other protesters camping out at Flamingo Park. "People were asking us to support sixteen thousand different causes. . . . The usual crazies are doing their crazy things, trying to drag VVAW into their crazy things," recalled Jan Barry.[83] Various groups, including the Black Panthers, asked VVAW to assume responsibility for security at rallies. The veterans had no desire to become the "police force" for the Left. The VVAW organizer Anne Bailey remembered: "They didn't really have any respect for our politics. They knew we were militant enough and we worked well together enough that we could provide security for their demos. We said we wouldn't do it, but we said, 'We'll train you to do it.'"[84]

All Last Patrol participants attended a lengthy meeting on Wednesday to decide what to do next. The veterans were split. Al Hubbard, who had recently been voted out as VVAW's executive secretary, appeared at the gathering. During Dewey Canyon III, the press had reported that Hubbard had lied about his rank in Vietnam. In Miami Beach, the enigmatic Hubbard once again insisted he had been a captain in Vietnam, and he proclaimed himself an "adviser to the national office."[85] Hubbard urged others at the meeting to take part in the actions planned by the Miami Convention Coalition (MCC), an ad hoc group organized by the antiwar leaders Rennie Davis and David Dellinger. The MCC planned to disrupt the convention Wednesday night. Hubbard still had plenty of followers, and several veterans agreed to take the fight into the streets. A larger contingent wanted to break camp after President Nixon's acceptance speech on Wednesday night and drive to Gainesville. The Gainesville Eight had been scheduled for arraignment on Thursday morning, and many of the veterans in Miami Beach wanted to rally behind their comrades.[86]

By the time the marathon planning meeting adjourned, President Nixon's speech was only a few hours away. Veterans began walking from Flamingo Park to the convention hall and assembled outside the convention site. Wanting to try something bolder, a group of VVAWers from California broke into the rear of the convention hall using wirecutters. They had been eying the buses that transported delegates up a steep ramp and into the back of the building. The veterans poured four quarts of motor oil on the ramp, which stalled the next bus. Within seconds, the system for ushering delegates into the convention center had malfunctioned. Because the stalled bus blocked access, the other buses lined up around the hall. Delegates inside the buses parked near the protesters shouted, "Gas 'em!" Riot police moved in and lobbed tear gas canisters at antiwar activists. A shift in winds sent the tear gas drifting into the convention hall.[87]

Inside the convention hall, three veterans in wheelchairs were planning an even more audacious confrontation. Bill Weiman, a double amputee from Boston, and Bobby Muller, a paraplegic from New York City, entered the convention floor using passes provided by Congressman Mc-Closkey. Ron Kovic borrowed a press pass from a TV producer from California to get inside the hall. Roger Mudd, covering the convention for CBS television news, arranged a two-minute interview with Kovic. The three veterans then met on the convention floor and locked their wheelchairs together. With balloons flying and crowds cheering, President Nixon began his acceptance speech. Five minutes later, the three veterans began shouting, "Stop the bombing! Stop the war!"[88] Security guards quickly surrounded the veterans and forced them to the nearest exit. The veterans kept chanting, raising clenched fists in defiance. Outraged delegates yelled obscenities and spat at the three men. Agents removed them from the auditorium and locked the doors so that the veterans could not get back in. A *Time* correspondent noticed the outburst: "Moments before Nixon proclaimed that the nation's Viet Nam veterans should be given 'the honor and respect they deserve and they've earned,' three such veterans in wheelchairs shouted 'Stop the bombing!'—and were summarily escorted from the hall by convention security personnel."[89] Despite their quick removal, Muller, Weiman, and Kovic considered their protest a stunning victory. "It had been the biggest moment of our lives, we had shouted down the president of the United States and disrupted his acceptance speech," wrote Kovic.[90]

Most networks and newspapers ignored the exploits of Muller, Weiman, and Kovic, but the three men became legends in VVAW circles. The thousand-plus VVAWers outside, heeding warnings from reliable sources of an impending police crackdown on antiwar activists, packed their belongings and drove out of Miami Beach that night. The veterans had mixed feelings about what they had experienced. Nobody could deny the effectiveness of the Silent March. But media coverage—while a sharp improvement over what it had been during the Winter Soldier investigation—fell far short of that accorded Dewey Canyon III. Most newspapers and broadcast news focused on the paltry turnout of antiwar activists in Miami Beach, an interpretation that dovetailed with President Nixon's promise that the war was winding down. In numerous instances, a motley assortment of resisters stole the spotlight from the veterans. At a time when Americans were more accepting than ever of public protest, a minority of antiwar activists resorted to more flamboyant and violent means to attract attention. On the night of President Nixon's acceptance speech, roving bands of protesters charged up Collins Avenue, shattering windows, slashing tires, and destroying automobiles.[91] More than a thousand protesters were arrested. The columnist John Osborne lamented in the *New Republic*: "The tragedy for the country, though not for the Nixon people, was that the miscellaneous Yippies, fags, dikes and extreme militants who monopolized the news during the first days of the convention obscured the steady discipline of the Vietnam Veterans Against the War. . . ."[92]

Worsening matters for VVAW was the absence of a consensus spokesperson. John Kerry had eloquently articulated the purpose and demands of VVAW during Dewey Canyon III, while keeping the antics of the self-promoting to a minimum. In Miami Beach, the wheelchair-bound veterans took center stage in many activities, but a "new" John Kerry never emerged. An organization with a membership as politically heterogeneous as VVAW required such a person. Joiners included Democrats, Trotskyists, Maoists, anarchists, and ex-GIs whose politics were no more complicated than a desire to bring their buddies home alive. But VVAW was full of people who avoided leadership as much as they rejected it. Years in the military had led most of the antiwar veterans to shun regimentation of any sort. Regardless of their political persuasion, most VVAWers were so anti-authoritarian by 1972 that the very idea of another John Kerry was anathema to them. Barry Romo recalled:

> We would go to a demonstration, like we did . . . at the Republican convention, and have over a thousand vets march five miles to the Fontainebleau Hotel, in total silence, in unison, in formation, without using anything but hand signals. Rocky Pomerance, head of the police chief's association, would later say that we were more disciplined than the state police. We could do that, but we couldn't say someone was the president. Only coordinators. So there was this duality. When we were demonstrating, we were disciplined. When we were outside of that, we were anarchistic, jealous, angry young males in 1970s America with adrenaline from delayed stress flowing.[93]

Leaving the mixed success of Miami Beach behind, the Last Patrol motorcades headed to Gainesville. On Thursday, August 24, the veterans marched through a monsoon-like downpour from their camp near the municipal airport to downtown Gainesville. Ron Kovic led the procession down University Avenue to the courthouse. One veteran played "Battle Hymn of the Republic" on a harmonica. Six of the Gainesville defendants appeared in court. Two of the men, Scott Camil and John Kniffin, had so much shrapnel in their bodies that they activated a metal detector in the court building. The six VVAW members declared themselves guilty of "committing war crimes against the people of Indochina" but pleaded innocent to the conspiracy charges.[94] When the arraignment was over, some of the veterans remained in Gainesville, but most marched back to the Last Patrol vehicles and headed home.[95] The Last Patrol drew to a close. For the Gainesville Eight, the battle had just begun.

Ironically, VVAW was at its largest just as the Vietnam War was grinding to a halt. "VVAW is Comet in Leftist Galaxy," blared a headline in the *Miami Herald* during the Democratic National Convention.[96] According to the VVAW national office, membership surpassed twenty-five thousand in the summer of 1972.[97] Observers, as well as most members, considered the war to be VVAW's raison d'être, so, with peace negotiations occurring in Paris during the late summer and fall, VVAW coordinators and activists became increasingly reflective about the future of their organization. The Colorado VVAW coordinator Brian Adams reasoned: "When the war in Indochina actually ends, much of the rationale for a purely veterans organization is negated."[98]

The possibility of peace aroused questions about VVAW's purpose. Should VVAW be disbanded, or was there reason for it to continue after the war? The more politically conscious members familiarized themselves with theories of imperialism. They read Mao, Lenin, Rosa Luxemburg, and Dee Brown's *Bury My Heart at Wounded Knee*, a recently published history of Native Americans. These radicals developed a broader understanding of war, capitalism, and colonialization. Ending the war was no longer simply a matter of "bringing buddies home." Those who wanted to keep VVAW intact focused their attention on the unrelenting B-52 air strikes, America's continued financing of repressive governments abroad, the need for amnesty for draft resisters, and the lack of VA benefits for Vietnam veterans. "There will be a continuing need for a veterans organization. Veteran service programs should and will continue," concluded Brian Adams.[99]

Another matter that triggered debates in virtually every chapter was the status of women. A number of VVAWers had reassessed their attitudes about women. "Sisters, don't let the men keep you in the kitchen. We need you! Without you, VVAW is only half an organization.... All power to the sisters!" declared Chicago's newsletter during the summer.[100] By the fall of 1972, some chapters were allowing women to join as full members. A vocal segment of veterans no longer wished to remain a "chauvinistic counterpart to a VVAW women's auxiliary."[101] The national steering committee considered revising VVAW's bylaws for the purpose of entitling women to all the privileges of full membership, including the right to hold national office. Questions arose about whether such a decision would undermine VVAW's integrity. In early 1973, amid much strife, VVAW would be rechristened "Vietnam Veterans Against the War/Winter Soldier Organization," thus offering women and nonveterans an opportunity to become fully enfranchised.[102]

The concept of the Winter Soldier Organization reflected the radicalization of VVAW. The left wing of VVAW shunned what it referred to as "vets' chauvinism," the glorification of having served in Vietnam. Opening the ranks to nonveterans would counter such elitist tendencies, they argued. Moderates did not necessarily object to the change, but they felt uncomfortable with the left wing's increasing clout. The Ohio coordinator Bill Crandell had mixed feelings as he watched VVAW move "leftward."[103] Crandell felt VVAW's strength lay in its plurality of political opinions. The organization started to unravel, he later concluded, when it began "sinking into sectarian conflict."[104] "Once we had recognized that we didn't want to be the traditional macho vets, we needed to focus that kind of nonsense somewhere else." Crandell recalled that many of his comrades became obsessed with "the correct line." "On some levels, it became almost a competition. . . . 'You think you're a leftist, well, I'm a Maoist.' 'Oh yeah, you think you're a Maoist? Well, Che Guevara's my man.'"[105]

The factional infighting within VVAW was ignored by the federal government, and the domestic intelligence program continued to single out the veterans. The FBI and the Nixon administration regarded VVAW as a monolithic organization of irrational, violence-prone agitators. Officials and agents stepped up the campaign of harassment in the summer and fall. Burglars broke into Scott Camil's home in Gainesville and stole files. Days later, someone ransacked the office of Camil's attorney, Carol Scott, removing her VVAW case files.[106] In New York, members' apartments were broken into and files were strewn about.[107] While there was no evidence to link the VVAW burglaries to the Nixon administration or any government agencies, the timing of the incidents—on the heels of the Watergate break-in—stirred suspicions. The White House counsel, John Dean, later testified before the Senate Watergate committee that Watergate was "an inevitable outgrowth" of "excessive concern over the political impact of demonstrators."[108] Obsessed with collecting intelligence on McGovern, President Nixon sought to link the senator with his "left-wing supporters."[109]

A year after the Watergate break-in, when various burglars began implicating the Nixon administration, the one "left-wing" organization repeatedly mentioned was VVAW. The Watergate burglar James McCord claimed that in the summer of 1972, "VVAW had offices in the Democratic National Headquarters" and that Democratic Party staffers were "working . . . with such groups as the VVAW."[110] McCord's allegations were false. VVAW never had such an office, and the organization was never affiliated with the Democratic Party. Nevertheless, Republicans continued their smear tactics. In GOP campaign literature titled "52 Reasons Why McGovern Must be Defeated," VVAW members were described as "dynamiters and gun shooters and plotters" who were "conspiring to blow up the Republican convention." The leaflet condemned McGovern for glorifying the veterans.[111]

Dirty tricks were rampant. A White House aide, Charles Colson, engaged in a crusade to revoke VVAW's tax-exempt status.[112] In cities across the country, urban antisubversive units (or "red squads"), usually the creation of local police departments, worked with the FBI to collect information on antiwar veterans.[113] At times, the subterfuge bordered on slapstick. In some cities, informers made money by selling VVAW literature to FBI agents.[114] The New Orleans chapter was so thoroughly saturated with spies that at one point it consisted entirely of government informants working for different agencies, each unaware of his comrades' true identities.[115] Attacks reached a new low when one culprit sprinkled itching powder in the bathroom of the national office.[116]

The Nixon administration's heavy-handed tactics helped the president trounce Senator George McGovern by a huge margin in the November elections. On November 7, President Nixon received 60.7 percent of the vote, slightly short of LBJ's record 61.1 percent landslide in 1964. The president carried every state except Massachusetts, receiving 521 electoral votes to McGovern's 17. Beleaguered antiwar activists were more discouraged than ever, but VVAW organizers remained philosophical about the elections. A report issued by VVAW's New York regional office before the elections reasoned that a McGovern victory would not result in a "fundamental change in the ruling structure of this country. The split between the two parties [over the war] represents the contradictory concerns of the Big Business establishment." Peace would come from continued grassroots resistance, not from the ballot box, the New York report concluded.[117]

VVAW had entered a period of stabilization in 1972, despite—or perhaps because of—an intense, clandestine campaign mounted against it by the federal government, coupled with the deescalation of the war in Southeast Asia. Growth had slowed by the summer. Paranoia, poor communications, a transient membership, and burnout took an enormous toll. But VVAW was still a force to be reckoned with in the fall of 1972. In a year that witnessed the decline or demise of many antiwar groups, VVAW maintained a strong presence in cities across the country, in some cases operating out of visible storefronts. The Last Patrol, while ultimately less captivating than Dewey Canyon III, was proof that members could still mount potent and creative national demonstrations.

The signing of the Paris Peace Accords in January 1973, which formally ended the war, posed new challenges. The next few years provided a test of VVAW's viability in a postwar world. In the face of a continued government onslaught, more staff departures, and its eventual takeover by a small ultraleft sect, VVAW withered into a paper organization. Yet it was a testament to the talent and persistence of its coordinators that VVAW did not immediately fold when Secretary of State Henry Kissinger and the North Vietnamese leader Le Duc Tho put pen to paper in Paris on January 27, 1973. An overall decline ensued, but some chapters actually experienced growth spurts after the peace accords, in part because of the national steering committee's decision to allow nonveterans to join. By 1974, the national office, now relocated to Chicago, could still mobilize two thousand protesters for a July 4 demonstration. The horror of war and betrayals by politicians cut more deeply into the psyches of VVAW members than those of most other war resisters. Even though the war was ending, in its aftermath there was much work left to be done. Many veterans believed there was still too much at stake to let go.

8

Making Peace

Decline did not come suddenly for VVAW. Membership had peaked at more than twenty-five thousand just a few months before U.S. and Vietnamese leaders signed the Paris agreement of January 1973, formally ending the Vietnam War. Although the effect of the treaty was swift and VVAW rapidly diminished in size, with numerous chapters folding, the cease-fire arrangement did not trigger the immediate collapse of the organization that some had predicted. In fact, VVAW would retain many characteristics of a mass movement for the next year and a half.

VVAW's continuation after the war owed much to its coordinators, who had the foresight to try to revamp VVAW into a veterans' advocacy network. They believed the VA had failed miserably to provide the most basic services to help Vietnam veterans cope with posttraumatic stress disorder and adjust to postwar life. What was needed now, more than ever, was a newly restructured VVAW that could fill the void. The rap groups, drug counseling programs, and volunteer efforts in VA hospitals, all dating back to 1970, were part of a larger struggle within VVAW to reach out to veterans who existed on the periphery of society.

The diligence of activists notwithstanding, VVAW never emerged as a nationwide veterans' rights group. The shift away from single-issue orientation was never completed. VVAW did not have the budget, the strength to withstand federal assaults, or a large enough core of volunteers to make the transition. Battles, both internal and external, took a toll. Harassment by federal agents, the costly Gainesville Eight trial, and factional splits reduced VVAW to a sect. Well-meaning attempts to achieve openness by allowing nonveterans to join backfired, prompting an influx of ultraleftists who wanted to station themselves at the vanguard of a revolutionary veterans movement.

Remarkably, VVAW would survive all of these travails. An obituary is still forthcoming. VVAW, smaller and less formal, adapted to postwar society, and its members—past and present—still shape the public's perception of America's longest war.

Two hundred B-52 bombers, each carrying thirty tons of explosives, began bombing the North Vietnamese cities of Hanoi and Haiphong on December 17, 1972. President Nixon referred to the attacks as "Operation Linebacker," a plan designed to force the Vietnamese to accept American terms for peace. Antiwar activists, the media, and much of the public dubbed it "the Christmas bombing." For twelve days and nights, American planes pulverized the two cities and the surrounding countryside, often striking civilian targets. Thousands of people were killed, but government officials in North Vietnam had learned of the operation in advance and evacuated more than a half million people from Hanoi.[1]

Among those still in the city during the bombings was an American delegation that included the folk singer Joan Baez, the Columbia University professor Telford Taylor, the Yale University theologian the Reverend Michael Alan, and the VVAW national coordinator Barry Romo. The four visitors brought Christmas cards and packages to American prisoners of war in Hanoi. Romo felt "stressed out" about journeying to a country at war with the United States—a war in which he had participated a few years earlier. The night "Operation Linebacker" began, he watched an American F-111 bomb downtown Hanoi, triggering a chorus of air raid sirens throughout the city. Romo and the other Americans joined their Vietnamese hosts inside a small underground bunker. "I stayed there one or two times during the bombing raids, and I couldn't take it. So I told the Vietnamese, 'Look, I'll . . . make sure everybody's down in there, but then I'm going upstairs.' You could hear the thunder, you could feel the ground move."[2]

For days, Romo wandered around Hanoi, witnessing scenes of devastation everywhere. A pile of rubble was all that remained of Bach Mai, Hanoi's largest hospital. Buried under the collapsed walls were the bodies of doctors, nurses, and hundreds of patients. An elementary school that had once housed children who had greeted Romo and the other Americans had been turned into a crater. The day after Christmas, bombs from B-52s pummeled Hanoi's busy Kham Thien Street, leaving fifteen hundred bodies in the ruins. During one intense air raid, Joan Baez recorded a song titled "Where Are You Now, My Son?," based on a Vietnamese woman she saw sifting through debris in search of her son.[3] Walking through the streets of Hanoi further radicalized the twenty-three-year-old Romo. He watched defiant Vietnamese citizens firing primitive K-44 carbines at Phantom jets. He drank Vietnamese beer with jubilant militia members. On the outskirts of town, antiaircraft batteries struck B-52s with deadly accuracy, and trucks rumbled past Romo carrying American pilots who had been shot down. Before Romo left Hanoi, a Vietnamese interpreter embraced him and said, "It is good that you are here to share in our suffering, because after the war you will also really share in our joy."[4]

Romo returned to the United States at the beginning of 1973 to resume work in a moribund antiwar movement. A number of organizations were defunct. Activists closed offices, packed old stationery, and tried to build new lives. The last act of the declining antiwar movement was a demonstration on the day of President Nixon's second inauguration, on January 20, 1973, which drew more than one hundred thousand protesters in Washington, D.C. An estimated five thousand VVAWers marched in the demonstration. Smaller protests occurred in all parts of the country, with VVAW maintaining a strong presence virtually everywhere.[5] Nevertheless, the antiwar leader Fred Halstead lamented: "The mass of American people considered U.S. involvement in the war virtually over, felt no urgency about it, and were not responding to antiwar calls."[6]

A week later, in Paris, Secretary of State Henry Kissinger and the North Vietnamese leader Le Duc Tho signed a cease-fire agreement, officially ending the war in Vietnam. The accords provided for withdrawal of U.S. troops by March, an immediate cease-fire, and the release of all American prisoners of war. "The United States will continue to recognize the Government of the Republic of Vietnam [the Thieu regime] as the sole legitimate government of South Vietnam," President Nixon announced.[7] Reactions in the antiwar movement were mixed. Many activists lauded the treaty and joined the American public in viewing it as an end to hostilities. Within a year, the two largest antiwar coalitions—the People's Coalition for Peace and Justice and the National Peace Action Coalition—would fold. But a sizable segment of the antiwar movement continued its work after the Paris agreement, emphasizing the need to end U.S. aid to the Thieu government in Saigon and to Cambodia's President Lon Nol, to pressure President Nixon to adhere to the peace accords, to cease the bombing of Cambodia, and to offer amnesty to draft resisters. Their struggle was an uphill one. "You had less of a mass movement, but you probably had a more effectively targeted movement," recalled an activist.[8]

VVAW leaders viewed the Paris agreement with skepticism. Their organization was one of a handful of antiwar groups that outlived the January 27 treaty, albeit with some immediate membership losses. "We are continuing to educate the public about our involvement in Indochina and about militarism at home. We feel that it is of utmost importance . . . that the lesson of Vietnam not be allowed to go untaught," editorialized *Free Fire*, the newsletter of the Burlington, Vermont, VVAW chapter.[9] *Veterans Voice*, the newsletter of the Kansas City VVAW office, added: "We must show by our words and deeds that we, veterans of the cursed war in Vietnam, Laos and Cambodia, realize that our struggle against U.S. oppression in Southeast Asia is not eased by the simple signing of a piece of paper."[10]

A number of members left VVAW after the peace accords. Jan Barry, the man who had founded VVAW and who led it until Dewey Canyon III, decided there was no point in maintaining his affiliation. "I was convinced, the day the war ended, there was no use for VVAW. What would you do with the organization?" Barry conceded the need to continue addressing "the historical amnesia, the . . . revisionism that goes on, and the inevitable next wars, plus the social aspect of how veterans were treated." But, like many of his comrades, he concluded that the most effective way to confront such problems after the signing of the peace accords was to become an independent activist.[11] Barry was not alone. Round-robin status reports collected by the national office from chapters across the country after the Paris Agreement indicated a declining interest in organizational activities. Much of the news was grim: "Alaska/Washington: little or no contact." "Arizona/New Mexico: . . . there has been minimal contact." "Colorado/Utah/Wyoming: Lost one of two chapters." "Connecticut/Rhode Island: With the exception of one chapter in Rhode Island and one woman in Connecticut, this region is defunct." "Louisiana: Communications sporadic. . . . problems with post office box of regional office." "Michigan: With the ending of communication, no address in Detroit, this region is dead." "New York City chapter is a disappointment. Should be one of the strongest in the country." "North and South Carolina: This important region is for all purposes defunct."[12] VVAW retained strong chapters in Kansas, Missouri, Illinois, Ohio, Wisconsin, Minnesota, upstate New York, Florida, and particularly California. Baltimore, Washington, D.C., San Francisco, Cincinnati, Denver, Los Angeles, and Chicago remained VVAW hotbeds.[13]

Still, activity slackened in early 1973. Members who did not quit re-duced their commitment. Exhaustion drove the national coordinator Steve Hawkins to resign in the spring. "I've come to the conclusion that having the national office in [my] home 24 hours a day, seven days a week, isn't the best situation for my personal and political development, as this has meant a total annihilation of personal life and privacy."[14] A VVAW national officer, Ed Damato, remembered a number of his com-rades succumbing to fatigue after the Paris Agreement. "The one thing that united the group was the word 'Vietnam.' That was our reason to exist. So of course there were people who were going to leave," Damato explained. He noted that organizers such as himself who were "politi-cized" during the war had a higher likelihood of staying in VVAW.[15] The Ohio VVAWer and future national coordinator Pete Zastrow, added: "VVAW always had a double focus of 'bring our brothers home' and 'pre-vent the next war.' But for a lot of people, the 'bring our brothers home' was by far the more important aspect of that dialectic."[16]

A sizable core of VVAW cadres never stopped working. In several parts of the country, small numbers of dedicated activists kept chapters alive. Annie Luginbill, coordinator of the Chicago Area Military Project (CAMP), one of the most successful military counseling services in the country, began working with VVAW's national office in Chicago as the war was ending. Every day, she joined dozens of other activists who occu-pied the second and third floors of an old building on Newport Street. She shifted her attention from "GI work to veterans' work," attended "na-tional steering committee meetings in church basements," and became "part of the VVAW family."[17]

Luginbill and other members mobilized veterans to help fashion VVAW into a viable, radical alternative to the American Legion. There was never a shortage of work. Building ties with other movements and drawing new sources of support became high priorities. Thus, in March VVAWers shipped medical supplies to the Oglala Sioux and their allies who had taken over the Wounded Knee historic site on the Pine Ridge In-dian Reservation in North Dakota. At the same time, two coordinators, Gary Staiger and Steve Hawkins, traveled to Japan to represent VVAW in antinuclear protests. In the spring, the national steering committee, in one of its most ambitious efforts, began formulating plans to build a clinic in the impoverished, predominantly African American community of Bogue Chito, Alabama. While VVAW officers reviewed blueprints for the clinic, the issue of amnesty for draft resisters simultaneously dominated the attention of antiwar veterans. Thirty VVAWers from ten states attended an international conference in Toronto, Canada, in May 1973, to implement a campaign for unconditional amnesty.[18]

Such far-reaching projects required more labor than VVAW's overworked staff could provide. To broaden the organization's waning base of support, leaders once again restructured the organization. The transformation began in the fall of 1972, when VVAW's staff voted to move the national office from New York City to Chicago. The veterans cited lower rents and a more convenient location as reasons for the change, but there were also underlying political tensions that prompted the transition. Chapter coordinators and rank-and-file joiners had long complained that the New York office was out of touch with the rest of the country. The new, more radical leadership that emerged in 1972 consciously sought to consolidate its power, and the new Chicago headquarters lacked the divisiveness that existed in New York and spelled a clear victory for the left wing.[19]

Another matter that reflected the changing currents was the question of whether to establish the long-debated Winter Soldier Organization (WSO), the proposed nonveteran branch of VVAW. At the January 1973 national steering committee meeting in Chicago, no clear consensus emerged. The "folks [who] saw WSO as the end of VVAW" and those who "felt it was too late in coming" were "so evenly balanced that a majority, in either direction, could not be attained," recalled one participant.[20] The divided body sent the matter back to chapter coordinators, who were expected to gauge the sentiments of members in their area and report back to the national steering committee at its April meeting in Placitas, New Mexico. By April, the pro-WSO forces had shored up enough support for the change, and membership was opened to nonveterans. While a sizable segment of critics questioned the wisdom of creating WSO, they failed to withstand charges of "veterans' chauvinism" and ultimately mounted a feeble resistance. Most chapters regarded WSO as an opportunity for VVAW to enlarge its ranks and allow women to participate as full members. "There are many strong, hard working non-vets in VVAW, but because of the name and nature of the organization, their work went by the wayside," lamented the Dayton Ohio VVAW newsletter.[21] Henceforth, the organization would go by the name Vietnam Veterans Against the War/Winter Soldier Organization (VVAW/WSO).

*

In Florida, the legal maneuvering surrounding the trial of the Gainesville Eight—the VVAWers accused of plotting to disrupt the 1972 Republican National Convention—continued into 1973. The trial aroused the attention of the media and proved to be one of the few issues that would unite the moderates and radicals in VVAW/WSO. "Free the Gainesville Eight!" became the rallying cry of the national office, and some chapters attracted new members who wanted to help with defense work. Antiwar luminaries from all parts of the country voiced their support for the eight men.

VVAW/WSO activists created a united front around the Gainesville Eight. But public displays of solidarity masked deep tensions between the national coordinators and the defendants. The leaders were dissatisfied with some of the eight, particularly Scott Camil, whose biting militancy intimidated some of his comrades. "Scott did a lot to try to be divisive. . . . But maybe he . . . just hated us," Ed Damato recalled.[22] For their part, the defendants had no desire to become martyrs for a shriveling cause. Camil resented what he regarded as attempts by the leadership to exploit the case for its own ends. He explained:

> The national office felt that they had a right to have a say in the strategy of the trial and what went on. And, based on our constitution, that's true. They did. On the other hand, the eight of us are the ones who are going to jail if it doesn't work, and our organization is so full of undercover people, why should we allow people from outside to come in and meet with us and our lawyers and know our strategy?[23]

The eight men on trial endured endless hardships. For more than a year, their lives were put on hold as they met with attorneys, spent weeks in the court room, and assisted in defense work. Nobody was immune to discouragement, but the ordeal took a particularly devastating toll on one defendant, Alton Foss. A native of Florida, Foss had served in the navy as a hospital corpsman in Vietnam. In 1966, a bullet shattered his leg during an ambush at Da Nang. The treatment he received at a Key West Naval Hospital afterward caused additional leg damage, making him eligible for 60 percent disability from the VA. Following nine other leg operations, Foss became "mentally . . . and physically addicted to narcotic drugs."[24] He obtained drugs from his mother, also an addict; physicians prescribed yet more drugs for him. He found work at a hospital, where he stole amphetamines from an operating room. Another job at a Miami drug company provided more amphetamines, as well as narcotics and psychedelics.

He took morphine and Demerol every day. The drug company fired him, prompting him to steal a motor vehicle full of drugs. A sympathetic judge gave him probation.[25]

Foss joined VVAW in early 1972, "fed up with the government people because they made me a cripple."[26] His history of drug addiction and mental problems made him an obvious target for undercover agents. In July, two infiltrators joined VVAW and befriended Foss. The three men took drugs and smoked marijuana together. Eventually, the informants revealed their real identities and convinced Foss that he had better "cooperate with us, or we get you on a drug bust." The FBI conducted hours of interviews with the paranoid veteran in a secluded motel room. Foss planned to "make a deal" until the week before the Republican National Convention, when FBI agents asked him "to be a witness against the other defendants in the conspiracy trial."[27] Foss refused. In the meantime, his world began to fall apart. Both of his parents had recently passed away, and his wife left him, taking their two sons. Shortly after Foss appeared before the grand jury in Tallahassee to answer charges of conspiracy, police arrested him for selling drugs to the two informants. Desperate and broke, Foss put his home up for the bond to get out of jail. "He'd call me at five o'clock in the morning, crying, really emotionally disturbed," recalled Foss's attorney.[28] On September 20, Foss went to the Gainesville Eight Defense Headquarters, slashed his left wrist with a razor, and drank two bottles of wood alcohol. His friends rushed him to a VA hospital, where he slowly recovered. He resolved to stay loyal to his VVAW "brothers" and prepared for a turbulent courtroom battle. The radical attorney William Kunstler volunteered to represent him.[29]

Foss and the other defendants faced a hostile judge and a well-financed prosecution. Before the trial, U.S. District Judge Winston Arnow, a retired Army major, enacted a "gag rule" banning public statements by participants in the trial. In pretrial hearings, Judge Arnow also forbade the defense to discuss the Watergate scandal in court, and he prohibited demonstrations within a block of the Federal Building.[30] The eight VVAWers were ultimately saved by a sloppy prosecution team. The depth of the government's ineptitude was revealed the opening day of the trial. On July 31, one defendant, Pete Mahoney, sitting in the court-supplied defense offices in the Federal Building, spied movement through a vent. A check of the adjacent utility closet revealed two FBI agents fumbling with telephone and electronic gear in the cramped space. One of the agents explained that the transmitter, amplifier, battery pack, receiver, earphones, and attaché cases were necessary for "checking the FBI lines."[31] When defense attorneys objected to the FBI's tactics, Judge Arnow scolded them for "making mountains out of molehills" and praised the FBI agents for being "perfectly candid and honest."[32]

Yet the prosecution's numerous errors quickly turned the trial in favor of the defendants. Several witnesses observed Prosecutor Guy Goodwin coaching the prosecution witness Bill Lemmer in the hall outside the courtroom. On the stand, Lemmer told of VVAW's alleged plans to organize assassination squads, instigate riots, and use slingshots loaded with "fried marbles" (marbles that had been heated so that they would shatter on impact) against the Miami police. Defense attorneys quickly discredited Lemmer and other government witnesses. One self-proclaimed "air force weapons instructor" who testified for the prosecution could not distinguish between the drastically different M-14 and M-16 rifles, nor could he tell the difference between a real M-16 and the toy M-16s that antiwar veterans used in guerrilla theater. Defense attorneys shot down the prosecution's claims that the VVAWers were planning to hide slingshots in their pant legs and underwear by showing the jury that such weapons could not fit inside those articles of clothing. FBI ballistics tests showed that fragments from "fried marbles" could not penetrate even the skins of rabbits. Pablo Fernandez, the Cuban informer who had attempted to sell weapons to VVAW members, testified that the veterans repeatedly refused his offers. Carl Becker, an FBI informant and a former VVAW regional coordinator, said that he never recalled "the use of the word riot" in any VVAW meetings, nor did he remember any mention of plans to use violence to disrupt the Republican National Convention.[33]

Worsening matters for the Nixon administration was the trial's widespread media coverage. Newspapers in the region were particularly sympathetic toward the defendants. "Conspiracy's Sorry Record" was the headline of an editorial in the *St. Petersburg Times*, while the *Gainesville Sun* referred to the affair as the "Saga of Taintsville."[34] An editorial in *The Charlotte Observer* in North Carolina sharply criticized the Justice Department: "We hope the government has more to go on than the word of one more dubious FBI informer."[35] The numerous Gainesville Eight stories also drew attention to the deepening Watergate scandal. "Antiwar Vets' Trial May Yield Watergate Data," announced *The Christian Science Monitor*.[36] A story in *The Louisville Times* ran under the headline "Judge Blocks Watergate Link to Trial of Vets."[37] Worried officials sought to downplay or ignore the case. In a pretrial hearing, former U.S. Attorney

General John Mitchell testified that he had "no recollection of any electronic surveillance relating to" VVAW and claimed he was "not even sure who the Gainesville Eight are."[38]

Making the ordeal more tolerable for the defendants were the many well-organized protests in Gainesville. A core of dedicated activists remained in the city during the entire trial. More than two hundred members from around the country leafleted the community, marched in front of A & P stores in support of the United Farm Workers, performed guerrilla theater, and participated in a "People's Fair" at Santa Fe Community College. The fair, which featured VVAW/WSO booths and rock music, attracted four hundred people from the area. The following day, August 4, a crowd of five hundred marched silently across town to the Federal Building. The radical luminary Tom Hayden, the folk singer Pete Seeger, and the Pentagon Papers defendant Anthony Russo spoke at a rally near the courthouse.[39]

One month after the trial began and fourteen months after the eight VVAW members were charged with conspiring to disrupt the Republican Convention, the case was turned over to the jurors. At 2:23 P.M. on August 31, after almost three and a half hours of deliberation, the forewoman, Lois Hensel, delivered the verdict of not guilty on all counts. The veterans and a crowd of their supporters in the courtroom cheered. A juror later said, "What was there to deliberate? They never showed us any evidence. We could have come back with a verdict in ten minutes."[40] Another juror added: "They had nothing on those boys."[41]

VVAWers across the country hailed the outcome as a great victory. The Wisconsin/Minnesota coordinator John Lindquist wrote: "We of VVAW can take pride in the acquittal of the Gainesville Eight. Just like the Vietnamese, we stood up to a much stronger force, Nixon and the Justice Department, and kicked their ass."[42] But the excitement was short-lived. Though the prosecution repeatedly erred in the courtroom and ultimately lost, the Justice Department fulfilled some of its aims with the Gainesville Eight trial. The endless hours of volunteer defense work absorbed the attention of activists who might have otherwise devoted their efforts to transforming VVAW/WSO into a viable, radical veterans' organization. "It took away from a lot of the energy. . . . And of course, everybody was found not guilty. But it took resources, money, and a lot of manpower to counteract that," recalled the VVAWer Jack McCloskey.[43] Even with assistance from a multitude of radical attorneys, VVAW/WSO spent $275,000 of its own money on the trial, thereby draining its bank account. The trial also ruined many of the southern chapters, which were already susceptible to infiltration by federal and local law enforcement agents. "What they did was pretty much undermine the entire southern part of the organization, which had been pretty active," explained Pete Zastrow.[44]

VVAW leaders chose to emphasize the positive aspects of the trial. A survey of chapter status reports collected in January 1974 by the national office failed to mention the collapse of southern chapters, except for a brief mention of Louisiana ("the region has become defunct") and North Carolina/South Carolina ("saw little, if any, sustained activity").[45] In April 1974, the national steering committee met in Milwaukee and offered an even grimmer update on the state of affairs in the South. States listed as "stagnant" included Missouri, Alabama, Mississippi, and Tennessee, while the once-bustling Florida chapter had fallen victim to "incredible internal hassles."[46] The prognosis for western chapters was equally dismal. With the exception of California and Colorado, VVAW/WSO had lost virtually its entire foothold in the western United States. National coordinators ignored the steady decline and remained optimistic. "In general, we have seen the organization continue to build during the past . . . months throughout the country. We seem to be reaching a period of stabilization," an internal report concluded.[47]

With the war over, members drifted away from VVAW. Bill Crandell paid his dues until 1975, but he had cut back significantly on his workload as a VVAW coordinator a few years earlier. "We were tired. Some of us had lived this as our daily lives for a long time." Still the Midwest coordinator by 1972, Crandell reached the point "where I held that responsibility and I wouldn't do anything with it. Mail would come and I wouldn't open it. I just couldn't face it because it didn't seem like it was going anywhere."[48] Numerous members disappeared, never to be heard from again. Al Hubbard, the former executive secretary, drove off into the Southwest, severing all contact with his comrades. Bill Weiman, the double-leg amputee from Boston who had gained fame during Dewey Canyon III and the Republican National Convention protests, took his wife and child to New Mexico. Joe Urgo, who remained a dedicated member of VVAW/WSO in New York City, later recalled: "The great majority of the average vets left because they were trying to settle down. Thousands moved into the two desertion points in the country: northern Vermont, close to Canada, and the Washington state area. Thousands disappeared into the woods."[49]

Despite the organization's heavy losses, enclaves of VVAW/WSO activists maintained busy schedules. Bill Davis, the national coordinator, recounted: "Our activities never seemed to cease. With the end of the war, our emphasis on veterans' benefits and the amnesty issue picked up. There was still plenty of work and plenty of people to do it."[50] Sporadic protests occurred in parts of the country. Predictably, most of the few thousand members who remained in VVAW/WSO moved left. Several chapters formed study groups. For many veterans, the writings of Marx, Lenin, and Mao provided a coherent historical framework to understand the dynamics of capitalism in general, and of the Vietnam War in particular. "What we lost in terms of numbers may have been made up for in terms of political savvy and direction," Pete Zastrow concluded.[51]

To rally support behind VVAW/WSO, coordinators planned more protests. VVAW/WSO organizers could still muster sizable crowds at their Veterans Day activities. A series of demonstrations late in January 1974, marking the anniversary of the signing of the Paris agreement, occurred in Chicago, Milwaukee, Denver, Miami, Kansas City, and New York City. Hundreds of people attended in each city. At the beginning of 1974, the national steering committee proposed a mass march in Washington, D.C., for July 4. The demonstration, it was hoped, would revive support for VVAW. The march turned out to be one of the most successful actions of the Watergate era. On July 4, an estimated 3,500 people formed a column that moved through the streets of Washington, D.C., carrying banners that reflected VVAW/WSO's demands: "Universal and Unconditional Amnesty"; "A Single-type Discharge for All Veterans"; "Implement the Peace Agreement—End All Aid to Thieu and Lon Nol"; "Kick Nixon Out!"[52]

The well-attended march did little to stall VVAW/WSO's decline. Membership rolls dwindled, due largely to the end of the war but also because of continued repression by authorities. Repeated attacks by police in March 1973 took a devastating toll on the once-thriving Los Angeles chapter. In the span of a few days, officers broke into the home of three VVAWers without a search warrant and ransacked the premises, disseminated bogus anti-VVAW/WSO leaflets allegedly written by an "ex-member," and clubbed a group of antiwar veterans on their way to a meeting with civil rights activists at a local church. "We're going to get you fuckers," one officer reportedly told a VVAW/WSO worker.[53]

In other parts of the country, being a VVAW/WSO member could be equally hazardous. FBI agents approached members in Kansas, Colorado,

New York, California, Florida, and Texas. In April 1973, Don Pennington, the regional coordinator for North and South Carolina, was sentenced to three months of hard labor for exchanging "some righteous words" with two MPs at Camp Lejeune in Jacksonville, North Carolina. Even though one of the MPs later testified that Pennington never uttered anything obscene, the VVAW/WSO coordinator was charged with using "vile and vulgar" language.[54] Six Marines stationed at Iwakuni, Japan, all members of VVAW/WSO, were arrested on July 4 for distributing copies of the Declaration of Independence to other Marines at a track meet.[55] Two days later, undercover police in Miami broke into the house of the Dade County VVAW/WSO coordinator Jim Hale and arrested him for possession of marijuana. The police "tore down articles" from Hale's wall and referred to his Vietnamese wife as "Viet Cong."[56]

What happened to Scott Camil after the Gainesville Eight trial is a disturbing example of the lengths to which authorities went to harass VVAW/WSO members. After the trial, Camil left Gainesville to recuperate. He took no solace in his courtroom victory. He still felt tremendous anger toward his close friend Emerson Poe, who turned out to be an FBI informer and witness for the prosecution. Later, Camil secretly returned to Gainesville, carefully avoiding most of the people he knew. "I needed some privacy. I got a friend to rent me a house and turn on the electricity and gas in his name."[57] He became intimately involved with a woman from Orlando. They saw each other regularly for three months and used drugs together. The woman introduced Camil to two male friends who persuaded him to accompany them to purchase drugs. He went with them, and, on the way home, one of the men held a gun to his neck. The man began striking Camil with the gun, and the veteran attempted to get out of the car. A shot rang out. A bullet penetrated Camil's back and exited his front. He jumped out of the car, landing on the pavement outside a restaurant. The bullet collapsed his lung and damaged his liver and kidney. As soon as he recovered, Camil learned that the two men worked for the Drug Enforcement Agency (DEA). He was charged with assaulting federal agents and possession and delivery of drugs. He endured another lengthy trial, which resulted in the jury finding him not guilty and recommending that the two DEA agents be indicted for attempted murder. The combination of several terrible experiences with authorities "effectively silenced me," Camil concluded.[58]

*

Informants and police raids hurt VVAW/WSO, but outside repression was no more damaging than the internecine battles that raged within. The more VVAW/WSO diminished in size, the longer and the more contentious its national steering committee meetings became. The creation of Winter Soldier Organization in 1973 relaxed membership qualifications, thus making it easier for small, ultraleft sects to penetrate the organization. In the San Francisco area, a group called Prairie Fire, the "above-ground" branch of the radical Weather Underground, began attracting members in 1973. Meanwhile, national coordinators in Chicago, as well as a growing segment of VVAW/WSO around the country, gravitated toward the Revolutionary Union (RU), a Maoist group later rechristened the Revolutionary Communist Party (RCP) in 1975 by its charismatic leader, Bob Avakian. Deepening rifts developed between various constituencies, erupting in a battle for the soul of VVAW/WSO. By 1975, what little vitality and viability existed in the organization had been shattered by an unbridgeable rift.[59]

Both sides issued lengthy position papers proclaiming the "correct line" and condemning their opponents. The pro–Prairie Fire factions in northern California initiated the "Anti-Imperialist Minority Focus" (AIMF). Jeanne Friedman, a longtime VVAW activist living in San Jose, drafted many of AIMF's statements. "Northern California was the dissident side. What happened was the RCP moved into VVAW at the national level first. . . . Structurally, it came down to a real organizational takeover [by the RCP]." Friedman disliked RU; years earlier, she had witnessed RU cadres at Stanford University recklessly encouraging students to abandon academics and organize workers in factories. When RU (and subsequently, the RCP) gained supporters in the national office, Friedman's friendships "with Barry [Romo] and the national office went down the toilet. I was the enemy."[60] In 1975, Friedman wrote an article titled "Struggle in VVAW/WSO" for a Santa Barbara underground newspaper, *Seize the Time*. She denounced RU for its attempts to transform VVAW/WSO into a purely veterans organization that ignored sexism, racism, and Third World liberation movements. She charged that the "secret cadre" in RU was seeking to jettison multi-issuism and concluded that RU "must be discredited and dumped" by "anti-imperialist forces in VVAW/WSO."[61]

The national office fired back with its own tract condemning the dissident faction as a "scum clique" of "opportunists" and "reactionaries."[62] Another pro-RU paper declared that VVAW/WSO should concentrate "on vets and GIs" and the "need to build [an] . . . organization around the struggles of vets at the VA and around unemployment." Vietnam veterans are the vanguard of revolutionary change and "are on the move . . . to lead that struggle," the paper concluded.[63] Like several of his comrades, the VVWA/WSO national coordinator, Bill Davis, initially supported RU. He later explained the issues surrounding the acrimonious split: "[VVAW/WSO] stayed pretty much mainstream and . . . focused on veterans, in spite of anti-imperialist focus groups who wanted to make it like, 'You can't be in VVAW unless you're anti-imperialist.' Well, so what? The average guy on the street doesn't have any idea what you're talking about. . . . Why should we focus on world struggles? We've got to focus on Vietnam veterans."[64] Added Barry Romo: "It was G.I. and vets' focus. That was where we had to go. . . . If we became something else, all we would become is this little petit bourgeois debating society, built upon guilt rather than action."[65]

The deepening fissure reached the heights of absurdity when the national office expelled "pseudo-chapters" in the San Francisco area, as well as in Buffalo, St. Louis, and Dayton, Ohio (the latter three were particularly active chapters). Ten VVAW/WSO members were also purged. To the segment of VVAW/WSO that embraced neither faction, the split made no sense. That two groups of people, seemingly on the same side of virtually every issue, should participate in such hostile exchanges with each other disheartened the less ideological veterans still in VVAW/WSO. The Wisconsin/Minnesota coordinator John Lindquist explained: "A lot of people dropped out of VVAW when the FBI messed with us," but VVAW/WSO lost "even a larger amount of people, over the long run," as a result of sectarian conflicts. "This whole thing around RU/RCP really turned off a lot of people. I basically just pulled back. I didn't run for regional coordinator." Lindquist instead devoted much of his time to assembling his own massive private research library on post-Vietnam syndrome (a condition later referred to as "posttraumatic stress disorder"). In 1979, he felt comfortable running for national coordinator of VVAW again. In spite of his disagreements with various leaders, he understood why some members had turned to Marx, Lenin, and Mao. "Even though I was dead-set against it, I honestly felt they needed to look at Marxist-Leninism."[66]

Terrible internal strife ravaged VVAW/WSO at a time when it could least afford such conflicts. The organization would survive, but only as a ineffectual fragment of its former self. Joe Urgo, himself a radical leftist by 1975, had helped build VVAW into a mass movement five years earlier.

He watched the collapse of VVAW/WSO with feelings of helplessness and despair. He recounted:

> It became hard to keep this thing going in a direction that made sense. . . . We were struggling to do the best we could. . . . The organization had to grow and it didn't know how to do it. It had to confront the state and we didn't really have the understanding that they were really out to hurt us. It had to confront some of the contradictions between the moderates and the radicals and try to figure out, 'Is there a common program that can unite people here?' And we didn't know how to do that. . . . It was a very difficult time.[67]

Unlike Students for a Democratic Society, the Black Panther Party, and a multitude of other radical organizations of the sixties and early seventies, VVAW never ceased to exist. It split, dwindled, and underwent additional transformations. Yet it did not fold. There was still a VVAW/WSO when North Vietnamese and NLF troops rolled into Saigon on April 30, 1975, and raised the Provisional Revolutionary Government flag on the balcony of the presidential palace. Antiwar veterans across the country cheered when radios, televisions, and newspapers reported the fall of South Vietnam to the Communists. In the meantime, a dedicated but diminishing core of activists persisted. VVAW/WSO members involved with the amnesty movement rejoiced when Presidents Ford and Carter offered clemency to draft resisters. VVAW/WSO's small clinic in Bogue Chitto, Alabama, was one of the few success stories amid the repression and infighting of the mid-seventies. The Martin Luther King Jr. Memorial Clinic opened its doors in the fall of 1973. Sympathizers presented a used ambulance to the clinic, and registered nurses screened patients for high blood pressure, tuberculosis, diabetes, malnutrition, anemia, rickets, and dental decay. Supplies were limited, but donations poured in from VVAW/WSO chapters all over the country. The St. Louis chapter was particularly effective at collecting medicine and raising money. Throughout the seventies, the clinic offered medical care to patients who had never encountered a doctor in their lives.[68]

Pockets of volunteers kept working into the late seventies. Having dropped "WSO" from their organization's name, VVAW members formed the Ashby Leach Defense Committee in 1976 to come to the aid of a Vietnam veteran who had held thirteen hostages at the offices of the Chessie System railroad in Cleveland. The company had refused to participate in a G.I. Bill program that would have increased his pay and benefits during his apprenticeship. Following a brief standoff on August 26, 1976, police arrested Leach, and VVAW hired a lawyer for him. After a three-month stay in jail, the veteran went on a VVAW-sponsored speaking tour.[69] The Ashby Leach incident failed to rejuvenate defunct chapters, but the groundswell of activity around the deadly aftereffects of Agent Orange offered some promise for a VVAW revival. Between 1962 and 1971, American planes had sprayed almost nineteen million gallons of herbicide over Vietnam. Beginning in the late 1970s, Vietnam veterans claimed that the toxic substances were responsible for a variety of health problems, from mysterious skin cancers to birth defects in their children. VVAWers pioneered early advocacy efforts for Agent Orange victims. They organized demonstrations in Milwaukee and Chicago in 1978, participated in the National Veterans Task Force on Agent Orange, and assisted veterans seeking to join one of the scores of lawsuits being filed around the country.[70]

The Ashby Leach affair and the Agent Orange compensation movement fanned VVAW's remaining embers. Nevertheless, by the late 1970s, the organization had been reduced to a handful of post office boxes scattered primarily in the Midwest and the Northeast. Another split in 1978 created two separate factions, Vietnam Veterans Against the War (VVAW) and an even smaller splinter group, Vietnam Veterans Against the War—Anti-Imperialist (VVAW AI), thus ending the RCP's ruinous influence over the national office. Only a handful of people noticed or cared about the latest schism. Even the coordinators who had survived the 1975 split were running out of stamina. Being a perennial activist provided no money and little stability. Revenue from dues and fundraisers no longer sustained the national office. To subsidize their way of life, VVAW officers accepted part-time work, which often led to full-time employment. Bill Davis recounted: "We decided we wanted things like jobs, lives, families."[71] Barry Romo did his best to keep VVAW from disappearing altogether. With the help of other veterans and friends around Chicago, he kept the national office going, largely out of his apartment. "For a lot of us, [VVAW represented] . . . years of political activity, putting your life on hold, getting beat by police, getting arrested, not finishing college, not having kids, running around the country. People spent more time in the streets of America than in the jungles of Nam, against their own government. People can't constantly do that."[72]

*

Through the years, VVAW has enjoyed intermittent revivals. In the eighties, the rise of the right, coupled with media portrayals of sixties radicals as "sellouts," left the remaining pockets of VVAWers feeling dispirited. The Cold War consensus crept back into American politics. Presidents spoke of overcoming the Vietnam syndrome. Against this discouraging backdrop, antiwar veterans discovered different ways of reconciling with the past. A surprising number of them weathered the eighties with their humanitarian principles intact. VVAW banners appeared at antinuclear rallies in the early 1980s and at demonstrations against the U.S. invasion of Grenada in 1983. The organization sent delegations to Central America to protest U.S. funding of the Nicaraguan Contras and the Salvadoran death squads. Nostalgic veterans from all parts of America sent donations to the national office. During the eighties, VVAW sporadically published its newspaper, retitled *The Veteran*. The dedication of the Vietnam Veterans Memorial in November 1982 drew former and current VVAW members to Washington, D.C. A few have written poems about the site. The 58,022 names engraved on the monument have reaffirmed members' opposition to the war. Bruce Weigl, a contributor to *Winning Hearts and Minds*, explained why he was present at the dedication ceremony: "I think we came, without really knowing it, to make the memorial our wailing wall. We came to find the names of those we lost in the war, as if by tracing the letters cut into the granite we could find what was left of ourselves."[73] The Persian Gulf War in 1991 sparked interest in VVAW. "The Gulf War reactivated a large group of people out there," recalled the national coordinator, Joe Miller.[74] Leaders reorganized VVAW, appointing coordinators to several regions around the United States. Old-timers stepped forward, volunteering to become national officers, fancying VVAW as a latter-day Abraham Lincoln Brigade.

Across the country, ex-VVAW members approached their fifties with shorter, grayer hair and a determination to make peace with their past. Some joiners have openly reminisced about the Vietnam War and the antiwar movement, while others have shunned such discussions. A growing number of former members have found respectable niches in society. The most visible former VVAW member is John Kerry. For years, the veteran lived in relative obscurity. He ran for the House of Representatives in Massachusetts's Fifth District, but his bid was sabotaged by a vengeful Charles Colson, President Nixon's former special assistant. "Nixon's hatchet man" (as the *Wall Street Journal* referred to Colson) planned a series of dirty tricks that effectively undermined Kerry's campaign, resulting in a victory for the Republican candidate, Paul Cronin. Colson's antics in the Kerry/Cronin race later came under the scrutiny of the press during the Watergate scandal.[75] Discouraged by his loss, Kerry attended Boston College Law School, graduating in 1976. Politics continued to exercise a hold on him. He worked as an assistant district attorney in Middlesex County and was elected lieutenant governor of Massachusetts in 1982. He ran for the United States Senate and won in 1984, and again in 1990. His most contentious Senate race occurred in 1996, when his opponent was Massachusetts's enormously popular Republican governor, William Weld. The campaign drained both men of millions of dollars—one of the costliest Senate races in U.S. history—and resulted in a victory for Kerry by a 52–45 percent margin.[76]

In the Senate, Kerry built a reputation as a tireless liberal, emerging as one of the most outspoken critics of U.S. policy in Central America and a proponent of fostering ties with Vietnam. Yet even his supporters have described him as "brooding and aloof."[77] In public, the senator rarely spoke of his service in Vietnam and never talked about his role in VVAW. He has consistently rejected interviews about his involvement in the war and his antiwar activities. "The things that probably really turned me I've never told anybody. Nobody would understand. These things are very personal. It was our youth," Kerry explained of his past.[78] In 1995, he married Teresa Heinz, the wealthy widow of Pennsylvania's Senator John Heinz. A year earlier, he had cosponsored a Senate resolution with Senator John McCain of Arizona, a Vietnam veteran and a former prisoner of war, urging President Bill Clinton to lift the U.S. embargo against Vietnam. On July 11, 1995, President Bill Clinton, standing beside Senators Kerry and McCain, announced the normalization of diplomatic relations between the two countries. "Whatever divided us before let us consign to the past. Let this moment, in the words of the Scripture, be a time to heal, and a time to build," the president declared.[79]

Elsewhere, ex-VVAWers have exercised considerable influence. In 1978, Bobby Muller, the paraplegic veteran from New York City who frequently spoke as a VVAW representative, founded Vietnam Veterans of America (VVA), "an advocacy organization devoted exclusively to the needs of Vietnam veterans."[80] Muller attempted to organize veterans of all political persuasions into his new group, but he remained steadfastly opposed to the war. He returned to Vietnam in 1981 with three other veterans, laying a wreath at the tomb of Ho Chi Minh, only to be red-baited by conservative veterans and attacked in newspapers back in the United

States.[81] Muller spent much of the 1980s traversing the United States, raising money, speaking about his experiences in Vietnam, and meeting veterans. Along the way, he discovered, much to his discouragement, that many VVA members lacked the political consciousness of his old VVAW comrades. "Everyone in combat I found was against the war when we came back—so I thought Vietnam vets were like me and my friends. I felt if we could bring us all together, we'd have something. It's a hard lesson to learn after I've traveled across the country that perhaps one third are like us, but a whole lot buy the conservative line."[82] Meanwhile, VVA grew rapidly. By the 1990s, it had a national membership of more than forty-five thousand Vietnam veterans, including one hundred members of Congress, and 525 chapters throughout the United States, Puerto Rico, the Virgin Islands, and Guam.[83]

Another one of VVAW's "wheelchair vets," Ron Kovic, drew attention to VVAW's oft-neglected past when he wrote his autobiography, *Born on the Fourth of July*. The book found instant critical acclaim when it first appeared in 1976. With poetic eloquence, Kovic recounted his combat experiences in Vietnam, resulting in his paralysis from the waist down. He described the squalid conditions in VA hospitals and his ultimate conversion to an antiwar activist. Hollywood battled over movie rights to the book for several years. Al Pacino originally agreed to play Kovic in the film version, which was to be scripted by a then-obscure screenwriter named Oliver Stone. The deal fell through after another film about a paraplegic veteran, *Coming Home*, failed to make large sums of money at the box office and "Pacino got cold feet."[84] The success of Stone's 1986 Vietnam War film *Platoon* resuscitated the project. Released in 1989, *Born on the Fourth of July* dramatized Kovic's turbulent life, culminating with the VVAW march on the Fontainebleau Hotel during the Republican National Convention of 1972. The film netted eight Academy Award nominations, including one for Tom Cruise's powerful performance as Ron Kovic. It ultimately won four Oscars and aroused renewed interest in VVAW.[85]

Other ex-members have pursued quieter endeavors. Jan Barry, the founder of VVAW, is a journalist who lives with his wife and children in Montclair, New Jersey. The antinuclear movement of the early 1980s thrust him into the role of activist once more. Although he is proud of his involvement in VVAW, he remains frustrated by the infighting that has so often crippled the group. As an organizer of VVAW's twenty-fifth anniversary in 1992, he encountered those divisions again. "People said they

wouldn't come if certain other people came. And I said, 'What's the purpose of having a get-together if you immediately say certain people can't
come?' I insisted this is an open organization and you don't keep these
animosities going when we're celebrating the fact that we had this organization."[86] VVAW's first vice-president, Carl Rogers, lives and works in
Santa Monica, where he is raising a son. He looks back on his VVAW days
with fond memories. His experiences in VVAW prepared him for a life-
time of involvement in humanitarian causes. "I have absolutely no regrets. We did the right thing at the right time."[87] The former executive
secretary Al Hubbard lives outside Santa Fe, New Mexico. Nearly everyone who knew him assumed he was dead. He has refused requests for interviews.[88]

Academia and law lured numerous VVAWers after the war. Bill Crandell went to graduate school at Ohio State University, where he completed his Ph.D. in U.S. history. He has held various positions, including
teacher, archivist, and full-time staffer at Vietnam Veterans of America.
For years, he has considered writing a book about VVAW. His involvement in VVAW "may be the proudest thing I've ever done. I'm not
ashamed of what I did in Vietnam anymore. I have been. But . . . I was
part of an organization that I think was central to ending the war. . . . We
did many important things, both to save lives and to restore America to
being America."[89] Idealism motivated the VVAW Arkansas coordinator
Don Donner to attend law school. He came "to the conclusion that if I
was going to continue to struggle with those in power, a law degree would
be useful." Cataclysmic events of recent years, such as the Cambodian
bloodbath under the Khmer Rouge in the late 1970s, the Iran-Iraq war of
the 1980s, and the Rwandan civil war in the 1990s, have tested his faith.
"During my days in the antiwar movement, I truly believed in the common humanity of man. I no longer do, and I deeply regret the loss of my
innocence." Though more pessimistic now than in his youth, Donner has
not relinquished his role as community activist in his hometown of
Fayetteville, Arkansas.[90]

While a large segment of VVAWers have come to terms with their service in Vietnam, the sectarian splits of the past still pit constituencies
against one another. The factions have so far resisted any sort of reconciliation. In 1978, Joe Urgo led the offshoot group Vietnam Veterans
Against the War—Anti-Imperialist (VVAW AI). He still feels such deep
hostility toward Barry Romo and the other individuals who became national officers in the mid-1970s that he has severed contact with them.

The acrimony has proved mutual. Both sides regarded themselves as the true heirs of VVAW's legacy. Throughout the 1990s, the national office continued to issue declarations condemning VVAW AI. "VVAW AI is actually the creation of an obscure, ultra-left sect called the Revolutionary Communist Party and is designed to pimp off of VVAW's history of struggle and continued activism," warned the spring 1991 *Veteran*.[91]

Other VVAWers from all parts of America have cast aside their differences to attend regular reunions. Every five years since 1987, members past and present have assembled to commemorate the founding of their organization. The 1992 reunion was particularly successful. Hundreds of veterans gathered in New York City on the last weekend in May. Mayor David Dinkins welcomed the participants with a lengthy letter of support. The event brought together a host of VVAW elders, including Jan Barry, Ed Damato, Joe Bangert, Jack McCloskey, W. D. Ehrhart, Barry Romo, and Pete Mahoney. Conspicuously absent were such key leaders as Mike Oliver, Al Hubbard, and Senator John Kerry, although Kerry's sister, Peggy, attended. At a rally in New York's Battery Park, the antiwar luminaries Daniel Berrigan and David Dellinger praised the veterans. "VVAW has always been at the cutting edge of the peace and justice movement!" Dellinger declared.[92] The gathering was often emotional, as veterans recounted the time they spent in Vietnam and in the streets of America. The San Francisco VVAWer Jack McCloskey received applause when he announced, "VVAW saved my life!"[93]

In the mid-1990s, VVAW still functioned as an organization, largely out of Barry Romo's Chicago apartment, with a support staff of several activists in the Midwest. In recent years, AIDS and Vietnam-related ailments have claimed some of VVAW's most committed activists. The New Jersey VVAWer Clarence Fitch's bout with AIDS came to an end in May 1990. A relative newcomer to VVAW, Fitch joined in 1978 and remained one of the organization's most committed activists in the 1980s, traveling to Nicaragua with a VVAW delegation and initiating a program that sent veterans to high school classes to talk about the Vietnam War.[94] Two other key VVAW figures, Jack McCloskey and Sheldon Ramsdell, died in 1996. McCloskey, a resident of San Francisco, served as VVAW's Pacific coordinator at the time of his death. He had suffered from numerous physical problems for several years. Ramsdell, a founding member of VVAW who was appointed "honorary vice president" in 1992, succumbed to AIDS shortly after McCloskey died.[95] Members have tried not allow the losses to deter them. Once a year, sometimes more frequently if finances allow,

VVAWers in Chicago conduct the "Homeless Vets Stand Down," where they provide counseling, meals, and various supplies to homeless veterans. Romo travels around the country and runs into ex-members, many of whom are eager to discuss "the old days." The national office regularly receives inquiries from early joiners, usually expressing astonishment that VVAW still exists. "We do have a culture that binds us together," Romo explained.[96]

Today, healing has become a high priority for the men and women who joined VVAW in the 1960s and 1970s. In recent years, this commitment has manifested itself in various forms. Return trips to Vietnam have become commonplace. A New York VVAWer, Dave Cline, brought supplies to Vietnam in December 1988 as part of a VVAW delegation, his first time back since he was medivaced out in 1967. The scars of war were still evident. "You come in for the landing, you see bomb craters full of water, and as the plane taxis you see all these old American planes off on the side rotting," he recalled.[97] John Lindquist, VVAW's Midwest coordinator, journeyed to Vietnam in December 1991 with his companion, the VVAW organizer Annie Bailey. He visited the site where his base once stood and delivered petitions to Foreign Minister Le Bang calling for normalized relations between Vietnam and the United States. En route to his old base, Lindquist met Huynh Dac Huong, the general who had commanded the artillery charge that shelled the bunker where he was stationed. "We knew you were a good man, so we missed," General Huong told Lindquist.[98] Even after the United States and Vietnam resumed diplomatic relations, VVAW delegations continued to visit Vietnam, thus fulfilling the promise of the medal thrower at Dewey Canyon III who vowed to rebuild Vietnam after the war.

Activism continues to play an important role for numerous VVAWers. Antiwar veterans have been involved with such groups as Swords to Plowshares in San Francisco; the National Veterans Legal Services Project in Washington, D.C.; Project Hearts and Minds in Monterey, California; Veterans for Peace, headquartered in Portland, Maine; the Midwest Committee for Military Counseling in Chicago; and the U.S.-Indochina Reconciliation Project in New York City. In 1982, the veteran Brian Wilson founded the Veterans Education Project (VEP), which sent veterans into high schools to talk about the Vietnam War. "Since I returned from Vietnam, nothing has given me the same sense of satisfaction, the same sense of purpose, or the same comfort of turning a terrible experience to a good purpose, as has my speaking to scores of high school classes in

Western Massachusetts," recalled the VVAWer Stephen Sossaman, who served with the 9th Infantry Division in Vietnam.[99]

For many veterans, the stark black granite walls of the Vietnam Veterans Memorial have come to symbolize the healing process. In February 1996, four veterans, all members of VVAW, all buddies since the early seventies, piled into a rented GMC van and drove across America. Their mission: to visit the Vietnam Veterans Memorial. One of the passengers, Mike Damron, a forty-nine-year-old former Marine tank commander and VVAW organizer from Arkansas, was dying of liver cancer. Reduced to a skeletal one hundred pounds, his last wish was to visit "the wall." The driver, John Kniffin, also had served as a tank commander in Vietnam and was one of the Gainesville Eight defendants. The four men endured the snowy highways of the hinterland with high spirits, vivid memories, and plenty of Simon and Garfunkel. When they reached the monument, arctic winds whistled through Washington, D.C. A shivering and frail Damron asked his three friends to leave him alone for fifteen minutes. He sat facing the reflective wall, reading the names in silence, dying. Back in the van, Damron whispered, "Fellas, I'm fading fast. I don't know how much time I have left. Let's all go home." The following week, he passed away at his home in Fayetteville. "He was actually killed in Vietnam back in 1966," declared one of his traveling companions.[100]

9

Reflections

The term "the sixties" summons flashbacks of Kent State, the Vietnam War, the rock festival at Woodstock, and a deeply divided America. The rise of VVAW in the late sixties and early seventies had a profound impact on the antiwar movement in the United States, yet the breadth of its influence remains largely neglected. VVAW transformed the movement by placing Vietnam veterans in the forefront of the nationwide struggle to end the Vietnam War. VVAW was simultaneously unique *and* a product of the times. The social and political trends of the era shaped the organization in varied and complex ways. Conditions were fertile for VVAW's blossoming, yet nothing like it had existed before. Since the American Revolution, there have always been small yet robust populations of politicized veterans. Continental Army soldiers joined Shays's Rebellion in the late 1780s. Civil War combatants held leadership positions in the Knights of Labor. World War I "doughboys" joined the Industrial Workers of the World and later the Communist Party. Spanish Civil War partisans maintained the Lincoln Brigade on American soil into the 1990s. World War II G.I.s later agitated against atomic weapons and the Vietnam War.

But none of these veterans fashioned an organization, based on their shared status as veterans, to collectively articulate grievances. The veterans organizations that did exist—namely, Veterans of Foreign Wars and the American Legion—offered little in the way of inspiration and were looked upon with contempt and suspicion by even moderate antiwar Vietnam veterans. VVAW leaders often lamented that they had no models or elder advisers to offer suggestions or provide direction. In contrast with Students for a Democratic Society (SDS), whose roots could be traced to the Student League for Industrial Democracy, VVAW had no real historic antecedents. The relatively small Veterans for Peace, defunct by 1970, failed set an example. In fact, Veterans for Peace, dominated by World War II and Korean War veterans, prompted Vietnam veterans in the New York City area to create an organization more responsive to the needs of soldiers who had served in Vietnam.

Nor did VVAW members profit initially from the large body of New Left and humanistic literature that influenced so many radicals. Intellectuals such as C. Wright Mills, Erich Fromm, and Herbert Marcuse failed to touch the veterans. Likewise, the poetry of Wilfred Owen and the writings of Mohandas Gandhi attracted few to the pacifist camp. The Civil Rights Movement, which converted countless students to the New Left, had a negligible influence on future VVAWers in the early 1960s. For most veterans, participation in the Vietnam War was the main factor that raised their political consciousness. There was nothing abstract or theoretical about the war in Southeast Asia to VVAW joiners. Close to two-thirds of the men surveyed at Dewey Canyon III said they had begun "to see a drastic change" in their views about U.S. involvement in Vietnam while serving in Vietnam.[1] Their direct involvement with "the atrocity that was" the Vietnam War (as one ex-G.I. dubbed it) endowed VVAWers with a legitimacy in the court of public opinion that few other antiwar activists possessed.[2] An unwritten, unspoken compact of trust existed between the veterans and a substantial portion of the millions of Americans who watched televised segments of the medal-throwing ceremony during Dewey Canyon III. The revelation that VVAW Executive Secretary Al Hubbard had lied about his rank and status in Vietnam was so potentially harmful to VVAW precisely because Hubbard's actions betrayed that trust. Yet his dishonesty caused minimal damage because the tide of popular support so strongly favored VVAW. That only 1,200 men—an infinitesimal percentage of Vietnam veterans—participated in Dewey Canyon III was irrelevant. To much of the country, the protest signified that Vietnam veterans were now among the growing and increasingly mainstream movement opposed to the war in Vietnam.

VVAWers were latecomers to the antiwar movement. Even as the war wound down, the organization enjoyed steady growth and widespread esteem. Part of VVAW's appeal was its large working-class membership. The memorable opening sentence of SDS's famed Port Huron Statement—"We are people of this generation, bred at least in modest comfort, housed now in universities, looking uncomfortably to the world we inherit"—was not applicable to VVAW.[3] Further studies of rank-and-file VVAW members will reveal that the antiwar movement, heretofore treated as a middle-class phenomenon, had a much broader constituency than has been previously assumed by "sixties" scholars. Half the veterans surveyed at Dewey Canyon III were raised in blue-collar households. At a Boston VVAW protest in October 1971, slightly fewer—43 percent—cited "labor" as the profession of their fathers. Almost 37 percent of Dewey Canyon III participants and nearly 39 percent at the Boston action listed their status as "unemployed."[4] The gritty veterans of VVAW represented a sharp contrast to the typically more affluent SDS radicals whose "comfort was penetrated by events too troubling to dismiss."[5]

The American reformer Henry Demarest Lloyd could have been describing VVAW when he referred to nineteenth-century populists as "a fortuitous collection of the dissatisfied."[6] VVAW served as a united front, bringing together a membership that embodied a broad segment of the political spectrum, from libertarian to Marxist. A myriad of motives prompted twenty-five thousand to thirty thousand people to join. VVAW chapters represented all things to all members: a vanguard group for Maoists; a campaign headquarters for Democrats; a vehicle for activists to plan large-scale demonstrations; a meeting place for rap groups; an information center for war crimes hearings; a gathering spot for poets; a rehabilitation home for drug addicts. In VVAW, veterans found an unconditional acceptance that had eluded them in other parts of the antiwar movement. "Going to Dewey Canyon III was the first time I ever felt comfortable in any sizable group of people. To this day, I hate to go into a room that's full of people," recalled the Kansas City VVAWer John Upton.[7]

The work of regional coordinators like Upton resulted in the expansion of VVAW beyond America's major metropolitan areas. Indeed, VVAW is one of the few examples of a small-scale organization that mushroomed into a mass movement. After 1970, VVAW served as the sole organizational option for antiwar Vietnam veterans. The thriving GI movement, which provided a steady supply of new members for VVAW, never produced one mass organization. David Cortright, author of *Soldiers in Revolt*, the earliest and the most influential book on dissent in the military during the Vietnam War, listed numerous small groups—many short-lived—that emerged as part of the G.I. movement: the G.I.-Civilian Alliance for Peace; G.I.s United Against the War in Vietnam; the American Servicemen's Union; the United States Servicemen's Fund; G.I.s for Peace; the Movement for a Democratic Military; the United Soldiers Union; the G.I. Coordinating Committee; the Concerned Officers Movement.[8] No consensus group emerged to offer cohesion or direction for the hundreds of thousands of dissident soldiers. For veterans, on the other hand, the choice was clear. VVAW was the only organized body of veterans that consistently opposed the Vietnam War. There are few examples of antiwar veterans collectively participating in effective acts of political resistance outside VVAW in the early 1970s.

Considering the anarchistic tendencies of most members, VVAW's very existence was a remarkable feat. The antiauthoritarian sentiments of most joiners proved a blessing and a curse. Membership restrictions, widespread suspicions, and petty rivalries averted takeovers by radical sects and moderate Democrats. There were always efforts by leftist groups such as the Progressive Labor Party and the Socialist Workers Party to control VVAW chapters. Similarly, Democratic doves courted VVAWers during Dewey Canyon III and the 1972 Democratic National Convention. Nevertheless, partisan attempts to expropriate VVAW consistently failed until the formation of the Winter Soldier Organization. The absence of membership qualifications and the ideological openness of VVAW/WSO left it vulnerable to takeovers by determined minorities. After 1974, ultra-Left factions enjoyed increasing authority and influence. Yet even the Revolutionary Communist Party cadres who had ascended to power by the mid-seventies were never able to tame the unruly elements in VVAW/WSO.

The politics of the era fashioned VVAW in ways that few activists comprehended at the time. The ideological evolution of VVAW paralleled that of other leftist groups. The organization followed the same course that one historian described as applying to SDS: "The three Rs for SDS began with reform, led to resistance, and have . . . ended at revolution."[9] Early VVAWers wore suits and ties, kept their hair short, debated on radio and television, and campaigned for dovish Democrats. They wanted nothing more than to end the war and bring Americans home. Their understanding of events in Southeast Asia was often limited to their experiences in Vietnam. These VVAWers distanced themselves from "irresponsible" militants in the antiwar movement, who either ignored or reviled the veterans. Donald Duncan, the ex-Green Beret who became an editor for the leftist magazine *Ramparts*, echoed the sentiments of most antiwar veterans in the late 1960s when he wrote: "In the long run, I don't think Vietnam will be better off under Ho's brand of communism. But it's not for me or my government to decide. That decision is for the Vietnamese."[10]

The thousands of VVAWers who entered the organization between the invasion of Cambodia in May 1970 and Dewey Canyon III a year later altered the style and tactics of their predecessors but retained a faith in American justice and institutions. This middle generation was more confrontational and spontaneous. Fatigues replaced formal attire, and the theater of action shifted into the streets. Petition drives in VA hospitals gave them their first taste of multi-issue politics. These veterans were confident that under the right circumstances, they would succeed in capturing the attention of Americans. That much of the public ignored the Winter Soldier Investigation in early 1971 genuinely shocked VVAWers; the failure of those war crimes hearings drove the veterans to mobilize for Dewey Canyon III. A dramatic event, held in Washington, D.C., would awaken complacent Americans and stimulate opposition to the war, VVAW coordinators reasoned. Their logic worked. The national spotlight fell on VVAW for one week in April 1971. The antiwar movement lionized the protesters. True believers felt vindicated.

A third wave of veterans, enjoying greater prestige by 1972, adopted a more radical perspective on the war and embraced the gospel of decentralization. The eclecticism of VVAW's early years gave way to consistent political theories. Deeper analyses of Asian and American history led to a more comprehensive understanding of the interplay among racism, sexism, class, and war. Like much of the New Left, the antiwar veterans used "imperialism"—a word applied chiefly to European countries before World War II—to describe American involvement in Vietnam. "We are opposed to the militarism and imperialism of those who govern in our name and we are appalled by their use of lies and deceit to mislead the public," editorialized the March 1973 issue of *Free Fire*, the Vermont VVAW chapter's newsletter.[11] The war in Southeast Asia was no longer regarded as an aberration but was seen as an unavoidable outcome of modern capitalism. Increasingly, it was felt that the vague humanitarian protest that had characterized VVAW's birth and ascent had failed to address the complexities of contemporary American society. A growing segment of antiwar veterans turned to Lenin and Mao for answers. Naturally, contradictions arose. VVAW officers shunned elitism and started the Winter Soldier Organization to open the ranks to nonveterans, but they simultaneously adopted a sort of veterans' nationalism. Veterans were always VVAW's number one priority. Activists pledged to provide services that the ailing VA system lacked. To sustain VVAW as a viable alternative to the American Legion after the Vietnam War, the national office emphasized the need to localize actions and strengthen regional chapters.

Ultimately, the cadres who sought to transform VVAW into a multi-issue organization failed at the task. As a collective body of veterans whose *raison d'être* was ending the Vietnam War, VVAW was highly successful. To continue existing after the war, however, VVAW needed to transform itself from a single-issue group to a mass movement with an array of grievances and demands. Though attempted, this transition was never completed. National coordinators failed to rally members around the objectives that dealt with matters other than ending the war in Vietnam. Even the name Vietnam Veterans Against the War was constraining. It rendered the group's single-issue status permanent. Moreover, decentralization left scores of chapters adrift. Few activists questioned the conventional wisdom of reducing the national office's authority and empowering local chapters. If anything, excessive centralization has been cited as a source of contention. In his cursory study of VVAW, John Helmer claimed that a "middle-class group, which holds leadership positions and publishes the chapter newsletters, has favored a national-level strategy," a policy that "sacrificed whatever possibility may initially have existed for a much larger and more representative organization along the lines of the . . . VFW or Legion." By exercising such thorough control, executive committee members were "able to contain the threat of local chapters splitting off on doctrinal or tactical grounds."[12]

A closer study of VVAW reveals that national officers were not as meddlesome as Helmer suggests. Regional coordinators and area VVAW organizers always enjoyed a tremendous amount of latitude. Leaders steered clear of micromanagement, perhaps to appease a recalcitrant rank and file. Before Dewey Canyon III, the New York headquarters distributed a manual titled "Guidelines for Organizing and Operating Chapters," which stated: "The actual operating of a local chapter of VVAW can and should . . . be as autonomous and diverse as possible. If an individual or group wishes to organize a chapter of VVAW, he need only advise the national office that they intend to do so."[13] As late as October 1972, the national steering committee conceded that there was "inadequate communication between individual members, chapters, regional and national levels concerning VVAW activities, structure, and policies."[14] Excessive decentralization led to a lack of cohesion at a time when VVAW could have developed into a feasible, multi-issue advocacy group, as Vietnam Veterans of America would later become. Still, it is safe to say that most VVAWers would have gladly sacrificed their organization for an end to the war. As former Army Information Specialist Alex Prim explained: "A lot of people who are in VVAW don't like to be in it. They would rather forget about Vietnam. Forget the war and spend more time with girls— rather than other veterans. But they feel they have to do this VVAW thing. . . . There's a war going on where our friends died. We understand what that means."[15]

Detractors have always cited numbers when criticizing VVAW. At the pinnacle of VVAW's success in 1972, membership rolls listed almost twenty-five thousand card carriers, or fewer than 1 percent of all eligible Vietnam era veterans. During the Winter Soldier hearings, military officials called into question VVAW's legitimacy by pointing out the relatively small number of testifiers in relation to the number of Americans in Vietnam. "These people tell you stories, but you're lucky if you can get two in eighty to sign a statement with actual dates, names, and facts," asserted an army colonel.[16] Two and a half months later, as veterans erected their encampment for Dewey Canyon III, VFW National Commander Herbert F. Rainwater fumed: "I can think of no time when I was so appalled as I was when nightly for a period of over one week every time I turned on the television set some newscaster, some politician or some private citizen was declaring that this group [Vietnam Veterans Against the War], less than a thousand strong, was representing the will of the average Vietnam veteran."[17] Colonel Harry G. Summers, a historian and the editor of *Vietnam* magazine, offered the most conservative appraisal when he estimated that VVAW, "which admitted college students and professors as well as veterans, peaked at about seven thousand members."[18] By emphasizing the low percentage of Vietnam veterans who paid dues to VVAW, opponents have sought to dismiss the significance and impact of the organization. To be sure, antiwar veterans were difficult to mobilize. Rallying his comrades was a task that left the national coordinator Pete Zastrow exhausted and frustrated. "Twenty-five thousand [members] is what the computer listing showed, but I'm not sure exactly what that meant. You could never get twenty-five thousand people out to the same thing. . . . I have a feeling that many of them probably did not much more than sign up for a membership card and put their name on paper."[19]

But numbers never tell the whole story. VVAW's influence was more far-reaching than its rolls indicate. If the antiwar movement triggered the disintegration of the Cold War consensus, then VVAW represented that breakdown at its most fundamental level. The veterans had served their country, many as combatants. "The warrior," observed the psychiatrist and rap group founder Robert Jay Lifton, "has been celebrated by virtually all known cultures for his individual courage, and for the collective glory he makes possible."[20] Americans were no exception. Presidents and the public have long held veterans in high esteem, at least in theory. The very existence of VVAW, like the G.I. movement that provided ample recruits, revealed that opposition to the war had extended to sectors where one would least expect to find it. The history of VVAW illuminates the collapse of morale in all branches of the armed forces in Vietnam after 1968. So acute was the crisis in the military that in his June 1971 essay in the *Armed Forces Journal*, retired Marine Corps Colonel Robert D. Heinl Jr. asserted, "By several orders of magnitude, the Army seems to be in the worst trouble. But the Navy has serious and unprecedented problems, while the Air Force . . . is itself facing disquieting difficulties."[21] All varieties of resistance, from sabotage to open mutiny, were widespread in the military by 1971. The deterioration of the armed forces benefited VVAW, which absorbed thousands of radicalized soldiers.

The predominantly young, white males who sought refuge in VVAW found a vibrant network of kindred spirits. VVAW offered shelter from jingoistic veterans groups, as well as from antiwar militants who did not fully understand what it meant to fight in Vietnam and lose buddies. Unlike earlier generations of veterans, VVAWers spoke openly about what they had been through in war and what it had done to them. They hoped that talking would enable them to find meaning in the most definitive period of their lives. Without knowing it at the time, the young veterans pioneered new forms of expression and rehabilitation. The rap groups and drug treatment sessions initiated by VVAW members would strongly influence similar services later offered by the Veterans Administration. In 1979, Congress allocated $12 million to the VA to open ninety new Vet Centers. Four years later, 135 such facilities existed. The Vet Center leaders (at least 10 percent of whom were affiliated at one time with VVAW, the remainder largely sharing VVAW's antiwar sentiments) have widely acknowledged that their counseling programs were based on techniques started by VVAW.[22] Robert Jay Lifton recalled: "When the Veterans Administration organized their outreach program, I was told that it was really based on our rap group model. And [VA counseling] of course reached hundreds of thousands, maybe millions, of veterans."[23]

Participation in rap groups was but one way of communicating. Some members discovered more creative methods of conveying the experience of war. A veterans' renaissance, centered around VVAW, emerged in the early 1970s. At the forefront of VVAW's cultural heyday were such poets as W. D. Ehrhart, Basil Paquet, Larry Rottman, Jan Barry, and Bruce Weigl and writers such as Ron Kovic and Larry Heinemann. Some of the most highly acclaimed literature about the Vietnam War has been written by VVAW members. *Winning Hearts and Minds*, the celebrated 1972 volume of poetry compiled by VVAWers, received much critical praise, as did *Free Fire Zone*, an anthology of short stories that appeared the following year. Some of the soldier-poets have become widely read and respected writers. The historian Bruce Franklin has written of W. D. Ehrhart: "Some consider him the preeminent figure in this [Vietnam War] literature—treasured for his nonfiction, enormously influential as the foremost anthologist of Vietnam War poetry, and himself an unsurpassed poet."[24]

Poetry, guerrilla theater, mock search-and-destroy missions, war crimes hearings, medal-throwing ceremonies, marches, rehabilitation programs—these were the weapons in VVAW's arsenal. More than any other individual or group, VVAW members succeeded at bringing the Vietnam War and its effects home to millions of Americans. In doing so, they won the reverence of friends and the animosity of opponents. Enemies in high places initially sought to debunk VVAW by claiming that members had falsified their credentials. Mark Lane's downfall came after he failed to perform background checks on the men he interviewed for *Conversations with Americans*, and some of his sources were later exposed as liars. Officials reasoned that the same tactic would have a devastating impact on VVAW. With the exception of Al Hubbard's dishonesty, however, there was no evidence of widespread fabrication among the members of VVAW. Joiners, by and large, were who they said they were. Officials opposed to VVAW considered other options. Violent methods were usually ruled out. In an effort to win the hearts and minds of the public, the presidential aide Charles Colson launched a series of front groups, such as Vietnam Veterans for a Just Peace. The results were disappointing. A Concerned Veterans for Nixon breakfast in July 1972 mustered only fifty guests.[25] Elsewhere, agents provocateurs plied their trade, often with mixed results. By 1972, government agencies looked increasingly to the South, VVAW's most vulnerable region. The summer of 1972 saw informants controlling Florida, Georgia, Alabama, Arkansas, Oklahoma, Louisiana, and Mississippi. Bill Lemmer and other undercover infiltrators tried, and failed, to encourage VVAWers to participate in violent acts at the Republican National Convention. Nevertheless, the Gainesville Eight conspiracy trial destabilized VVAW by absorbing the organization's money, resources, and labor at a critical time.

The Gainesville Eight trial and the Senate Watergate hearings highlighted the Nixon administration's obsession with the antiwar veterans. Repeated references to VVAW by the Watergate burglars during Senator Sam Ervin's televised Watergate hearings indicate that the organization was a unwitting catalyst for the break-in; the burglars had entered the Democratic National Committee offices searching for information to link Senator George McGovern to the antiwar movement. A year after the incident, the White House "plumber" and CREEP chieftan James McCord testified about VVAW offices in the Democratic National Headquarters, plans by Democrats to sponsor a national VVAW speaking tour, and ties linking the "violence-oriented" VVAW, the McGovern campaign, and the Democratic National Committee.[26] Subsequent Watergate accounts focused on extent of the Nixon administration's knowledge of CREEP activities and the sequence of events during and after the burglary. Seldom have the Watergate histories asked *why* the break-ins occurred; therefore, VVAW's role in the scandal has been largely ignored. An exhaustive treatment of the subject would be remiss without considering the Nixon administration's preoccupation with VVAW.

For the same reasons they alarmed authorities, VVAWers energized liberals and radicals alike. The *Washington Post* columnist William Raspberry explained VVAW's appeal when he commended the men who discarded their medals during Dewey Canyon III. These protesters were a breed apart, Raspberry opined, because they "weren't trying to stop the war in order to forestall being sent to Vietnam. They've been and to that degree they're safe. They were saying stop the war—not because I don't want to get hurt but because the war is tragic and senseless and wrong."[27] The men and women who joined VVAW and committed their lives to the organization idealistically regarded themselves as present-day "winter soldiers," in the tradition of the American revolutionaries at Valley Forge "who stayed after they had served their time."[28] Their contributions sparked a social movement that had virtually no precedent.

VVAWers kept the antiwar movement alive at a time when so many Americans had surrendered to cynicism and complacency. The politics of identity heightened members' awareness and forged a struggle for veterans' rights. And yet even the most radical members conformed to Cornell

University Professor Theodore Lowi's characterization of sixties activists as "extreme reformists": "They used radical action to gain attention, but their demands and hopes were for the present society to live by its own ideals."[29] The antiwar veterans overcame self-pity, avoided bitterness, and substituted passive withdrawal for active confrontation. In doing so, they contributed significantly to ending the war in Vietnam.

Notes

NOTES TO CHAPTER 1

1. SAC, FBI, New York (100-160644), Memorandum to Director, FBI, September 20, 1967, 1. Author's FOIA files.

2. SAC, FBI, New York (100-160644), Report on Vietnam Veterans Against the War, October 20, 1967, 1. Author's FOIA files.

3. SAC, FBI, New York (100-160644), Memorandum to Director, FBI, September 20, 1967, 1. Author's FOIA files.

4. FBI, New York, "Vietnam Veterans Against the War: Report disseminated to the local intelligence agencies in accordance with Bureau Policy," section D. Author's FOIA files.

5. FBI files obtained by the author through the Freedom of Information Act reveal constant surveillance of VVAW by the FBI through May 1968, just before VVAW disbanded. The FBI would reopen the investigation when VVAW reemerged toward the end of 1969. Author's FOIA files.

6. The best descriptions of the Spring Mobilization to End the War in Vietnam come from Tom Wells's *The War Within* (Berkeley: University of California Press, 1994), 132–135; Charles DeBenedetti and Charles Chatfield's *An American Ordeal: The Antiwar Movement of the Vietnam Era* (Syracuse: Syracuse University Press, 1990), 175–176; and Fred Halstead's *Out Now! A Participant's Account of the American Movement Against the Vietnam War* (New York: Monad Press), 280–286. Figures for the turnout at the demonstration come from several sources. Tom Wells writes that "more than 300,000" turned out; the *New York Times* (April 16, 1967) estimate was 100,000, while the April 16 issue of the *Boston Globe* carried the headline "400,000 March in New York Against War."

7. Wells, *War Within*, 62, 112.

8. DeBenedetti and Chatfield, *An American Ordeal*, 175–176.

9. *Veterans Stars and Stripes for Peace*, September 1967.

10. Wells, *War Within*, 56–57, 144.

11. Richard Moser, "From Deference to Defiance: America, the Citizen-Soldier and the Vietnam era," Ph.D. diss., Rutgers University (1992), 59. DeBenedetti and Chatfield, *An American Ordeal*, 157.

12. Wells, *War Within*, 99.

13. Ibid., 99–100. Halstead, *Out Now!*, 175.

14. Donald Duncan, "The Whole Thing Was a Lie!" *Ramparts*, February 1966, 13–24. The following year saw the publication of Duncan's book *The New Legions* (New York: Random House), a thorough account of his service in Vietnam, as well as his subsequent opposition to the war. It was one of the earliest books about the Vietnam War experience.

15. Duncan, "Whole Thing," 23–24. Vincent Noble, "Political Opposition in the Age of Mass Media: GIs and Veterans Against the War in Vietnam," Ph.D. diss., University of California Irvine (1987), 231.

16. VVAW, *25 Years Fighting for Veterans Peace and Justice* (Chicago: VVAW, 1992), 7.

17. Duncan, "Whole Thing," 24.

18. Moser, "Deference to Defiance," 60.

19. Nancy Zaroulis and Gerald Sullivan, *Who Spoke Up? American Protest Against the War in Vietnam, 1963–1975* (Garden City, N.Y.: Doubleday, 1984), 80. Moser, "Deference to Defiance," 60. Noble, "Political Opposition," 235. Most literature that refers to the Veterans for Peace in Vietnam acknowledges that the majority of members were World War II and Korean War veterans. Donald Mosby (a.k.a. McDonald Moore), editor of the organization's newspaper, *Veterans Stars and Stripes for Peace*, agrees that the majority members were veterans of those two wars. Unfortunately, Veterans for Peace kept poor records regarding its membership. Donald Mosby interview.

20. Mosby interview. Halstead, *Out Now!*, 137.

21. Wells, *War Within*, 133. *Veterans Stars and Stripes for Peace*, September 1967. Barry Romo interview.

22. Jan Barry interview. Wells, *War Within*, 140–141.

23. Barry interview.

24. Ibid.

25. Al Santoli, *Everything We Had: An Oral History of the Vietnam War by Thirty-three American Soldiers Who Fought It* (New York: Random House, 1981), 4–5. Barry interview.

26. Bell Gale Chevigny, "Vietnam: The Worst Years of Our Lives," *Village Voice*, 15 February 1968, 14.

27. Barry interview.

28. Santoli, *Everything We Had*, 6–7. Barry interview.

29. Santoli, *Everything We Had*, 10. Chevigny, "Worst Years," 14.

30. Ibid.

31. Barry interview.

32. Chevigny, "Worst Years," 24.

33. Santoli, *Everything We Had*, 7–9.

34. Barry interview.

35. Santoli, *Everything We Had*, 7–9. Barry interview.

36. Barry interview.

37. Ibid.

38. Jan Barry, "Vietnam Veterans' Voice," unpublished, circa October 1967, VVAW Papers, Box 11, SHSW, Madison.

39. Barry interview. "By-Laws of the Vietnam Veterans Against the War," unpublished, circa 1967, VVAW Papers, Box 1 SHSW, Madison.

40. Carl Rogers interview.

41. Rogers interview. Bill Adler, ed., *Letters from Vietnam* (New York: E. P. Dutton, 1967), 170.

42. The information on Rogers is culled from a pamphlet titled "Viet-Nam Veteran Speaks Out: Carl Rogers," which appeared in early 1968. VVAW Papers, Box 11 SHSW, Madison.

43. Ibid.

44. Sheldon Ramsdell interview.

45. Wells, *War Within*, 150, 162.

46. "Marchers Confront War Makers at the Pentagon," *Veterans Stars and Stripes for Peace*, November/December 1967, 1.

47. Ramsdell interview. Barry interview. Todd Gitlin, *The Sixties: Years of Hope, Days of Rage* (New York: Bantam Books, 1987), 233. Halstead, *Out Now!*, 314, 334–339. Wells, *War Within*, 195–199.

48. *New York Times*, November 19, 1967.

49. Barry interview.

50. Rogers interview.

51. FBI Agent D. J. Brennan, "Vietnam Veterans Against the War Internal Security Memorandum," to W. C. Sullivan, November 19, 1967. Author's FOIA files. According to the memorandum, Secretary McNamara's assistant, William C. Hunt, requested information "only on the organization and its coordinator" for the sake of expediency. But Hunt further advised FBI agents that "the Army is checking all names in the advertisement through records at Fort Holabird, Maryland."

52. FBI Agent D. J. Brennan, "Vietnam Veterans Against the War Internal Security Memorandum," to W. C. Sullivan, November 20, 1967. Author's FOIA files.

53. William C. Hunt, letter to J. Edgar Hoover, December 20, 1967. Author's FOIA files.

54. Ibid. J. Edgar Hoover, letter to William C. Hunt, December 26, 1967. Author's FOIA files.

55. "Viet Vets Organize," *Veterans Stars and Stripes for Peace*, September 1967, 2.

56. Ibid.

57. Bell Gale Chevigny, "A Farewell to Arms: 'Over There' Is Here," *Village Voice*, March 14, 1968, 22.

58. Barry interview.

59. Barry interview. "History of the Vietnam Veterans Against the War," n.d. (circa early 1972), issued by National Office, and "Viet-Nam Veterans Organize Against the War" (circa early 1968), Box 1, VVAW Papers, SHSW, Madison.

60. William Crandell, "They Moved the Town: Organizing Vietnam Veterans Against the War," in Melvin Small and William D. Hoover, eds., *Give Peace a Chance* (Syracuse, N.Y.: Syracuse University Press, 1992), 142.

61. William Crandell interview.

62. Chevigny, "A Farewell," 22, 56.

63. Ramsdell interview.

64. Chevigny, "A Farewell," 56.

65. Ibid.

66. Rogers interview.

67. Chevigny, "A Farewell," 56.

68. Murray Polner, *No Victory Parades: The Return of the Vietnam Veteran* (New York: Holt, Rinehart and Winston, 1971), 59.

69. Mike McKusker interview.

70. Barry interview.

71. VVAW, *25 Years*, 7.

72. Robert Armstrong, Eugene, Oregon, to Jan Barry, New York, 8 April 1968, Box 11, VVAW Papers, SHSW, Madison.

73. Polner, *No Victory*, 87.

74. For a good biographical sketch on Thich Nhat Hanh, see John Prados, *The Hidden History of the Vietnam War* (Chicago: Ivan R. Dee, 1995), 99–101. McKusker interview.

75. McKusker interview.

76. Ibid.

77. Halstead, *"Out Now!"*, 426.

78. *Vietnam GI*, July 1969.

79. Halstead, *Out Now!*, 428. *Vietnam GI*, July 1969.

80. Barry interview.

81. Gitlin, *The Sixties*, 295.

82. Rogers interview.

83. Eugene McCarthy, *The Year of the People* (Garden City, N.Y.: Doubleday), 1969, 69.

84. Polner, *No Victory*, 60.

85. Ibid.

86. McCarthy, *Year of the People*, 74.

87. The original "Vietnam Veterans for McCarthy" advertisement is contained in Box 16, VVAW Papers, SHSW, Madison.

88. With the exception of a few respondents who supported Robert Kennedy

and one Socialist Workers Party candidate, the questionnaires indicated unanimous support for McCarthy. See "Background Questionnaires," Box 11, VVAW Papers, SHSW, Madison.

89. Wilkinson and Kennedy questionnaires are contained in Box 11, VVAW Papers, SHSW, Madison.

90. For a useful discussion of the differences between Kennedy and McCarthy, see Terry H. Anderson, *The Movement and the Sixties* (Oxford: Oxford University Press, 1995), 204–206.

91. "Keep the Heat On," *Vietnam GI*, May 1968, 4.

92. Polner, *No Victory*, 87.

93. McKusker interview.

94. Zaroulis and Sullivan, *Who Spoke Up?*, 166.

95. Jan Barry, Carl Rogers, and Robert Bradley Kennedy, "Viet-Nam Veterans Proposal to the Continuations Committee of the Coalition for an Open Convention," June 1968, Box 13, VVAW Papers, SHSW, Madison.

96. McCarthy, *Year of the People*, 197. Rogers interview.

97. Rogers interview. McKusker interview.

98. Anderson, *The Movement*, 216–221.

99. Ibid. "A Viet-Nam Veteran Asks: Where Is the Democracy I Fought to Preserve?" 1968, Box 13, VVAW Papers, SHSW, Madison.

100. John A. Talbott, M.D., "Letter from Viet-Nam Veteran to the Delegates of the Democratic Convention," Box 16, VVAW Papers, SHSW, Madison.

101. McKusker interview.

102. Anderson, *The Movement*, 222.

103. McKusker interview.

104. The VVAW member, John Durant, is quoted in Polner, *No Victory*, 47.

105. Rogers interview.

106. Ramsdell interview.

107. Polner, *No Victory*, 47.

108. Barry interview.

109. *Vietnam GI*, July 1969.

110. VVAW, "Rough History of the VVAW," Box 1, VVAW Papers, SHSW, Madison.

111. Barry interview.

112. Rogers interview.

113. Halstead, *Out Now!*, 432–435.

114. "GIs, Vets Share Platform at SF Antiwar Rally," *Veterans Stars and Stripes for Peace*, October 1968, 1.

115. Mosby interview.

116. "GIs, vets share," *Veterans Stars and Stripes for Peace*, October 1968, 1.

117. "Jeff Sharlet Dies," *Vietnam GI*, July 1969.

NOTES TO CHAPTER 2

1. The caller's quote is from Barry interview.

2. For Moratorium events, see Wells, *War Within*, 371.

3. Rayford Henderson and Bruce Ford, "Background Questionnaire," Box 11, VVAW Papers, SHSW, Madison.

4. Lewis Delano, "Background Questionnaire," Box 11, VVAW Papers, SHSW, Madison. McKusker interview. Barry interview.

5. David Cortright, *Soldiers in Revolt: The American Military Today* (Garden City, N.Y.: Anchor Press/Doubleday, 1975), 53. Moser, 133. Halstead, 425.

6. Cortright, *Soldiers in Revolt*, 54. In the spring of 1971, Colonel Robert Heinl said that "some 144 underground newspapers [were] published or aimed at U.S. military bases." A March 1972 study by the Department of Defense estimated the total number at 245, while the historian David Cortright, who studied the G.I. movement, collected a comprehensive list identifying 259 such newspapers. See Cortright, *Soldiers in Revolt*, 55.

7. Ibid.

8. McKusker interview.

9. Peter Martinsen, "Background Questionnaire," Box 11, VVAW Papers, SHSW, Madison.

10. McKusker interview.

11. Madelyn Moore interview.

12. Vietnam Veterans Against the War, *The Winter Soldier Investigation: An Inquiry into American War Crimes* (Boston: Beacon Press, 1972), 152.

13. Scott Moore interview.

14. Ibid.

15. DeBenedetti and Chatfield, *An American Ordeal*, 265.

16. Barry interview.

17. Citizens Commission of Inquiry on U.S. War Crimes, "National Committee for a Citizens' Commission of Inquiry on U.S. War Crimes" brochure, circa January 1970, courtesy Michael Uhl.

18. Barry quote in Wells, *War Within*, 404.

19. John Duffet, ed., *Against the Crime of Silence: Proceedings of the Russell International War Crimes Tribunal* (New York: O'Hare Books, 1968), 9.

20. The three Vietnam veterans at the Russell Tribunal were Donald Duncan, David Tuck, and Peter Martinsen. Duncan, discussed at length in Chapter 1, later hosted VVAW's Winter Soldier Investigation in Detroit in January and February 1971. Martinsen was active for years in the Los Angeles chapter of VVAW. It is not known whether Tuck, an activist from Cleveland, was affiliated with VVAW.

21. Barry interview.

22. Ibid. Minutes from VVAW Meeting, January 24, 1970, Box 8, VVAW Papers, SHSW, Madison.

23. Joe Urgo interview.

24. Ibid.

25. Ibid. Urgo worked at the Atlantic City airport detachment when President Nixon and Henry Kissinger were considering dropping nuclear bombs on the Ho Chi Minh trail in the fall of 1969. The detachment was placed on twenty-four-hour alert, and the nuclear-loaded F–106s, on status DEFCON 2 (green-light readiness for attack), were positioned outside the hangars for takeoff. Urgo telephoned the Associated Press in New York to ask what was happening, yet the AP employee who took his call knew of no major crises. Urgo remembered: "In Seymour Hersh's book, *The Price of Power*, . . . he recounts this story and has a footnote with my name on it because I'm the only GI he found that could actually confirm that this thing really happened." Nixon and Kissinger scrapped what the president ominously dubbed "the November 1 ultimatum." Urgo interview. Also see: Seymour Hersh, *The Price of Power: Kissinger in the Nixon White House* (New York: Summit Books, 1983), 120, 126, 129.

26. Pat O'Haire, "R.A.W. Feelings," *New York Daily News*, August 28, 1970.

27. William Overend, "Who Is Al Hubbard?" *National Review*, June 1, 1971, 589, 607.

28. Madelyn Moore interview.

29. Al Hubbard, "A Viable VVAW." *First Casualty*, August, 1971.

30. Urgo interview. VVAW, "Rough History," 2.

31. McKusker interview.

32. O'Haire, "R.A.W. Feelings."

33. Urgo interview.

34. Madelyn Moore interview.

35. Urgo interview.

36. "From Vietnam to a VA Hospital: Assignment to Neglect," *Life*, May 28, 1970, 24–33.

37. Ibid.

38. Richard Nixon, "Rationale for the Invasion of Cambodia (April 30, 1970)," in Marvin E. Gettleman et al., eds., *Vietnam and America: A Documented History* (New York: Grove Press, 1995), 451–455.

39. Ibid., 441. Richard Nixon, *RN: The Memoirs of Richard Nixon* (New York: Grosset & Dunlap, 1978), 388.

40. Anderson, *The Movement*, 350.

41. VVAW, "Rough History," 2.

42. I. F. Stone, *The Killings at Kent State: How Murder Went Unpunished* (New York: Vintage Books, 1971), 34–36.

43. *Akron Beacon Journal*, May 24, 1970.

44. Tim Butz interview.

45. Ibid.

46. Urgo interview.

47. Ron Kovic, *Born on the Fourth of July* (New York: Simon & Schuster, 1976), 134–135.

48. W. D. Ehrhart, *Passing Time: Memoir of a Vietnam Veteran Against the War* (Jefferson, N.C.: McFarland), 88.

49. Richard E. Peterson and John A. Bilorusky, *May 1970: The Campus Aftermath of Cambodia and Kent State* (Berkeley: Carnegie Commission on Higher Education, 1970), 1–10. Anderson, *The Movement*, 350.

50. Crandell, "They Moved," 143. Crandell interview.

51. Robert Hanson interview. For membership figure, see VVAW, "Rough History," 2.

52. Hanson interview. Interestingly, Hanson's mother was the first African American female officer in the desegregated United States Navy. She was admitted March 8, 1945.

53. The Friedman quote is contained in Joan Morrison and Robert K. Morrison, eds., *From Camelot to Kent State: The Sixties Experience in the Words of Those Who Lived It* (New York: Times Books, 1987), 86–87. Anderson, *The Movement*, 351.

54. *New York Times*, May 9, 1970. Urgo interview.

55. Anderson, *The Movement*, 351.

56. Wells, *War Within*, 426.

57. Halstead, *Out Now!*, 544–545.

58. Senator Charles Goodell, telegram to the New York State Headquarters of American Veterans for Peace Coalition, May 19, 1970, Box 15, VVAW Papers, SHSW, Madison. For other accounts of the march, see: *Syracuse Herald-Journal*, May 20, 21, 1970. *Ithaca Journal*, May 21, 1970.

59. Jack Deacy, "The Veterans," *New York Daily News*, May 27, 1970.

60. Ibid.

61. Barry interview.

62. Jeremy Rifkin, Tod Ensign, and Louise Hellinger, "Letter to CCI Members," June 4, 1970, Rare and Manuscript Collections, Carl A. Kroch Library, Cornell University, Ithaca, New York. Courtesy Michael Uhl. James Simon Kunen, *Standard Operating Procedure* (N.Y.: Avon, 1971), 22.

63. McKusker interview.

64. Ibid. *New York Post*, August 1, 1970.

65. *Philadelphia Inquirer*, August 1, 1970.

66. Madelyn Moore interview.

67. O'Haire, "R.A.W Feelings."

68. Henry Lesnick, ed., *Guerrilla Street Theater* (New York: Avon Books, 1973), 11–25, 251.

69. Scott Moore, letter to Operation RAW participants, n.d. (circa August 1970), Box 15, VVAW Papers, SHSW, Madison.

70. Al Hubbard, Operation RAW Schedule of Events, September 1, 1970, Box

15, VVAW Papers, SHSW, Madison. Scott Moore and Al Hubbard, Operation RAW Report, Box 15, VVAW Papers, SHSW, Madison.

71. *Congressional Record*, April 23, 1971, S5551-S552.

72. James Carroll, "The Friendship that Ended the War," *New Yorker*, October 21 & 28, 1996, 146.

73. John Kerry, Boston Massachusetts, to the author, January 31, 1996.

74. 71. *Congressional Record*, April 23, 1971, S5551-S552.

75. *The New York Times*, April 23, 1971.

76. Urgo interview.

77. Memorandum from Philadelphia Federal Bureau of Investigation to the FBI, Washington, D.C., "Vietnam Veterans Against the War, Operation Raw, September 4–7, 1970," July 22, 1970, 1. Memorandum from SAC, Cincinatti, to Director, FBI, "Proposed Peace March from Morristown, New Jersey, to Valley Forge, Pennsylvania, September 4–7, Sponsored by Vietnam Veterans Against the War." July 24, 1970, 1–2. Author's FOIA files.

78. Memorandum from SAC, New York, to Director, FBI, "Proposed Peace March from Morristown, New Jersey, to Valley Forge, Pennsylvania, September 4–7, Sponsored by Vietnam Veterans Against the War," August 7, 1970, 2–3. Author's FOIA files.

79. Memorandum from SAC, New York, to Director, FBI, "Proposed Peace March from Morristown, New Jersey, to Valley Forge, Pennsylvania, September 4–7, Sponsored by Vietnam Veterans Against the War," September 1, 1970, 2. Author's FOIA files.

80. Memorandum from SAC, Cincinatti, to Director, FBI, "Proposed Peace March from Morristown, New Jersey, to Valley Forge, Pennsylvania, September 4–7, Sponsored by Vietnam Veterans Against the War." August 7, 1970, 2. Author's FOIA files.

81. Ibid.

82. Memorandum from SAC, New York, to Director, FBI, "Proposed Peace March from Morristown, New Jersey, to Valley Forge, Pennsylvania, September 4–7, Sponsored by Vietnam Veterans Against the War," September 1, 1970, 2. Author's FOIA files.

83. Hubbard, Operation RAW Schedule. Hubbard footage is contained in *Different Sons* (videocassette), directed by Jack Ofield, produced by Arthur Littman, Bowling Green Films, 1970.

84. Joel Greenberg interview. Ramsdell interview. Dave Braum, "Operation Raw Statement." Solicited from Al Hubbard, October 13, 1970. Box 15, VVAW Papers, SHSW, Madison.

85. Jerry Hutlin, "Operation Raw Statement." Solicited from Al Hubbard, October 13, 1970. Box 15, VVAW Papers, SHSW, Madison.

86. Greg Makota, "Operation Raw Statement." Solicited from Al Hubbard, October 13, 1970. Box 15, VVAW Papers, SHSW, Madison.

212 | Notes to Chapter 2

87. Joseph Bremman, "Operation Raw Statement." Solicited from Al Hubbard, October 13, 1970. Box 15, VVAW Papers, SHSW, Madison.

88. Don Saunders, "Operation Raw Statement." Solicited from Al Hubbard, October 13, 1970. Box 15, VVAW Papers, SHSW, Madison.

89. Crandell, "They Moved," 144. *New York Times*, September 5, 1970.

90. *New York Times*, September 5, 1970. Moore and Hubbard, Operation RAW Report. *Different Sons*. Crandell, "They Moved," 144.

91. Urgo interview. Scott Moore interview. Moore and Hubbard, Operation RAW Report.

92. Crandell interview.

93. VVAW flier, "A U.S. Infantry Company Just Came Through Here," is contained in Box 15, VVAW Papers, SHSW, Madison. Moore and Hubbard, Operation RAW Report.

94. Jeffrey Kirk, "Operation Raw Statement." Solicited from Al Hubbard, October 13, 1970. Box 15, VVAW Papers, SHSW, Madison.

95. *New York Times*, September 6, 1970.

96. Ibid.

97. The "motley crew" quote is from *Different Sons*.

98. Hanson interview.

99. Wells, *War Within*, 455.

100. "It doesn't feel like" and "hawk to dove" are in *Different Sons*.

101. Honking motorists are in *New York Times*, September 7, 1970.

102. Madelyn Moore interview. Also see: *New York Times*, September 4–8, 1970.

103. Hanson interview.

104. Barry interview. Wells, *War Within*, 455.

105. Mike McKusker provided the author with the details of the People's Army Jamboree protests that occurred in mid-August 1970.

106. "Many of these in the march today" is from *Different Sons*.

107. *New York Times*, September 8, 1970.

108. "I don't blame those fellows" is from *Different Sons*.

109. Urgo interview. *New York Times*, September 8, 1970. *Different Sons*.

110. Hubbard quotation is from *Different Sons*. The other descriptions are found in: Crandell, "They Moved," 144–145. "Operation RAW: Viet Vet March Stirs Thought," GI Press Service, September 7, 1970. *New York Times*, September 8, 1970. Urgo interview.

111. Manuel Dones, "Operation RAW Statement," solicited from Al Hubbard, October 13, 1970, Box 15, VVAW Papers, SHSW, Madison.

112. Urgo interview.

113. Ed Damato interview.

114. Barry interview.

NOTES TO CHAPTER 3

1. Scott Camil interview.
2. Camil interview. Scott Camil, "Undercover Agents' War on Vietnam Veterans," in Bud Scultz and Ruth Scultz, eds., *It Did Happen Here* (Berkeley: University of California Press, 1989), 320.
3. Camil, "Undercover Agents," 320.
4. Camil interview.
5. Ibid.
6. Ibid.
7. Ibid. Camil, "Undercover Agents," 321.
8. Tod Ensign, "Organizing Veterans Through War Crimes Documentation," in Viet Nam Generation, *Nobody Gets Off the Bus*, ed. Dan Duffy and Kalí Tal (Woodbridge, Conn.: Viet Nam Generation, 1994), 146.
9. Ibid, 145.
10. Ibid.
11. Ibid.
12. Tod Ensign interview.
13. Ibid.
14. Kunen, *Standard Operating Procedure*, 24. Ensign, "Organizing Veterans," 146. Ensign interview.
15. Michael Uhl, "War Crimes Chronology" (Draft), March 11, 1995, 3. Author's collection, courtesy of Michael Uhl.
16. Michael Foot and Isaac Kramnick, eds., *The Thomas Paine Reader* (New York: Penguin Books 1987), 116.
17. Michael Uhl, Walpole, Maine, to the author, March 31, 1995. *New York Times*, September 8, 1970.
18. Peter Collier, *The Fondas: A Hollywood Dynasty* (New York: G. P. Putnam's Sons, 1991), 192.
19. John Frook, "Nag, Nag, Nag! Jane Fonda has Become a Nonstop Activist," *Life*, April 23, 1971, 54. Barry interview.
20. Mark Lane interview.
21. Ensign, "Organizing Veterans," 146. Uhl, "War Crimes Chronology," 24. Michael Uhl, Walpole, Maine, to the author, March 31, 1995.
22. Butz interview.
23. Ensign interview.
24. Crandell, "They Moved," 147–148.
25. Ibid., 147.
26. William Crandell, "What Did America Learn from the Winter Soldier Investigation," in Viet Nam Generation, *Nobody Gets Off the Bus*, 143.
27. Michael Uhl, Walpole Maine, to the author, December 1, 1995.

28. Barry interview.

29. Frook, "Nag, Nag, Nag!," 52c.

30. Ed Damato, one-time VVAW president, first heard about the VVAW and Operation RAW during Fonda's appearance on the *Dick Cavett Show*. During another appearance, Fonda mentioned VVAW, which lured Robert Hanson to the cause (see Chapter 2).

31. Frook, "Nag, Nag, Nag!," 52c. Interestingly, Fonda incurred the hatred of prowar Americans more than a year before traveling to North Vietnam and posing alongside communist antiaircraft guns. Other antiwar entertainers, such as Peter Boyle, Donald Sutherland, and Harry Belafonte, failed to evoke such animosity.

32. Wesley Swearingen, *FBI Secrets: An Agent's Exposé* (Boston: South End Press, 1995), 127–129. Fonda quote is from *Newsweek*, November 16, 1970, 65.

33. Lane interview.

34. Ibid.

35. Ensign, "Organizing Veterans," 146.

36. Ibid.

37. Ibid.

38. Barry interview.

39. Michael Uhl, Walpole, Maine, to the author, February 22, 1996.

40. Ensign interview.

41. Ibid.

42. Kunen, *Standard Operating Procedure*, 25. When asked about the Citizens' Commission of Inquiry on U.S. War Crimes in Vietnam, Mark Lane said that he knew of the organization but paid little attention to it. Lane remarked: "I didn't follow what they [CCI] were doing. . . . I don't actually recall very much. I don't think it [the split] was really significant. I don't think it interfered with what VVAW was doing." Lane interview.

43. Ibid.

44. Wells, *The War Within*, 462.

45. Urgo interview. Barry offered a similar explanation in Tom Wells' *The War Within*, 461–462. However, a cursory glance at CCI and VVAW documents from the period undermines VVAW's explanation that VVAW and CCI fought over the location of the Winter Soldier Investigation. In fact, CCI organizers handled all the paperwork for the Winter Soldier Investigation facilities in Detroit and in Windsor, Canada. Jeremy Rifkin had some doubts about the site. "The problem Jeremy had was that they wanted to do it in Detroit, not in Washington," Ensign recalled. "He thought that was stupid. But he went along with it." Ensign interview.

46. Butz interview.

47. Barry interview.

48. Ibid.

49. Ibid.

50. Jan Barry, New York City, to the members of VVAW and CCI, December 6, 1970. Rare and Manuscript Collections, Carl A. Kroch Library, Cornell University, Ithaca, New York. Courtesy Michael Uhl.

51. Madelyn Moore interview.

52. Michael Uhl, Walpole Maine, to the author, February 22, 1996.

53. "The Winter Soldier Investigation" pamphlet, n.d. (circa December 1970), Box 16, VVAW Papers, SHSW, Madison. Butz interview. Lane interview. Hanson interview.

54. Ken Campbell interview.

55. Jon Floyd interview.

56. Rusty Sachs interview.

57. Camil interview.

58. Lane interview.

59. "Conversations with Americans," reviewed by Neil Sheehan, *New York Times Book Review*, December 27, 1970, 5.

60. Mark Lane, *Conversations with Americans* (New York: Simon & Schuster, 1970), 27.

61. Sheehan, review "Conversations with Americans," 5.

62. Sheehan offered evidence in the form of Pentagon and military records showing that a former infantryman, Michael Schneider, an ex-Marine, Terry Whitmore, and a navy medical corpsman, Garry Gianninoto, had lied to Lane about their experiences in Vietnam. Sheehan, "Conversations with Americans," 5, 19.

63. Lane interview.

64. Urgo interview.

65. Lane interview.

66. Lane reported that after he collected documents proving that all of his interviewees were who they said they were, his publisher apologized. "Simon & Schuster paid me a substantial sum of money to make up for the fact they never published the paperback, based upon false statements, which they admitted were false, and they paid me a sum of money, gave me my rights back to the paperback, and that was that. But since that time, for years, no major publisher has, based on Simon & Schuster's position, ever published a book of mine," he recalled. However, Lane's 1991 book, *Plausible Denial*, an account of the CIA's involvement in the Kennedy assassination, was published by a small press in New York City and appeared on the *New York Times*'s nonfiction best-seller list for three weeks. Lane interview.

67. Crandell, "They Moved," 146.

68. *Playboy*, February 1971, 65.

69. Madelyn Moore interview.

70. Joe Urgo interview. VVAW, "History" (n.d., circa February 1971), Box 1, VVAW Papers, SHSW, Madison.

71. Hanson interview.

72. Crandell, "They Moved," 147.

73. VVAW, "History."

74. "The Winter Soldier Investigation" pamphlet, n.d. (circa December 1970), Box 16, VVAW Papers, SHSW, Madison. Urgo interview.

75. *Detroit Free Press*, January 28 1971. Lane interview.

76. *Congressional Record*, April 6, 1971, 9948.

77. Ibid., 9951.

78. Ibid., 9979.

79. Ibid., 9971.

80. Ibid., 9958.

81. Ibid., 10042.

82. VVAW, *Winter Soldier Investigation*, 54, 46.

83. Peter Michelson, "Bringing the War Home," *New Republic*, February 27, 1971. *Congressional Record*, April 6, 1971, 9949, 9958, 10005, 10047.

84. Ibid., 9949.

85. Ibid., 9950.

86. VVAW, *Winter Soldier Investigation*, 102.

87. *Congressional Record*, April 6, 1971, 9986.

88. Vietnam Veterans Against the War, "The Winter Soldier Investigation" (press release), n.d. (circa February 1971), summarizes the lack of media attention and mentions the testimony on Laos and the violation of the Christmas truce that the veterans discussed at length on the first day of the hearings. Box 16, VVAW Papers, SHSW, Madison See also *Congressional Record*, April 6, 1971, 9947–9967.

89. A sampling of headlines from the *Detroit Free Press* includes: "Canada Keeps Out 5 Viet Witnesses in 'Crimes Trial,'" January 28, 1971; "Ex-GIs to Tell of Atrocities," January 31, 1971; "Five Ex-Marines Tell of 1969 Laos Invasion," February 1, 1971; "Probe Sought on Atrocity Charges," February 2, 1971.

90. A sampling of headlines from the *Chicago Sun Times*: "Ex-Marines Tell Ground Fighting in Laos in 1969," February 1, 1971; "'Just Blew Kids Away'— Winter Soldiers Tell War Horror Stories," February 1, 1971; "Winter Soldiers Tell Gruesome War Stories in Detroit," February 1, 1971; "2 Call for Winter Soldier Probe," February 2, 1971; "Cong Prisoners Wired, Jolted with Electricity—Ex-GI," February 2, 1971.

91. Barry interview.

92. "Veterans Assess Atrocity Blame," *The New York Times*, February 7, 1971.

93. Crandell, "They Moved," 147.

94. Todd Gitlin, *The Whole World Is Watching: Mass Media in the Making and Unmaking of the New Left* (Berkeley: University of California Press, 19800, 192. Gitlin further writes: "According to my anonymous informant [at CBS], the veterans' charges were 'not confirmable.' Maybe they were not confirmable in prin-

ciple (because all other witnesses were dead, say); more likely they were not confirmable because the network's version of 'news' does not go in much for independent investigation. Most important of all, antiwar veterans were not legitimate sources of jarring news" (192). Also see: Peter Michelson, "Bringing the War Home," *New Republic*, February 27, 1971. VVAW, "The Winter Soldier Investigation" (press release).

95. In his analysis of the media's reaction (or lack thereof) to the Winter Soldier Investigation, Todd Gitlin theorized: "In the end, the media chiefs kept what seemed to them an even keel. It was only when the administration pushed them and the rest of the Eastern Establishment too far—with the Agnew barrage, the enemies list, the prior restraint against newspapers publishing the Pentagon papers, the Fielding break-in, and the Watergate burglary—that the media ended up sympathetic to the legitimate political system's revolt against Nixon's transgressions." Gitlin, *The Whole World Is Watching*, 192.

96. Ensign interview.

97. "The Winter Soldier Investigation" pamphlet, n.d. (circa December 1970), Box 16, VVAW Papers, SHSW, Madison.

98. Kunen, *Standard Operating Procedure*, 27. Kenneth J. Campbell and Elliott L. Meyrowitz, "Vietnam Veterans and War Crimes Hearings," in Melvin Small and William Hoover, eds., *Give Peace a Chance: Exploring the Vietnam Antiwar Movement*, 135. In his "War Crimes Chronology" (draft), the CCI activist Michael Uhl surveyed the newspapers that had covered CCI's National Veterans' Inquiry (December 1–3, 1970) in Washington, D.C. Newspapers that ran stories about the event included the *New York Times*, the *Pittsburgh Press*, the *New York Post*, the *Evening Bulletin* (Philadelphia, the *St. Louis Post Dispatch*, the *Washington Daily News*, the *Los Angeles Times*, the *Times* (London), the *Florida Times Union*, the *Charlotte Observer*, the *Chicago Daily News*, the *Cleveland Press*, the *Detroit News*, the *Daily Freeman* (Kingston, N.Y.), and the *San Francisco Chronicle*. Two articles about the NVI appeared immediately after the event in the *New York Times*, compared to one article in the same newspaper about the Winter Soldier Investigation, one week later. Even though NVI received more generous national coverage than the Winter Soldier Investigation, Jules Whitcover wrote a column in the *Los Angeles Times* (December 8, 1970), days after the NVI adjourned, headlined "New Vietnam Atrocity Charges Little Noticed." See "War Crimes Chronology" (draft) by Michael Uhl (author's possession), 13–14. Damato interview.

99. Wells, *The War Within*, 490.

100. Ibid., 489.

101. Robert Jay Lifton, *Home from the War: Vietnam Veterans: Neither Victims nor Executioners* (New York: Simon and Schuster, 1973), 316.

102. *Congressional Record*, April 6, 1971, 10049.

103. Ibid., 10048.

104. Damato interview. Vietnam Veterans Against the War, "The Winter Soldier Investigation" (press release).

105. Ibid.

106. "Remarks of the Honorable Michael J. Harrington (D-Mass.) at News Conference of Vietnam Veterans Against the War, Friday, February 5, 1971," Box 16, VVAW Papers, SHSW, Madison.

107. *Chicago Sun-Times*, February 2, 1971.

108. *Congressional Record*, April 6, 1971, 9947–10055.

109. *Cincinnati Enquirer*, February 2, 1971. Stanley Karnow, *Vietnam: A History* (New York: Viking Press, 1983), 629–632.

110. Zaroulis and Sullivan, *Who Spoke Up?*, 347.

111. Gitlin, *The Sixties*, 411.

112. Barry interview. Urgo interview.

113. McKusker interview.

114. Camil, "Undercover Agents," 321.

115. Ibid.

116. Camil interview.

117. Ibid.

118. John Kerry and the Vietnam Veterans Against the War, *The New Soldier* (New York: Collier, 1971), 38.

NOTES TO CHAPTER 4

1. Wells, *War Within*, 315, 423, 307.

2. Art Goldberg, "Vietnam Vets: The Antiwar Army," *Ramparts*, 12.

3. Lifton, *Home from the War*, 76.

4. Al Hubbard, "The Winter Soldier Offensive (Phase–3): Dewey Canyon III—A Limited Incursion into the Countries of Congress, the Supreme Court, and the Fourth Estate," Box 13, VVAW Papers, SHSW, Madison. Lampooning the rhetoric of the Nixon administration, Hubbard further declared: "The incursion designated 'Dewey Canyon 3' will penetrate into the country of Congress for the limited purpose of ascertaining if any pretense of Constitutional Democracy exists in this country."

5. "Minutes from the First Semi-Annual Meeting of the VVAW National Steering Committee Meeting," Box 8, VVAW Papers, SHSW, Madison. Crandell, "They Moved," 148.

6. "VVAW Regional Coordinators," contained in VVAW Newsletter #1, March 1971, Box 11, VVAW Papers, SHSW, Madison.

7. Ibid. Urgo interview. In the newly restructured VVAW, the national officers (e.g., president, vice president, executive secretary, secretary), sat on the national steering committee (NSC) with the twenty-six regional coordinators. The NSC became the main governing body within VVAW, establishing a constitu-

tion and by-laws and providing leadership and direction for the organization. Each national officer and regional coordinator was given a vote on the NSC. The new, loose structure of the organization gave regional coordinators the power to "make all decisions relative to VVAW operations, consistent with VVAW philosophy and policy as determined by the National Steering Committee in their respective geographic area of responsibility." (See "Minutes from the First Semi-Annual Meeting of the VVAW National Steering Committee Meeting.")

8. *New York Times*, April 23, 1971.

9. Urgo interview.

10. Camil interview.

11. Urgo interview.

12. Ibid.

13. Barry Romo interview.

14. Ibid.

15. Barry Romo, "Project 100,000—'He Was Dead and I Was Going Home,'" from VVAW, *25 Years*, 31.

16. Romo interview.

17. Romo, "Project 100,000," 31.

18. Ibid.

19. Romo interview.

20. Ibid.

21. Ibid.

22. "Objectives of VVAW," from VVAW Newsletter #1, March 1971.

23. Urgo interview.

24. *New York Times*, March 17, 1971.

25. See Chapter 1.

26. Jan Barry and other early members of VVAW had mailed their medals to the government. Barry sent his decorations to Secretary of Defense Robert McNamara. Barry interview. DeBenedetti and Chatfield, *An American Ordeal*, 309.

27. Romo interview.

28. *New York Times*, March 17, 1971.

29. Kerry, *New Soldier*, 138.

30. Romo interview. *New York Times*, March 17, 1971.

31. Many years later, Romo insisted the Steering Committee voted to throw the medals at Dewey Canyon III, yet VVAW Newsletter #1 (March 1971) announced that "medals will be formally returned, in a body bag, to Congress." Joe Urgo, Jan Barry, and Scott Moore later recalled that the matter was left up in the air at the meeting and that, ultimately, the decision to throw the medals was made during the demonstration itself. Romo, Urgo, Barry, and Moore interviews.

32. Damato interview.

33. John Upton interview. John Lindquist interview. Floyd interview. Campbell interview. *Hóa Bính* (Colorado VVAW Newsletter), August 1971, 2, Box 12, VVAW Papers, SHSW, Madison. Romo interview.

34. Halstead, *Out Now!*, 587.

35. Ibid., 591. Wells, *War Within*, 461, 479–480. By early 1969, the largest antiwar coalition in the country, the National Mobilization to End the War in Vietnam (the Mobe), was on its deathbed. In the summer of 1969, a group of activists representing a broad segment of liberal and Left politics, met in Cleveland and started the New Mobilization to End the War in Vietnam (the New Mobe). Within a year, the New Mobe had gone the way of the old Mobe. The Trotskyist SWP and some of its allies founded the National Peace Action Coalition (NPAC) at a conference on June 19–21, 1970. Meanwhile, a group of eighty "independent radicals" met September 11–13, 1970, in Milwaukee, and launched the National Coalition Against War, Racism, and Repression (NCAWRR). In early February 1971, NCAWRR was reconstituted as the People's Coalition for Peace and Justice (PCPJ). See DeBenedetti and Chatfield, *An American Ordeal*, 281, 294–295, 301–302.

36. Butz interview.

37. Halstead, *Out Now!*, 592. Butz interview. Wells, *War Within*, 473.

38. Butz interview.

39. John O'Connor and Rod Kane, "Strictly Undercover" (unpublished manuscript, 1992), 66 (courtesy of John O'Connor). The quip "an ice pick in every Trot" is a sardonic reference to the murder of Leon Trotsky with an ice pick by an agent of Joseph Stalin.

40. Butz interview.

41. Wells, *War Within*, 490.

42. Ibid., 482.

43. Ibid., 489.

44. O'Connor and Kane, "Strictly Undercover," 96.

45. Camil, "Undercover Agents," 323.

46. Crandell, "They Moved," 150.

47. John O'Connor interview.

48. Ibid.

49. O'Connor and Kane, "Strictly Undercover," 43.

50. O'Connor interview.

51. Butz interview.

52. O'Connor interview.

53. Butz interview.

54. The underground Denver newspaper *Chinook* (April 29, 1971) published a Liberation News Service story about Robert F. Tatman, an FBI informant in Philadelphia, who announced at a VVAW rally on April 16, "My downfall as an effective informer came when I found myself agreeing with what I heard said at

various rallies." In *Home from the War,* the psychiatrist Robert J. Lifton recalled an FBI informant, "either part American Indian or possibly Puerto Rican," who attended a rap group meeting at the VVAW offices in New York City. He later confessed to the veterans that he was an FBI informer "but had liked everyone he met and felt very badly about the whole thing." He was subsequently never seen again. Lifton, *Home from the War,* 93.

55. Damato interview.

56. VVAW Newsletter #1, March 1971.

57. Ibid.

58. Barry interview.

59. Lifton, *Home from the War,* 75.

60. Robert J. Lifton interview.

61. Arthur Egendorf, *Healing from the War: Trauma and Transformation After Vietnam* (Boston: Houghton Mifflin Company, 1985), 115.

62. Ibid., 91.

63. Lifton, *Home from the War,* 73.

64. Jack McCloskey interview.

65. Ibid. The early New York and San Francisco rap groups influenced later psychological services for veterans. In 1979, Congress funded Operation Outreach for the Veterans Administration, which featured therapy sessions modeled after the VVAW rap groups. The Disabled American Veterans initiated a similar program.

66. Lifton interview.

67. McCloskey interview.

68. Lifton, *Home from the War,*97.

69. McCloskey interview.

70. O'Connor and Kane, "Strictly Undercover," 130–131, 136.

71. Ibid., 136–137. O'Connor interview.

72. O'Connor and Kane, "Strictly Undercover," 118.

73. Romo interview.

74. O'Connor and Kane, "Strictly Undercover," 117, 131–132.

75. Hanson interview.

76. *Newsweek,* May 3, 1971, 25.

77. O'Connor and Kane, "Strictly Undercover," 146.

78. Ibid., 141.

79. Wells, *War Within,* 489.

80. Urgo interview.

81. Ibid.

82. Wells, *War Within,* 489.

83. *New York Times,* April 17, 1971.

84. *New York Times,* April 19, 1971.

85. *New York Times,* April 17, 1971.

86. Crandell, "They Moved," 148.

87. O'Connor and Kane, "Strictly Undercover," 144.

88. Crandell, "They Moved," 148.

89. O'Connor interview.

90. Ibid.

91. Urgo interview.

92. O'Connor and Kane, "Strictly Undercover," 149.

93. Wells, *War Within*, 491.

94. Hubbard, "The Winter Soldier Offensive (Phase–3)."

95. Crandell, "They Moved," 154. Press releases, issued by the national office, reflected VVAW's frustration: "For four years now they [VVAW members] have been trying to speak out—on national television shows, with a four-day march last Labor Day from Morristown, N.J., to Valley Forge, Pa., and with the Winter Soldier Investigation, a hearing into War Crimes held in Detroit last February—and each time they have received scant coverage from the national press." Vietnam Veterans Against the War, "Dewey Canyon III" press release, n.d. (circa mid-March 1971), Box 13, VVAW Papers, SHSW, Madison.

96. Vietnam Veterans Against the War Connecticut Office Newsletter #2, Box 12, VVAW Papers, SHSW, Madison.

97. *New York Daily News*, March 27, 1971.

98. Butz interview.

99. Vietnam Veterans Against the War: "Dewey Canyon III" press release, n.d. (probably late March 1971), Box 13, VVAW Papers, SHSW, Madison.

NOTES TO CHAPTER 5

1. O'Connor and Kane, "Strictly Undercover," 145.

2. Crandell, "They Moved," 148.

3. *Greely (Colorado) Tribune*, April 19, 1971. *Chinook* (Denver), April 29, 1971. Crandell interview. Romo interview. Floyd interview. Vietnam Veterans Against the War Connecticut Office Newsletter #2, Box 12, VVAW Papers, SHSW, Madison. *Providence Journal*, Rhode Island, April 26, 1971. McKusker interview. Lindquist interview.

4. Figures from Hamid Mowlana and Paul H. Geffert, "Vietnam Veterans Against the War: A Profile Study of the Dissenters," in Kerry, *The New Soldier*, 172–174.

5. Ibid., 125. Exact times of events for Dewey Canyon III are contained in "Dewey Canyon III Schedule" (n.d., circa early April 1971), Box 13, VVAW Papers, SHSW, Madison.

6. Camil interview. O'Connor and Kane, "Strictly Undercover," 150.

7. O'Connor and Kane, "Strictly Undercover," 150.

8. Camil interview.

9. Art Goldberg, "Vietnam Vets: The Antiwar Army," *Ramparts*, 12.

10. Ibid.

11. Kerry, *New Soldier*, 26. Barry interview.

12. Hanson interview.

13. Kerry, *New Soldier*, 104.

14. *Washington Post*, April 21, 1971.

15. Ibid.

16. Crandell, "They Moved," 149.

17. *St. Louis Globe-Democrat*, April 21, 1971. *Washington Post*, April 21, 1971.

18. Ibid.

19. Goldberg, "Vietnam Vets," 12.

20. Ibid.

21. Camil interview.

22. Goldberg, "Vietnam Vets," 12. Barry interview.

23. *Staten Island Advance* (Staten Island, N.Y.), April 20, 1971.

24. Ibid. Rusty Sachs interview.

25. Don Yurman, "Veterans in Washington," *Chinook* (Denver), April 29, 1971, 5.

26. Ibid.

27. Ibid.

28. *Cleveland Plain Dealer*, April 21, 1971.

29. *Washington Post*, April 21, 1971.

30. *Milwaukee Sentinel*, April 21, 1971.

31. *Chicago American*, April 21, 1971.

32. *New York Times*, April 22, 1971. Romo interview.

33. *Cleveland Plain Dealer*, April 22, 1971.

34. Kerry, *New Soldier*, 59.

35. Goldberg, "Vietnam Vets," 12.

36. Ibid. *Milwaukee Sentinel*, April 21, 1971.

37. Ibid.

38. Urgo interview.

39. Camil interview.

40. Urgo interview.

41. Romo interview.

42. Kerry, *New Soldier*, 58.

43. Zaroulis and Sullivan, *Who Spoke Up?*, 356. The president's comments were reported widely in the press the next day. For example, see Yurman, "Veterans in Washington," 5.

44. Ibid. Yurman, "Veterans in Washington," 5.

45. *New York Times*, April 21, 1971. O'Connor and Kane, "Strictly Undercover," 158.

46. Ibid.

47. Urgo interview.

48. Crandell, "They Moved," 150. Crandell interview.

49. Butz interview.

50. *Washington Post*, April 22, 1971.

51. Jonathan Schell, *The Time of Illusion* (New York: Alfred A. Knopf, 1976), 148.

52. *Washington Post*, April 22, 1971.

53. Kerry, *New Soldier*, 64.

54. Ibid., 76. *New York Times*, April 22, 1971.

55. Yurman, "Veterans in Washington," 8.

56. Kerry, *New Soldier*, 76.

57. Goldberg, "Vietnam Vets," 13.

58. Halstead, *Out Now!*, 610. One short-haired orator gave a fiery speech denouncing Presidents Lyndon Johnson and Richard Nixon as "unfit to sleep in Washington." A few VVAWers who did not recognize the man grabbed him after his talk and accused him of being a police agent. They stopped browbeating him when another member pointed out that he was Carl Rogers, founding vice president of the organization. After drifting away from VVAW after the 1968 Democratic National Convention in Chicago, Rogers had founded the GI-Servicemen's Link to Peace, a G.I.-rights group that offered legal counseling and assisted fledgling coffeehouses near bases. The "Link," as Rogers called it, folded within a year. Rogers went to work for his old friend Dick Fernandez at Clergy and Laymen Concerned about Vietnam (CALCAV). Rogers handled media relations and edited CALCAV's newsletter, the *American Report*. He attended Dewey Canyon III to reunite with old comrades, only to realize that most VVAWers had joined the organization years after he left it. Rogers interview.

59. Ibid., 606.

60. Goldberg, "Vietnam Vets," 13.

61. Wells, *War Within*, 494. Madelyn Moore interview.

62. Kerry, *New Soldier*, 86. O'Connor and Kane, "Strictly Undercover," 166.

63. Crandell, "They Moved," 150.

64. *Washington Post*, April 22, 1971.

65. Damato interview.

66. Romo interview.

67. Halstead, *Out Now!*, 606.

68. Ibid.

69. Urgo interview.

70. Yurman, "Veterans in Washington," 8.

71. O'Connor interview.

72. Zaroulis and Sullivan, *Who Spoke Up?*, 356.

73. *Washington Post*, April 22, 1971.

74. John W. Dean III, *Blind Ambition: The White House Years* (New York: Simon & Schuster, 1976), 42.

75. Wells, *War Within*, 493.

76. Ibid., 493–494.

77. Ibid., 494.

78. *Washington Post*, April 22, 1971.

79. Ibid.

80. *Washington Daily News*, April 22, 1971.

81. H. R. Haldeman, *The Haldeman Diaries: Inside the Nixon White House* ((New York: G. P. Putnam's Sons, 1994), 278. Mitchell requested the order be dissolved "on the grounds that there was only one more night left and it wasn't worth pursuing."

82. *Detroit News*, April 23, 1971.

83. Ibid.

84. Haldeman, *Haldeman Diaries*, 278.

85. *Washington Post*, April 23, 1971.

86. Ibid. Crandell, "They Moved," 150.

87. Yurman, "Veterans in Washington," 8.

88. *Washington Post*, April 23, 1971.

89. Ibid.

90. Ibid. Crandell, "They Moved," 150.

91. *Cincinatti Enquirer*, April 23, 1971. *New York Times*, April 23, 1971.

92. *Congressional Record* (Senate), April 23, 1971. *New York Times*, April 23, 1971.

93. Madelyn Moore interview.

94. Barry interview.

95. Halstead, *Out Now!*, 606.

96. Wells, *War Within*, 495. Halstead, *Out Now!*, 610.

97. Among those who presented testimony that was ignored was Mike McKusker. He later recalled: "[Kerry] spoke to the Senate, the House of Lords, he being a clean-shaven Naval officer—and now he's a member of the House of the House of Lords—and I spoke to the House of Representatives, the House of Commons, and I was an enlisted man, the grunt. And that was our division all the way down the line. John made this speech that he had xeroxed and sent all over the fucking world. I just had a few remarks that showed up in the Congressional Record and that was it." McKusker interview.

98. Wells, War Within, 495.

99. Barry interview.

100. Damato interview.

101. Yurman, "Veterans in Washington," 11.

102. Washington Post, April 23, 1971.

103. Washington Post, April 24, 1971.

104. Overend, "Who Is Al Hubbard?" 589.

105. Ibid.

106. Barry interview.

107. Bill Crandell estimated that "as many as 3,000" veterans took part in the ceremony. Fred Halstead placed the number at the much more conservative level of 600 in *Out Now!*, 607. *Newsday* (April 24, 1971) tallied 1,500 to 2,000. The *New York Daily News* estimated 1,000. Other figures: *Washington Post* (April 24, 1971): 600 to 1,000; *New York Times* (April 24, 1971): 700; Washington, D.C., Park Police: 800.

108. Jean O'Connor interview.

109. *Newsday*, April 24, 1971.

110. Camil interview.

111. Camil, "Undercover Agents," 322.

112. Kerry, *New Soldier*, 142.

113. Ibid., 134.

114. VVAW, *25 Years*, 41.

115. Goldberg, "Vietnam Vets," 13–14.

116. Ibid., 16–17. VVAW, *Only the Beginning*, produced and directed by VVAW, 1972.

117. Ibid.

118. Ibid.

119. Damato interview.

120. Upton interview.

121. Crandell, "They Moved," 151.

122. *Newsday*, April 24, 1971.

123. Hanson interview.

124. Sachs interview.

125. *Washington Post*, April 24, 1971. Bill Branson interview.

126. Barry Romo, "It's the Memories, Not the Merit: A Medal for Men's Lives," in VVAW, *25 Years*, 41.

127. Ibid.

128. Yurman, "Veterans in Washington," 11.

129. Ibid.

130. Ibid.

131. Kerry, *New Soldier*, 134.

132. Upton interview. For the tally of the medals thrown, see "A Garbage Heap of Honor," *Newsday*, April 24, 1971.

133. Rogers interview.

134. Damato interview.

135. Romo interview.

136. Crandell interview.

137. *Washington Post*, April 24, 1971.

138. Wells, *War Within*, 496.
139. Ibid.
140. Halstead, *Out Now!*, 607.
141. Kerry, *New Soldier*, 152.
142. *New Kensington Dispatch*, April 21, 1971.
143. Crandell interview.
144. *Boston Globe*, April 20, 1971.
145. *Christian Science Monitor*, April 22, 1971.
146. *Cleveland Plain Dealer*, April 21, 1971.
147. *Philadelphia Daily News*, April 22, 1971.
148. *Akron Beacon Journal*, April 26, 1971.
149. Haldeman, *Haldeman Diaries*, 278.
150. John Helmer, *Bringing the War Home: The American Soldier in Vietnam and After* (New York: Free Press, 1974), 68.
151. Zaroulis and Sullivan, *Who Spoke Up?*, 358.
152. DeBenedetti and Chatfield, *An American Ordeal*, 310.
153. Helmer, *Bringing the War Home*, 93.

NOTES TO CHAPTER 6

1. Romo interview.
2. DeBenedetti and Chatfield, *An American Ordeal*, 310.
3. Zaroulis and Sullivan, *Who Spoke Up?*, 368–369.
4. Wells, *War Within*, 515–516.
5. DeBenedetti and Chatfield, *An American Ordeal*, 320.
6. Ibid. SANE dropped from 24,700 members in 1969 to 21,500 members in 1972. During the same period, WILFP was down from 12,300 to 8,000, CALCAV from 31,200 to 23,000.
7. VVAW, *25 Years*, 42. Cortright, *Soldiers in Revolt*, 80.
8. Anderson, *The Movement*, 377–378. David Cortright, "GI Resistance During the Vietnam War," in Melvin Small and William D. Hoover, eds., *Give Peace a Chance*, 124–125.
9. Colonel Robert D. Heinl Jr., "The Collapse of the Armed Forces," *Armed Forces Journal* (June 1971), 38.
10. Anderson, *The Movement*, 378.
11. Wells, *War Within*, 526. Urgo interview.
12. *First Casualty*, August 1971, 11.
13. McKusker interview. Overend, "Who Is Al Hubbard?", 589.
14. David King, "The Veterans' March to Boston," *New Republic*, June 12, 1971, 11–12.
15. Vietnam Veterans Against the War, "Guidelines to Marches and Guerrilla Theater," courtesy Tom Thompson.

16. Helmer, *Bringing the War Home*, 94. *New York Times*, May 22, 1971.

17. Crandell interview.

18. Anderson, *The Movement*, 356.

19. Gitlin, *The Sixties*, 417.

20. McCloskey interview. *First Casualty*, August 1971, 8, 9. VVAW, "History," n.d. (circa early 1972), Box 1, VVAW Papers, SHSW, Madison.

21. A helpful account of VVAW's Cairo Project is Scott Moore's "Lifeline to Cairo," *First Casualty*, August 1971, 1, 3. Moore interview.

22. Ibid.

23. Ibid.

24. Craig Scott Moore, "A Report to the Executive Committee of VVAW Concerning a Month's Trip to the Field and Other Observations," n.d. (circa August 1971), Box 8, VVAW Papers, SHSW, Madison.

25. Ibid.

26. Ibid.

27. Scott Moore interview.

28. Barry interview.

29. Michael Uhl, "The Citizens Commission of Inquiry on U.S. War Crimes in Vietnam: Chronology of background and key events taken from organization's records stored at the Department of Manuscripts & University Archives, Olin Library, Cornell University," 13. Contains excerpt of "Sailor" John McGarraty's letter, dated August 8, 1971. Courtesy of Michael Uhl.

30. Rod Kane, *Veteran's Day: A Combat Odyssey* (New York: Simon and Schuster, 1990), 157.

31. *New York Times*, August 30, 1971. *H=a B8nh* (Colorado Vietnam Veterans Against the War newsletter), November 1971, 10, Box 12, VVAW Papers, SHSW, Madison.

32. Sachs interview.

33. Pete Zastrow interview.

34. *First Casualty*, August 1971.

35. Moore, "Lifeline to Cairo," 3.

36. *First Casualty*, August, 1971, 10.

37. Texas Regional Office, Vietnam Veterans Against the War, Austin Texas, to Texas Area Coordinators, August 22, 1971. Box 13, VVAW Papers, SHSW, Madison.

38. Kunen, *Standard Operating Procedure*, 24.

39. Linda Van Devanter, *Home Before Morning: The Story of an Army Nurse in Vietnam* (New York: Beaufort Books, 1983), 29–30.

40. Ibid., 95.

41. Ibid., 222.

42. Ibid., 212.

43. Ibid., 230–231.

44. Ibid., 231.

45. VVAW, *25 Years*, 10.

46. Jean O'Connor interview.

47. Clayborne Carson, *In Struggle: SNCC and the Black Awakening of the 1960s* (Cambridge, Mass.: Harvard University Press, 1981), 147.

48. Abe Peck, *Uncovering the Sixties: The Life and Times of the Underground Press* (New York: Pantheon Books, 1985), 208.

49. Robin Morgan, ed. *Sisterhood Is Powerful* (New York: Vintage Books, 1970), xxxix.

50. "By-Laws of Vietnam Veterans Against the War, Inc.," Article I, Membership, 2, Box 8, VVAW Papers, SHSW, Madison. On women in the Detroit office, see *VVAW Newsletter*, Detroit, Michigan, April 1972, Box 12, VVAW papers, SHSW, Madison.

51. Anne Bailey interview.

52. Ibid.

53. Linda Alband interview.

54. Jeannie Friedman interview.

55. Egendorf, *Healing from the War*, 129.

56. Lifton, *Home from the War*, 271.

57. Egendorf, *Healing from the War*, 130.

58. Overend, "Who Is Al Hubbard?," 589. On the Fort Pierce vigil, see "Vets Plan Vigil for Black GI," *New York Post*, August 26, 1970.

59. Hanson interview.

60. Wallace Terry, "Bringing the War Home," in Clyde Taylor, ed., *Vietnam and Black America: An Anthology of Protest and Resistance* (Garden City, N.Y.: Anchor Press/Doubleday, 1973), 200–208.

61. Ibid., 212.

62. Morrison and Morrison, *From Camelot to Kent State*, 77.

63. Cortright, "GI Resistance," 119.

64. Terry, "Bringing the War Home," 206.

65. Ibid., 207.

66. Footage contained in *Winter Soldier*, 1972, produced by Winterfilm.

67. Kunen, *Standard Operating Procedure*, 24.

68. Hanson interview.

69. For Latino involvement in VA hospital protests, see Goldberg, "Vietnam Vets," 16–17, and Jack Deacy, "The Veterans," *New York Daily News*, May 27, 1970.

70. Charley Trujillo, ed., *Soldados: Chicanos in Vietnam* (San Jose, Calif.: Chusma House Publications, 1990), 35.

71. Ibid., ii.

72. Romo interview. Unfortunately, VVAW never maintained any reliable records on the race, ethnicity, or gender of its members.

73. Ibid.

74. *Hóa Bình* (Colorado Vietnam Veterans Against the War newsletter), November 1971, 10.

75. Romo interview.

76. Vince Muscari, "Cut Off da Ear if You're a Queer," *First Casualty*, October 1971, 2.

77. Bulletin of fall VVAW activities, n.d. (circa September 1971), Box 15, VVAW Papers, SHSW, Madison.

78. Ed Damato, letter to VVAW members, December 19, 1971, Box 15, VVAW Papers, SHSW, Madison.

79. Urgo interview. There is a great deal of compelling information on the speaking tour of the six VVAW and CCI members in Europe, but I have decided not to include it here. The six participants were: Larry Rottman, coordinator of the New Mexico VVAW region; Ken Campbell and Nathan Hale, both from the Philadelphia chapter; Randy Floyd, coordinator of the Texas region; Danny Notley; and Bart Osborn. Ken Campbell and Randy Floyd interviews. See also: *First Casualty*, December 1971, 2, 8; and "Statement Given to the PRG Delegation in Paris," July 7, 1971, Box 10, VVAW Papers, SHSW, Madison.

80. Joe Urgo, "A Trip to Hanoi," *First Casualty*, October 1971, 5.

81. Upton interview.

82. VVAW list of 1971 actions, Bulletin of fall VVAW activities, n.d. (circa early 1972), Box 15, VVAW Papers, SHSW, Madison. For an outstanding account of the Arkansas Operation Raw, see Nancy Saunders' "Through the Looking Glass, Part One: The Arkansas RAW March—October 30 & 31, 1971," in the *Ozark Gazette* (Fayetteville, Arkansas), October 28, 1996, 1, 9.

83. See combined reports from "Vets Day Across the Nation," *Hóa Bình*, November 1971, 15, and *First Casualty*, December 1971, 10.

84. Barry interview.

85. W. D. Ehrhart, *Passing Time: Memoir of a Vietnam Veteran Against the War* (Jefferson, N.C.: McFarland, 1986), 224–225.

86. Barry interview.

87. Jan Barry, Basil T. Paquet, and Larry Rottman, eds., *Winning Hearts and Minds: War Poems by Vietnam Veterans* (Brooklyn, N.Y.: First Casualty Press/McGraw-Hill, 1972), v.

88. Ehrhart, *Passing Time*, 224–225. Lifton, *Home from the War*, 131. Money received from McGraw-Hill financed a less successful book of short stories titled *Free Fire Zone*, which appeared in 1973. By this time, Jan Barry had abandoned First Casualty Press. *Free Fire Zone* was edited by Paquet, Rottman, and an ex-marine, Wayne Karlin. The editors talked of publishing "a third volume, *Postmortem*, . . . a collection which examines America's policies and attitudes towards Asia through the eyes of the men who implemented them," but the collection never materialized. See *Free Fire Zone: Short Stories by Vietnam Veterans* (New York: McGraw-Hill/First Casualty Press, 1973), vii.

89. Ehrhart, *Passing Time*, 163. VVAW, *25 Years*, 15.

90. Wells, *War Within*, 532. *New York Times*, December 29, 1971.

91. Zaroulis and Sullivan, *Who Spoke Up?*, 374.

92. *Newsweek*, January 10, 1972, 20.

93. Vietnam Veterans Against the War, "Christmas Eve" press release, December 25, 1971, Box 15, VVAW Papers, SHSW, Madison. Zaroulis and Sullivan, *Who Spoke Up?*, 374. Butz interview. Wells, *War Within*, 531–532.

94. *Newsweek*, January 10, 1972, 20.

95. Morrison and Morrison, *From Camelot to Kent State*, 87.

96. Terry DuBose, "'Operation Peace on Earth'—Killeen Texas Itinerary," Box 15, SHSW, Madison.

NOTES TO CHAPTER 7

1. Vietnam Veterans Against the War, Inc., newsletter (New York City), May 15, 1972, Box 11, VVAW Papers, SHSW, Madison.

2. Vietnam Veterans Against the War Newsletter, Philadelphia Chapter, March 1972, Box 13, VVAW Papers, SHSW, Madison.

3. Long Beach Vietnam Veterans Against the War, June 1972, 2. *Hóa Bính*, August 1971, 2. Detroit VVAW Newsletter, April 1972, 7. Providence, RI, VVAW Newsletter #2, n.d., circa July 1971. Dayton VVAW Newsletter, July 5, 1972, 1. Box 12, Box 13, VVAW Papers, SHSW, Madison.

4. McCloskey interview.

5. A good account of Billy Dean Smith and Gary Lawton and of the activities surrounding their imprisonment is contained in *Favorite Sons* (Southern California VVAW newsletter), n.d. (probably March 1972), vol. 1, no. 2, 5, Box 12, VVAW Papers, SHSW, Madison.

6. For a list of spring 1972 VVAW actions, see "We Are Everywhere," *First Casualty*, July 1972, 10–12, and Vietnam Veterans Against the War, Inc., Newsletter (New York City), May 15, 1972, Box 11, VVAW Papers, SHSW, Madison.

7. Zaroulis and Sullivan, *Who Spoke Up?*, 378, 383.

8. Ibid., 385, 389.

9. *Favorite Sons* ("A publication of Vietnam Veterans Against the War, California, Hawaii, Nevada."), vol. 1, no. 2 (n.d., circa March 1972), 3, 6.

10. Jeb Stuart Magruder, *An American Life: One Man's Road to Watergate* (New York: Atheneum, 1974), 199–200, 250.

11. Don Donner, Fayetteville, Arkansas, to the author, November 6, 1996.

12. Ibid. John Kifner, "Informer Appears Key to U.S. Case Against 6 Antiwar Veterans," *New York Times*, August 14, 1972.

13. The CBS journalist Mike Wallace claimed Lemmer was "orphaned when he was a kid—three years old, I believe." But newspaper accounts, as well as Lemmer's obituary, indicate that his mother, Zettie Mae Lemmer, remained part of

his life. See Mike Wallace interview with Bill Lemmer and Barbara Stocking, *CBS Morning News* transcript, CBS Television Network, September 5, 1973, Box 14, VVAW Papers, SHSW, Madison.

14. Ibid. Kifner, "Informer Appears Key to U.S. Case Against 6 Antiwar Veterans."

15. Mike Wallace interview with Bill Lemmer. Frank Donner, "The Confession of an FBI Informer," *Harpers*, December 1972, 54.

16. Donner, "The Confession," 56.

17. Ibid., 55.

18. Ibid.

19. Ibid., 56. Kifner, "Informer Appears Key to U.S. Case Against 6 Antiwar Veterans."

20. Mike Wallace interview with Bill Lemmer. Donner, "The Confession of an FBI Informer," 54.

21. James McCord's testimony before Senate Select Committee on Presidential Campaign Activities (May 18, 1973), chaired by Senator Sam Ervin, is contained in Jan Barry, "Watergate & the VVAW," *Win*, June 2, 1973, 7.

22. Nancy Miller, "Watergate South," *Computers and People*, December 1974, 18.

23. Ibid.

24. Interview with Jeb Stuart Magruder on *CBS Morning News*, January 18, 1973. Cited in Barry, "Watergate & the VVAW," 9.

25. Prados, *Hidden History of the Vietnam War*, 282–283.

26. *Newsweek*, July 31, 1972, cited in Barry, "Watergate & the VVAW," 8.

27. Nancy Miller, "Through the Looking Glass, Part Five: 'Maybe,'" *Ozark Gazette* (Fayetteville, Ark.), January 27, 1997, 9. On the eleven agencies, see the *Miami Herald*, June 10, 1973.

28. Camil, "Undercover Agents," 323.

29. Ibid., 325.

30. Ibid., 325–326. Camil interview. Camil's ordeal is also summed up in the *St. Louis Post-Dispatch*, October 29, 1972. Also see: Jack Anderson, "Vets Suspect Watergate Antics," syndicated column, July 11, 1973.

31. Philadelphia VVAW Newsletter, March 1972, 5, Box 13, VVAW Papers, SHSW.

32. McCloskey interview.

33. Miller, "Watergate South," 20.

34. Magruder's quotes are excerpted from his testimony before the Ervin Committee in Miller, "Watergate South," 22.

35. Ibid.

36. *Miami Herald*, May 26, 1973.

37. *Miami Herald*, May 23, 1973. Prados, *Hidden History of the Vietnam War*, 290. Interestingly, after his unsuccessful attempts to sell weapons to VVAW ac-

tivists, Fernandez was asked by the Watergate burglar Eugenio Martinez to incite riots at the Democratic National Convention. The *Miami Herald* (May 23, 1973) reported: "Martinez offered [Fernandez] $700 a week to infiltrate protest groups at last summer's Democratic convention and embarrass George McGovern 'for the Republican Party.'"

38. *New York Times*, August 8, 1973.

39. *Miami Herald*, June 8, 1973.

40. Lucian K. Truscott IV, "To Discredit the Vets," *Village Voice*, May 31, 1973.

41. Don Donner, Fayetteville, Arkansas, letter to the author, December 5, 1996. When former Secretary of State Dean Rusk visited the University of Arkansas, Lemmer lured the VVAWer Mike Damron into a scheme to send a letter to a local newspaper threatening to bomb the building where Rusk planned to speak. Police quickly arrested Damron. Lemmer was the only other person who knew about the threatening letter. Next, Lemmer constructed an incendiary device and convinced a seventeen-year-old student, Mark C. Vanciel, to place it in the historic Old Main building at the University of Arkansas. The police immediately captured Vanciel and left Lemmer alone. Outside Kansas City, police arrested a group of activists for marijuana possession. Lemmer was the only one released on bail. See Donner letter, and Frank Donner (no relation), "The Confession," 57.

42. Donner, "The Confession," 58.

43. Alband interview. Bailey interview. Kifner, "Informer Appears Key to U.S. Case Against 6 Antiwar Veterans," *New York Times*, August 14, 1972.

44. Donner, "The Confession," 62.

45. Don Donner, Fayetteville, Arkansas, letter to the author, December 5, 1996.

46. Donner, "The Confession," 54.

47. Kifner, "Informer Appears Key to U.S. Case Against 6 Antiwar Veterans." Prados, *Hidden History of the Vietnam War*, 284. Don Donner, Fayetteville, Arkansas, letter to the author, December 5, 1996.

48. Helmer, *Bringing the War Home*, 96.

49. The National Collective of Vietnam Veterans Against the War, "Minutes of the Vietnam Veterans Against the War National Steering Committee Meeting, September 29-October 2, 1972," Box 8, VVAW Papers, SHSW, Madison.

50. *First Casualty*, July 1972, 7.

51. De Benedetti and Chatfield, *An American Ordeal*, 336. Prados, *Hidden History of the Vietnam War*, 284.

52. Robert Sanford, "Tallahassee Eight—Warriors for Peace," *St. Louis Post-Dispatch*, October 29, 1972.

53. Ibid.

54. Donner, "The Confession," 54.

55. Ever unstable, Bill Lemmer, residing in Wyoming at the time the indict-

ments were handed down, was fired from two different jobs as a result of his "inability to work with other people." See *Arkansas Gazette* (Fayetteville, Ark.), August 17, 1973.

56. Frank J. Donner, *The Age of Surveillance: The Aims and Methods of America's Political Intelligence System* (New York: Vintage Books, 1981), 374.

57. Lucian Truscott IV, "Vietnam Veterans Against the War," *Saturday Review*, October 7, 1972, 15. *St. Louis Post-Dispatch*, October 29, 1972.

58. Vietnam Veterans Against the War, Inc., Dayton Ohio Newsletter #15, July 28, 1972, 1, Box 13, VVAW Papers, SHSW, Madison.

59. John Lindquist interview.

60. *Washington Post*, August 19, 1972. *New York Times*, August 20, 1972.

61. Kovic, *Born on the Fourth of July*, 170.

62. Camil, "Undercover Agents," 319.

63. Lindquist interview.

64. Ibid. Prados, *Hidden History of the Vietnam War*, 285.

65. Peter Goldman, "This Is What It Was Like," *Newsweek*, September 4, 1972, 32.

66. Truscott, "Vietnam Veterans Against the War," 16.

67. Romo interview. Lindquist interview. Lee Winfrey, "Viet Vets and Nazis in Clash," *Tallahassee Democrat*, August 21, 1972. Mike Baxter and John Camp, "500 Drive Back at Hotel; Vets Quell Nazis at Park," *Miami Herald*, August 21, 1972.

68. Bill Davis interview.

69. Zaroulis and Sullivan, *Who Spoke Up?*, 392.

70. *Cincinnati Enquirer*, August 21, 1972.

71. Kovic, *Born on the Fourth of July*, 170. *Washington Post*, August 19, 1972.

72. *New York Times*, August 22, 1972.

73. Ibid. Prados, *Hidden History of the Vietnam War*, 287. *Miami Herald*, August 22, 1972.

74. Truscott, "Vietnam Veterans Against the War," 16. Hunter S. Thompson, *Fear and Loathing: On the Campaign Trail '72* (New York: Warner Books, 1973), 387.

75. Prados, *Hidden History of the Vietnam War*, 287.

76. Thompson, *Fear and Loathing*, 383–384.

77. Ibid., 387.

78. Ibid., 388.

79. Theodore H. White, *The Making of the President 1972* (New York: Atheneum, 1973), 242.

80. Kurt Vonnegut Jr., "In a Manner That Must Shame God Himself," *Harper's*, November 1972, 61.

81. Truscott, "Vietnam Veterans Against the War," 16.

82. Thompson, *Fear and Loathing*, 392.

83. Wells, *War Within*, 553.

84. Bailey interview.

85. Truscott, "Vietnam Veterans Against the War," 21.

86. Ibid. Prados, *Hidden History of the Vietnam War*, 288–289.

87. Prados, *Hidden History of the Vietnam War*, 288. *Miami Herald*, August 24, 1972.

88. *Washington Post*, August 24, 1972.

89. "A New Majority for Four More Years?" *Time*, September 4, 1972, 9.

90. Kovic, *Born on the Fourth of July*, 184.

91. Phil Tracy, "Smiling Through with the G.O.P.," *Commonweal*, September 8, 1972, 23.

92. John Osborne, "Beach Party for the President," *New Republic*, September 2, 1972, 23. Echoing Osborne, *U.S. News and World Report* (September 4, 1972, 22) noted: "In contrast with some protesters—who harangued and jostled Convention delegates, set fire to flags and bunting, and screamed obscenities—about 1,200 Vietnam Veterans Against the War staged a silent, well-disciplined 'protest march' near the Convention's headquarters hotel, the Fontainbleau."

93. Romo interview.

94. *St. Petersburg Times*, August 25, 1972.

95. Prados, *Hidden History of the Vietnam War*, 289.

96. *Miami Herald*, July 9, 1972.

97. Ibid.

98. Brian Adams, "Thoughts on the Future of VVAW," 6, in "Committee on VVAW Internal Problems and Politics, NSC Meeting, Palo Alto, California, September 29-October 2, 1972," Box 8, VVAW Papers, SHSW, Madison.

99. Ibid.

100. Chicago VVAW, "Hot News off the Wires of the VVAW Press Service," (n.d., circa July 1972), 4, Box 10, VVAW Papers, SHSW, Madison.

101. Adams, "Thoughts on the Future of VVAW," 6.

102. Bill Hager, "From the Region," *Favorite Sons*, June 1973, 3, Box 12, VVAW Papers, SHSW, Madison.

103. Crandell interview.

104. Crandell, "They Moved," 151.

105. Crandell interview.

106. Jack Anderson, "Vets Suspect Watergate Antics," syndicated column, July 11, 1973.

107. Prados, *Hidden History of the Vietnam War*, 289–290.

108. Wells, *War Within*, 549.

109. Ibid., 548.

110. Truscott, "To Discredit the Vets," *Village Voice*, May 31, 1973.

111. Donner, *Age of Surveillance*, 374.

112. Ibid., 350.

113. Ibid., 370.

114. Zastrow interview.

115. Prados, *Hidden History of the Vietnam War*, 289.

116. Ibid., 289–290.

117. The National Collective of Vietnam Veterans Against the War, "Minutes of the Vietnam Veterans Against the War National Steering Committee Meeting, September 29-October 2, 1972," 12–13, Box 8, VVAW Papers, SHSW, Madison.

NOTES TO CHAPTER 8

1. Gabriel Kolko, *Anatomy of a War: Vietnam, the United States and the Modern Historical Experience* (New York: New Press, 1985), 441. Marilyn B. Young, *The Vietnam Wars, 1945–1990* (New York: HarperCollins, 1991), 278–279.

2. Romo interview.

3. Joan Baez, *And a Voice to Sing With: A Memoir* (New York: Summit Books, 1987), 193–221.

4. Romo interview. Barry Romo, "Report from Hanoi: Vietnam Revisited," *Winter Soldier*, April 1973, 3.

5. Romo interview. Halstead, *Out Now!*, 699–700.

6. Ibid., 692.

7. *New York Times*, January 25, 1973.

8. Wells, *War Within*, 567.

9. *Free Fire*, Burlington, Vermont, VVAW Newsletter, Box 13, VVAW Papers, SHSW, Madison.

10. *Veterans Voice*, Kansas City, Missouri, VVAW Newsletter, Box 12, VVAW Papers, SHSW, Madison.

11. Barry interview.

12. Vietnam Veterans Against the War, "Internal Notes: Overview and Breakdown on Regions," n.d. (circa spring 1973), Box 8, VVAW Papers, SHSW, Madison.

13. Ibid. Vietnam Veterans Against the War, "National Steering Committee Meeting, Placitas, New Mexico, April 19–April 23, 1973," 2–5. Courtesy Tom Thompson.

14. VVAW, "National Steering Committee Meeting, Placitas, New Mexico, April 19-April 23, 1973," 7.

15. Damato interview.

16. Zastrow interview.

17. Annie Luginbill interview.

18. *Winter Soldier*, April 1973, 7. *Winter Soldier*, May 1973, 7, 12. *Winter Soldier*, July 1973, 7. VVAW, "National Steering Committee Meeting, Placitas, New Mexico, April 19-April 23, 1973," 7.

19. In an interview with the author, a national steering committee member, Linda Alband, discussed at length the radical currents within the organization

that opposed Hubbard and other New York leaders and ultimately drove the national office to relocate to Chicago.

20. Bill Hager, "From the Region," *Favorite Sons*, June 1973, 3, Box 12, VVAW Papers, SHSW, Madison.

21. Dayton, Ohio, VVAW/WSO News, May 9, 1973, 1, Box 13, VVAW Papers, SHSW, Madison.

22. Damato interview.

23. Camil interview.

24. *Pensacola Journal* (Pensacola, Fla.), April 24, 1973.

25. *Miami Herald*, October 8, 1972.

26. *Pensacola Journal*, April 24, 1973.

27. *Miami Herald*, October 8, 1972.

28. Ibid.

29. Ibid.

30. *Gainesville Sun*, July 14, 1973. *Louisville Times*, June 21, 1973. *Gainesville Sun*, July 17, 1973.

31. *New York Times*, August 1, 1973.

32. Prados, *Hidden History of the Vietnam War*, 291.

33. Ibid., 293. *Miami Herald*, May 26, 1973. *Arkansas Gazette* (Fayetteville, Ark.), August 17, 1973.

34. *St. Petersburg Times*, August 10, 1972. *Gainesville Sun*, July 17, 1973.

35. *Charlotte Observer*, August 29, 1972.

36. *Christian Science Monitor*, June 14, 1973.

37. *Louisville Times*, June 21, 1973.

38. *Mobile Register* (Mobile, Ala.), April 26, 1973.

39. For a useful summary of VVAW protests during the Gainesville Eight trial, see "Free the Gainesville 8: The Trial and Demonstrations," *Winter Soldier*, September 1973, 9.

40. *Winter Soldier*, October 1973, 3. Prados, *Hidden History of the Vietnam War*, 292–293.

41. Prados, *Hidden History of the Vietnam War*, 293.

42. John Lindquist, "The Gainesville 8 Are Free," Milwaukee VVAW Newsletter, September 1973, 1, Box 12, VVAW Papers, SHSW, Madison.

43. McCloskey interview.

44. Zastrow interview.

45. Vietnam Veterans Against the War/Winter Soldier Organization, "11th National Steering Committee Meeting, Yellow Springs, Ohio," 2, Box 8, VVAW Papers, SHSW, Madison.

46. Vietnam Veterans Against the War/Winter Soldier Organization, "12th VVAW/WSO National Steering Committee Meeting, 11 to 15 April, 1974," 1–4, Box 8, VVAW Papers, SHSW, Madison.

47. Ibid., 3.

48. Crandell interview.

49. Urgo interview.

50. Davis interview.

51. Zastrow interview.

52. *Winter Soldier*, May 1974, 3. *Winter Soldier*, August 1974, 10. For a list of protests in early 1974, see *Winter Soldier*, March 1974, 12–13.

53. *Winter Soldier*, April 1973, 10.

54. *Winter Soldier*, May 1973, 13.

55. *Winter Soldier*, August 1973, 5.

56. *Winter Soldier*, September 1973, 3.

57. Camil, "Undercover Agents," 330.

58. Ibid., 330–333.

59. Davis and Romo interviews.

60. Friedman interview. Disagreements with the national office were not confined to the San Francisco Bay area. The Buffalo chapter, in a position paper titled "Tell No Lies, Claim No Easy Victories," charged the Revolutionary Union with "direct efforts at manipulation within the organization. A clear example is the formation of new chapters and regions of VVAW/WSO by the RU. This serves to push a particular line through a mechanical manipulation of 'democratic' processes, rather than applying principled political struggle and education of the masses." (See note 61). The St. Louis chapter focused its attacks on *Winter Soldier*, the monthly newspaper of VVAW/WSO: "Increasingly, the content of *Winter Soldier* does not relate to concerns of our primary constituency which we continue to regard as veterans, GIs, and those who share our goals and concerns. . . . a member of the St. Louis chapter . . . did not write a letter to the editor because he felt that *Winter Soldier* was no longer a forum for rank and file members." See St. Louis Chapter/Alabama Region, "Criticisms of *Winter Soldier* with Regard to Language, Content & Rigidity of Editorial Positions," Box 9, VVAW Papers, SHSW, Madison.

61. Jeanne Friedman "Struggle in VVAW/WSO," from *Seize the Time*, reprinted by the Northern California Anti-Imperialist Caucus, 1975, Box 15, VVAW Papers, SHSW, Madison.

62. Tom Zangrilli, Barry Romo, and Ron Schneck, untitled position paper on the recent expulsion of the Anti-Imperialist Minority Faction, 1–2, Box 15, VVAW Papers, SHSW, Madison.

63. VVAW/WSO Collective, untitled paper on the 1975 VVAW/WSO split, 3, Box 15, VVAW Papers, SHSW, Madison.

64. Davis interview.

65. Romo interview.

66. Lindquist interview.

67. Urgo interview.

68. Operation County Fair Newsletter, February 1974, 1–2. Operation

County Fair, "Medicine for the People," May 1974, 1–4, Box 15, VVAW Papers, SHSW, Madison.

69. *Chicago Sun-Times*, March 3, 1977.

70. Vietnam Veterans Against the War, "Chemical Time Bomb in Vietnam Veterans," and Vietnam Veterans Against the War, "Agent Orange Investigation," Box 13, VVAW Papers, SHSW, Madison.

71. Davis interview.

72. Romo interview.

73. Young, *Vietnam Wars*, 328.

74. Joe Miller interview.

75. Lucian K. Truscott IV, "The Men from CREEP Were Busy All Over," *Village Voice*, June 7, 1973.

76. William M. Welch, "Clash of Political Titans Turns Scrappier in Mass. Senate Race," *USA Today*, November 5, 1996.

77. Ibid.

78. James Carroll, "A Friendship That Ended the War," *New Yorker*, October 21 and 28, 1996, 146.

79. Ibid., 155–156.

80. Vietnam Veterans of America, "A Short History of VVA," pamphlet (Washington, D.C.: Vietnam Veterans of America, 1996).

81. Bettina Moss, "The Vietnam Veterans Adviser," *Penthouse*, July 1989, 90.

82. Myra MacPherson, *Long Time Passing: Vietnam and the Haunted Generation* (Garden City, N.Y.: Doubleday, 1984), 615. Many VVAWers were involved in starting VVA. One, John Upton, a former Kansas/Missouri VVAW coordinator, was so disgusted with VVA's constant focus on the Prisoner of War/Missing in Action issue that he left VVA. Using recording equipment in his basement, he launched the Vietnam Veterans Radio Network, a weekly, half-hour program of music and history. The show is syndicated to various radio stations in the United States, Canada, and Belgium and is broadcast worldwide via shortwave radio from Radio for Peace International in Costa Rica. John Upton, Kansas City, Missouri, to the author, August 31, 1995.

83. VVA, "Short History."

84. Norman Kagan, *The Cinema of Oliver Stone* (New York: Continuum Books, 1995), 145–146.

85. Ibid., 163.

86. Barry interview.

87. Rogers interview.

88. The author has tried repeatedly to reach Hubbard. At one point, in April 1995, Hubbard agreed to provide a written response to a series of questions provided by the author. No reply ever came from Hubbard, and repeated attempts to contact him have ended in failure.

89. Crandell interview.

90. Don Donner, Fayetteville, Arkansas, to John App, San Juan Capistrano, California, April 19, 1995, 5–6. Courtesy of Don Donner.

91. *Veteran*, Spring 1991, 12.

92. Joe Miller, "Remembrance and Recommitment at VVAW's 25th Anniversary," *Veteran* (Spring 1992), 6–9.

93. Ibid., 9.

94. VVAW New York/New Jersey Chapter, "In Loving Memory of Clarence Fitch, 1948–1990" (n.d., circa 1990), courtesy of Ben Chitty.

95. *San Francisco Chronicle*, March 17, 1996. *San Francisco Chronicle*, March 30, 1996.

96. Romo interview.

97. *Penthouse*, July 1989, 90.

98. Lindquist interview. John Lindquist, "Sixth VVAW Delegation Visits Vietnam," *Guidon*, Spring 1992, 3–4. Courtesy of Barry Romo.

99. VVAW, *25 Years*, 27.

100. A moving and thorough account of Mike Damron's visit to the Vietnam Veterans Memorial is Mike Masterson's "The Last Mission," *Northwest Arkansas Times* (Fayetteville, Ark.), March 10, 1996.

NOTES TO CHAPTER 9

1. Kerry, *New Soldier*, 174.

2. Lifton, *Bringing the War Home*, 210.

3. Tom Hayden, "The Port Huron Statement," from Diane Ravitch, ed., *The American Reader* (New York: Harper Perennial, 1991), 321.

4. Helmer, *Bringing the War Home*, 97–98.

5. Hayden, "Port Huron," 321.

6. Helmer, *Bringing the War Home*, 99.

7. Upton interview.

8. Cortright, *Soldiers in Revolt*, 50–94.

9. Alan Adelson, *SDS: A Profile* (New York: Scribner's, 1971), 203.

10. Donald Duncan, "The Whole Thing Was a Lie!," *Ramparts*, February 1966, 24.

11. *Free Fire* (Vermont VVAW newsletter), March 1973, 1, Box 13, VVAW Papers, SHSW, Madison.

12. Helmer, *Bringing the War Home*, 98–99.

13. Vietnam Veterans Against the War, Inc., "Guidelines for Organizing and Operating Chapters," n.d. (circa late 1970 or early 1971), Box 9, VVAW Papers, SHSW, Madison.

14. Minutes of the VVAW NSC Meeting, Palo Alto, California, September 29–October 2, 1972, Box 8, VVAW Papers, SHSW, Madison.

15. Kerry, *New Soldier*, 152.

16. *Detroit Free Press*, January 31, 1971.

17. Helmer, *Bringing the War Home*, 68.

18. Colonel Harry G. Summers Jr., *Vietnam War Almanac* (New York: Facts on File Publications, 1985), 351.

19. Zastrow interview.

20. Lifton, *Home from the War*, 25.

21. Gettleman et al., *Vietnam and America*, 327.

22. MacPherson, *Long Time Passing*, 230, 236. Lifton interview.

23. Lifton interview.

24. Bruce Franklin, introduction to W. D. Ehrhart *Busted: A Vietnam Veteran in Nixon's America* (Amherst, Mass.: University of Massachussetts Press, 1995).

25. *Washington Post*, July 29, 1972.

26. Lucian K. Truscott IV, "To Discredit the Vets," *The Village Voice*, May 31, 1973.

27. William Raspberry, "Some Good Things About War Protest," *Washington Post*, April 27, 1971.

28. *Congressional Record*, April 6, 1971, 9948.

29. *New York Times*, September 26, 1982.

Bibliography

MANUSCRIPT COLLECTIONS

Citizens' Commission of Inquiry on U.S. War Crimes in Vietnam (CCI) Papers. Rare and Manuscript Collections, Carl A. Kroch Library, Cornell University, Ithaca, New York. Courtesy Michael Uhl.

Hoover Institution on War, Revolution, and Peace, Stanford University, Palo Alto, California.

Social Action Collection, State Historical Society of Wisconsin, Madison.

Social Protest Project, The Bancroft Library, University of California, Berkeley.

Vietnam Veterans Against the War National Office Papers and Film Archive, Chicago, Illinois.

Vietnam Veterans Against the War Papers, State Historical Society of Wisconsin, Madison.

SECONDARY WORKS

Adelson, Alan. *SDS: A Profile*. New York: Scribner's, 1971.

Adler, Bill, ed. *Letters from Vietnam*. New York: E. P. Dutton, 1967.

Anderson, Terry. *The Movement and the Sixties*. Oxford: Oxford University Press, 1995.

Baez, Joan. *And a Voice to Sing With: A Memoir*. New York: Summit Books, 1987.

Barry, Jan, ed. *Peace Is Our Profession: Poems and Passages of War Protest*. Montclair, N.J.: East River Anthology, 1981.

Barry, Jan, Basil T. Paquet, and Larry Rottmann, eds. *Winning Hearts & Minds: War Poems by Vietnam Veterans*. Brooklyn, N.Y.: First Casualty Press/McGraw-Hill, 1972.

Baskir, Lawrence M., and William A. Strauss. *Chance and Circumstance: The Draft, the War and the Vietnam Generation*. New York: Alfred A. Knopf, 1978.

Berrigan, Daniel. *America Is Hard to Find*. New York: Doubleday, 1972.

Boyle, Richard. *GI Revolts: The Breakdown of the U.S. Army in Vietnam*. San Francisco: United Front Press, 1973.

Camil, Scott. "Undercover Agents' War on Vietnam Veterans." In Bud Scultz and

Ruth Scultz, eds. *It Did Happen Here*. Berkeley: University of California Press, 1989.

Carson, Clayborne. *In Struggle: SNCC and the Black Awakening of the 1960s*. Cambridge, Mass.: Harvard University Press, 1981.

Churchill, Ward and Jim Vander Wall. *The COINTELPRO Papers: Documents from the FBI's Secret War Against Domestic Dissent*. Boston: South End Press, 1990.

Collier, Peter. *The Fondas: A Hollywood Dynasty*. New York: G. P. Putnam's Sons, 1991.

Cortright, David. *Soldiers in Revolt: The American Military Today*. Garden City, N.Y.: Anchor Press/Doubleday, 1975.

Crandell, William. "They Moved the Town." In *Give Peace a Chance: Exploring the Vietnam Antiwar Movement*, ed. Melvin Small and William D. Hoover. Syracuse, N.Y.: Syracuse University Press, 1992.

Crowell, Joan. *Fort Dix Stockade: Our Prison Camp Next Door*. New York: Links Books, 1974.

Dean, John. *Blind Ambition: The White House Years*. New York: Simon & Schuster, 1976.

DeBenedetti, Charles, with Charles Chatfield. *An American Ordeal: The Antiwar Movement of the Vietnam Era*. Syracuse, N.Y.: Syracuse University Press, 1990.

Dellinger, Dave. *More Power Than We Know*. New York: Anchor Press, 1975.

——. *Vietnam Revisited: From Covert Action to Invasion to Reconstruction*. Boston: South End Press, 1986.

Donner, Frank J. *The Age of Surveillance: The Aims and Methods of America's Political Intelligence System*. New York: Vintage Books, 1981.

Duffet, John, ed. *Against the Crime of Silence: Proceedings of the Russell International War Crimes Tribunal*. New York: O'Hare Books, 1968.

Duncan, Donald. *The New Legions*. New York: Random House, 1967.

Egendorf, Arthur. *Healing from the War: Trauma and Transformation After Vietnam*. Boston: Houghton Mifflin, 1985.

Ehrhart, W. D. *Busted: A Vietnam Veteran in Nixon's America* Amherst, Mass.: University of Massachusetts Press, 1995.

——. *Going Back: An Ex-Marine Returns to Vietnam*. Jefferson, N.C.: McFarland, 1987.

——. *In the Shadow of Vietnam: Essays, 1977–1991*. Jefferson, N.C.: McFarland, 1991.

——. *Passing Time: Memoir of a Vietnam Veteran Against the War*. Jefferson, N.C.: McFarland, 1986.

——. *Vietnam-Perkasie: A Combat Marine Memoir*. Jefferson, N.C.: McFarland, 1983.

Emerson, Gloria. *Winners and Losers*. New York: Random House, 1976.

Foner, Phillip S. *American Labor and the Indochina War.* New York: International Publishers, 1971.

Foot, Michael, and Isaac Kramnick, eds. *The Thomas Paine Reader.* New York: Penguin Books, 1987.

Gardner, Fred. *The Unlawful Concert: An Account of the Presidio Mutiny Case.* New York: Viking Press, 1970.

Gettleman, Marvin E., et al., eds. *Vietnam and America: A Documented History.* New York: Grove Press, 1995.

Giesler, Chuck. *Profile of a Protest.* Lansing, Mich.: Allstar Printing, 1972.

Gioglio, Gerald. *Days of Decision: An Oral History of Conscientious Objectors in the Military During the Vietnam War.* Trenton, N.J.: Broken Rifle Press, 1989.

Gitlin, Todd. *The Sixties: Years of Hope, Days of Rage.* New York: Bantam Books, 1987.

————. *The Whole World Is Watching: Mass Media in the Making and Unmaking of the New Left.* Berkeley: University of California Press, 1980.

Gottlieb, Sherry Gershon. *Hell No, We Won't Go!: Resisting the Draft During the Vietnam War* New York: Viking, 1991.

Greene, Bob. *Homecoming: When the Soldiers Returned from Vietnam.* New York: Ballantine Books, 1990.

Haldeman, H. R. *The Haldeman Diaries: Inside the Nixon White House.* New York: G. P. Putnam's Sons, 1994.

Halstead, Fred. *GIs Speak Out Against the War: The Case of the Ft. Jackson 8.* New York: Pathfinder Press, 1970.

————. *Out Now! A Particpant's Account of the American Movement Against the Vietnam War.* New York: Monad Press, 1978.

Heath, Louis G., ed. *Mutiny Does Not Happen Lightly: The Literature of the American Resistance to the Vietnam War.* Metuchen, N.J.: Scarecrow Press, 1976.

Helmer, John. *Bringing the War Home: The American Soldier in Vietnam and After.* New York: Free Press, 1974.

Hersh, Seymour. *The Price of Power: Kissinger in the Nixon White House.* New York: Summit Books, 1983.

Kagan, Norman. *The Cinema of Oliver Stone.* New York: Continuum Books, 1995.

Kane, Rod. *Veteran's Day: A Combat Odyssey.* New York: Simon and Schuster, 1990.

Karlin, Wayne, Basil T. Paquet, and Larry Rottmann, eds. *Free Fire Zone: Short Stories by Vietnam Veterans.* New York: McGraw Hill/First Casualty Press, 1973.

Karnow, Stanley. *Vietnam: A History.* New York: Viking Press, 1983.

Kerry, John, and the Vietnam Veterans Against the War. *The New Soldier.* New York: Collier, 1971.

Kirk, Donald. *Tell It to the Dead: Memories of a War.* Chicago: Nelson-Hall, 1975.

Kolko, Gabriel. *Anatomy of a War: Vietnam, the United States, and the Modern Historical Experience.* New York: New Press, 1991.

Kovic, Ron. *Born on the Fourth of July.* New York: Simon & Schuster, 1976.

Kunen, James Simon. *Standard Operating Procedure.* New York: Avon, 1971.

Kutler, Stanley I., ed. *Encyclopedia of the Vietnam War.* New York: Simon & Schuster/Macmillan.

———. *The Wars of Watergate: The Last Crisis of Richard Nixon.* New York: Norton, 1990.

Lane, Mark. *Conversations with Americans.* New York: Simon & Schuster, 1970.

Lang, Daniel. *Patriotism Without Flags.* New York: W. W. Norton, 1974.

Lesnick, Henry, ed. *Guerrilla Street Theater.* New York: Avon Books, 1973.

Levy, Charles J. *The Spoils of War.* Boston: Houghton Mifflin, 1974.

Lifton, Robert Jay. *Home from the War: Vietnam Veterans: Neither Victims nor Executioners.* New York: Simon and Schuster, 1973.

Loory, Stewart H. *Defeated: Inside America's Military Machine.* New York: Random House, 1973.

Lynd, Alice. *We Won't Go: Personal Accounts of War Objectors.* Boston: Beacon Press, 1968.

McCarthy, Eugene. *The Year of the People.* Garden City, N.Y.: Doubleday, 1969.

MacPherson, Myra. *Long Time Passing: Vietnam and the Haunted Generation.* Garden City, N.Y.: Doubleday, 1984.

Magruder, Jeb Stuart. *An American Life: One Man's Road to Watergate.* New York: Atheneum, 1974.

Mason, Steve. *Warrior for Peace.* New York: Simon & Schuster, 1989.

Morgan, Robin, ed. *Sisterhood Is Powerful.* New York: Vintage Books, 1970.

Morrison, Joan, and Robert K. Morrison. *From Camelot to Kent State: The Sixties Experience in the Words of Those Who Lived It.* New York: Times Books, 1987.

Moser, Richard R. "From Deference to Defiance: America, the Citizen-Soldier and the Vietnam Era." Ph.D. diss., Rutgers University, 1992.

Nixon, Richard M. *RN: The Memoirs of Richard Nixon.* New York: Grosset & Dunlap, 1978.

Noble, Vincent. "Political Opposition in the Age of Mass Media: G.I.s and Veterans Against the War in Vietnam." Ph.D. diss., University of California Irvine, 1987.

O'Connor, John, and Rod Kane. "Strictly Undercover." Unpublished manuscript, 1992. Courtesy of John O'Connor.

Peck, Abe. *Uncovering the Sixties: The Life and Times of the Underground Press.* New York: Pantheon Books, 1985.

The Pentagon Papers as Published by the New York Times. New York: Bantam Books, 1971.

Peterson, Richard E., and John A. Bilorusky. *May 1970: The Campus Aftermath of*

Cambodia and Kent State. Berkeley: Carnegie Commission on Higher Education, 1970.

Polner, Murray. *No Victory Parades: The Return of the Vietnam Veteran*. New York: Holt, Rinehart & Wilson, 1971.

Powers, Thomas. *The War at Home: Vietnam and the American People*. New York: Grossman Publishers, 1973.

Prados, John. *The Hidden History of the Vietnam War*. Chicago: Ivan R. Dee, 1995.

Prasad, Devi. *They Love It but Leave It: American Deserters*. London: Farmer and Sons, 1971.

Radine, Lawrence B. *The Taming of the Troops: Social Control in the U.S. Army*. Westport, Conn.: Greenwood Press, 1977.

Rees, Steve. "A Questioning Spirit: GIs Against the War." In Dick Cluster, ed., *They Should Have Served That Cup of Coffee*. Boston: South End Press, 1979.

Retzer, Joseph David. "War and Political Ideology: The Roots of Radicalism Among Vietnam Veterans." Ph.D. diss., Yale University, 1976.

Sale, Kirkpatrick. *SDS*. New York: Random House, 1973.

Santoli, Al. *Everything We Had: An Oral History of the Vietnam War by Thirty-three American Soldiers Who Fought It*. New York: Random House, 1981.

Schell, Jonathon. *The Time of Illusion*. New York: Alfred A. Knopf, 1976.

Scultz, Bud, and Ruth Scultz, eds. *It Did Happen Here*. Berkeley: University of California Press, 1989.

Seidenberg, Willa, and William Short. *A Matter of Conscience: G.I. Resistance During the Vietnam War*. Andover, Mass.: Addison Gallery of Art, 1992.

Severo, Richard, and Lewis Milford. *The Wages of War: When American Soldiers Came Home—From Valley Forge to Vietnam*. New York: Simon and Schuster, 1989.

Small, Melvin, and William D. Hoover, eds. *Give Peace a Chance: Exploring the Vietnam Antiwar Movement*. Syracuse, N.Y.: Syracuse University Press, 1992.

Stapp, Andy. *Up Against the Brass*. New York: Simon and Schuster, 1970.

Stavis, Benedict. *We Were the Campaign: New Hampshire to Chicago for McCarthy*. Boston: Beacon Press, 1969.

Stone, I. F. *The Killings at Kent State: How Murder Went Unpunished*. New York: Vintage Books, 1971.

Summers, Jr., Colonel Harry G. *Vietnam War Almanac*. New York: Facts on File Publications, 1985.

Swearingen, Weley. *FBI Secrets: An Agent's Exposé*. Boston: South End Press, 1995.

Taylor, Clyde, ed. *Vietnam and Black America: An Anthology of Protest and Resistance*. Garden City, N.Y.: Anchor Press/Doubleday, 1973.

Terry, Wallace, II. *Bloods: An Oral History of the Vietnam War by Black Veterans*. New York: Random House, 1984.

Thompson, Hunter S. *Fear and Loathing: On the Campaign Trail '72*. New York: Warner Books, 1973.

Tollefson, James W. *The Strength Not to Fight: An Oral History of Conscientious Objectors of the Vietnam War.* Boston: Little, Brown and Company, 1993.

Trujillo, Charley, ed. *Soldados: Chicanos in Vietnam.* San Jose, California: Chusma House Publications, 1990.

Van Devanter, Lynda. *Home Before Morning.* New York: Beaufort Books, 1983.

Viet Nam Generation. *Nobody Gets Off the Bus: The Viet Nam Generation Big Book*, ed. Dan Duffy and Kalí Tal (Woodbridge, Conn.: Viet Nam Generation, Inc., 1994).

Vietnam Veterans Against the War. *The Winter Soldier Investigation: An Inquiry into American War Crimes.* Boston: Beacon Press, 1972.

Vietnam Veterans Against the War. *25 Years Fighting For Veterans Peace and Justice.* Chicago: Vietnam Veterans Against the War, 1992.

Waterhouse, Larry. G., and Marrian G. Wizard. *Turning the Guns Around: Notes on the GI Movement.* New York: Praeger, 1971.

Watts, Max, and David Cortright, eds. *Left Face: Soldier Unions and Resistance Movements in Modern Armies.* New York: Greenwood Press, 1991.

Wells, Tom. *The War Within: America's Battle over Vietnam.* Berkeley: University of California Press, 1994.

White, Theodore H. *The Making of the President 1972.* New York: Atheneum, 1973.

Williams, Reese, ed. *Unwinding the Vietnam War: From War into Peace.* Seattle: Real Comet Press, 1987.

Young, Marilyn B. *The Vietnam Wars, 1945–1990.* New York: HarperCollins, 1991.

Zaroulis, Nancy, and Gerald Sullivan. *Who Spoke Up? American Protest Against the War in Vietnam, 1963–1975.* Garden City, N.Y.: Doubleday, 1984.

FILMS

Born on the Fourth of July (Director, Oliver Stone, 1989).

Different Sons (Director, Jack Ofield, 1971).

Forrest Gump (Director, Robert Zemekis, 1994).

I'll Never Do That Again (Documentary film, 1987).

Only the Beginning (Documentary film, produced by Vietnam Veterans Against the War, 1972).

The War at Home (Documentary film, 1981).

Winter Soldier (Documentary film, produced by the Winterfilm Cooperative, 1972).

INTERVIEWS

Linda Alband, April 27, 1995
Anne Bailey, August 25, 1995
Jan Barry, March 5, 1995
Bill Branson, August 23, 1995
Tim Butz, September 16, 1995
Scott Camil, June 15, 1995
Ken Campbell, March 11, 1996
William Crandell, June 16, 1995
Ed Damato, July 18, 1995
Bill Davis, August 26, 1995
Tod Ensign, March 16, 1996
Jon Randy Floyd, March 12, 1996
Jeanne Friedman, April 27, 1995
Joel Greenberg, August 25, 1995
Robert Hanson, April 29, 1995
Mark Lane, April 2, 1996
Robert Jay Lifton, May 22, 1996
John Lindquist, August 25, 1995

Annie Luginbill, August 24, 1995
Jack McCloskey, April 27, 1995
Mike McKusker, September 28, 1995
Joe Miller, July 18, 1996
McDonald Moore, June 29, 1995
Madelyn Moore, January 5, 1996
Scott Moore, November 5, 1995
Jean O'Connor, May 3, 1996
John O'Connor, May 3, 1996
Ray Parish, August 26, 1995
Greg Payton, July 17, 1995
Carl Rogers, May 12, 1995
Barry Romo, August 23, 1995
Rusty Sachs, April 11, 1996
John Upton, September 18, 1995
Joe Urgo, August 3, 1995
Pete Zastrow, October 28, 1996

CORRESPONDENCE

Don Donner, Fayetteville, Arkansas. November–December, 1996.
Tom Thompson, Oracle, Arizona. February 17, 1995
Michael Uhl, Walpole, Maine. February 1995–December 1996.

NEWSPAPERS AND PERIODICALS

Akron (Ohio) Beacon Journal
Arkansas Gazette (Fayetteville, Arkansas)
Boston Globe
Charlotte Observer
Chicago American
Chicago Sun-Times
Chicago Tribune
Chinook (Denver)
Christian Science Monitor
Cincinnati Enquirer
Cleveland Plain Dealer
Commonweal
Computers and People

Detroit Free Press
Detroit News
First Casualty
Gainesville (Florida) Sun
Greely (Colorado) Tribune
Guidon
Harpers
Ithaca (New York) Journal
Life
Louisville Times
Miami Herald
Milwaukee Sentinel
Mobile (Alabama) Register

Nation
National Review
New Republic
New York Daily News
New Yorker
New York Times
Newsday
Newsweek
Ozark Gazette (Fayetteville, Arkansas)
Pensacola (Florida) Journal
Penthouse
Philadelphia Daily News
Playboy
Providence (Rhode Island) Journal
Ramparts
St. Louis Post-Dispatch

St. Petersburg (Florida) Times
San Francisco Chronicle
Saturday Review
Staten Island (New York) Advance
Syracuse (New York) Herald-Journal
Tallahassee Democrat
Time
U.S. News and World Report
Veteran
Veterans Stars and Stripes for Peace
Vietnam Generation
Vietnam GI
Village Voice
Washington Post
Win
Winter Soldier

Index

About the Author

The son of antiwar activists, Andrew E. Hunt first encountered Vietnam Veterans Against the War while still a young boy in the early 1970s, when hundreds of members of the Southern California chapter assembled for their annual meeting/campout in his family's sprawling backyard.

Hunt received a Ph.D. in history from the University of Utah. He currently teaches contemporary American history at the University of Waterloo in Ontario, Canada, where he lives with his wife, Lori, daughter, Madeline, and son, Aidan.